The Virtue of Bonhoeffer's Ethics

Princeton Theological Monograph Series

K. C. Hanson, Charles M. Collier, D. Christopher Spinks,
and Robin Parry, Series Editors

Recent volumes in the series:

Koo Dong Yun
The Holy Spirit and Ch'i *(Qi):*
A Chiological Approach to Pneumatology

Stanley S. MacLean
Resurrection, Apocalypse, and the Kingdom of Christ:
The Eschatology of Thomas F. Torrance

Brian Neil Peterson
Ezekiel in Context: Ezekiel's Message Understood in Its Historical
Setting of Covenant Curses and Ancient Near
Eastern Mythological Motifs

Amy E. Richter
Enoch and the Gospel of Matthew

Maeve Louise Heaney
Music as Theology: What Music Says about the Word

Eric M. Vail
Creation and Chaos Talk: Charting a Way Forward

David L. Reinhart
Prayer as Memory: Toward the Comparative Study of Prayer
as Apocalyptic Language and Thought

Peter D. Neumann
Pentecostal Experience: An Ecumenical Encounter

Ashish J. Naidu
Transformed in Christ:
Christology and the Christian Life in John Chrysostom

The Virtue of Bonhoeffer's Ethics

A Study of Dietrich Bonhoeffer's Ethics *in Relation to Virtue Ethics*

JENNIFER MOBERLY

with a foreword by Stephen Plant

☙PICKWICK *Publications* · Eugene, Oregon

THE VIRTUE OF BONHOEFFER'S ETHICS
A Study of Dietrich Bonhoeffer's *Ethics* in Relation to Virtue Ethics

Princeton Theological Monograph Series 194

Copyright © 2013 Jennifer Moberly. All rights reserved. Except for brief quotations in critical publications or reviews, no part of this book may be reproduced in any manner without prior written permission from the publisher. Write: Permissions, Wipf and Stock Publishers, 199 W. 8th Ave., Suite 3, Eugene, OR 97401.

Pickwick Publications
An Imprint of Wipf and Stock Publishers
199 W. 8th Ave., Suite 3
Eugene, OR 97401

www.wipfandstock.com

ISBN 13: 978-1-61097-945-0

Cataloguing-in-Publication data:

Moberly, Jennifer.

The virtue of Bonhoeffer's ethics : a study of Dietrich Bonhoeffer's *Ethics* in relation to virtue ethics / Jennifer Moberly ; foreword by Stephen Plant.

xvi + 254 pp. ; 23 cm. Includes bibliographical references and index.

Princeton Theological Monograph Series 194

ISBN 13: 978-1-61097-945-0

1. Bonhoeffer, Dietrich, 1906–1945. Ethics. 2. Bonhoeffer, Dietrich, 1906–1945. Ethik. 3. Christian ethics. 4. Virtues. I. Plant, Stephen. II. Series. III. Title.

BJ1253.B6153 M63 2013

Manufactured in the U.S.A.

For Bonnie and Karl, with thanks and love

Contents

Foreword by Stephen Plant   ix

Preface   xi

Acknowledgments   xiii

List of Abbreviations   xv

1 Introduction   1

2 Bonhoeffer and "Virtue Ethics"   15

3 Virtue Ethics in the Christian Tradition   53

4 Bonhoeffer's *Ethics* as Virtue Ethical   99

5 Mode of Ethical Discourse   141

6 Divine Command and/or Virtue Ethics   163

7 Conclusion   219

Bibliography   233

Index   247

Foreword

Jennifer Moberly's book takes us to the beating heart of Dietrich Bonhoeffer's theology. From his first to his last theological writings Bonhoeffer wanted theology to engage with the truly central questions of the Christian life: What does it mean for the Church to be the body of Christ? How does God give himself to us and how may we receive God? How do we read the Bible? How do we follow Jesus? How do we live together in community? What is the will of God? Who is Jesus Christ for us today? Each of these questions about the Christian life involves *both* theology *and* ethics, what Christians think and what they do.

This basic insight about the ways good thinking and good living inform each other is one that Jennifer Moberly's book never loses sight of. Her book is, therefore, not *simply* a book that helps makes sense of Bonhoeffer's writings on ethics, but is a book about how to think and live well in light of the Gospel of Jesus Christ. This is its first virtue.

A second virtue of Jennifer Moberly's book is that it helps those who would attend to Bonhoeffer's theological ethics to think *clearly* about them. There has sometimes been a tendency in writing about Dietrich Bonhoeffer to make ethical use of his life and thought before it has been properly understood. Bonhoeffer is not the only twentieth century theologian of whom that is true, but the "temptation" to conscript Bonhoeffer to the cause of this or that theological trend has proved particularly hard to resist because of the attraction of his costly involvement in the defining events of his century. Moberly's reading of Bonhoeffer is an exercise in the unfashionable virtue of solid and thoughtful scholarship. Her book attends carefully to the complex textual issues that Bonhoeffer's *Ethics* presents, bringing to bear on it considerable linguistic skill. She sets the text of Bonhoeffer's *Ethics* not only within his historical and intellectual context, but crucially also sets his thinking within broader streams of Catholic and Protestant moral theology. Moberly's book is the product of years of patient work, but wears its expertise lightly. By these means Bonhoeffer's faithfulness to Christian tradition—and his creative interpretation of it for his own place and time—are both brought into perspective.

Foreword

A final virtue of Moberly's book is that, based on its close and careful engagement with Bonhoeffer's moral theology, it makes an original contribution concerning the ethics of virtue, the ethics of obedience to divine command and their interrelationship. By describing, analyzing and developing Bonhoeffer's proposals Moberly challenges what can, at times, seem like a consensus view that these two approaches to ethics are always and everywhere at odds with each other. Her constructive proposal—that virtue ethics, properly understood, can complement an ethics of command—has significance not only for interpreting Bonhoeffer but for all who seek to follow Jesus Christ.

Moberly's book is being published as the final volumes of the Dietrich Bonhoeffer works in English are being prepared for the press. The completion of a complete scholarly edition of Bonhoeffer's works in German for Gütersloher Verlagshaus and of a complete English translation published by Fortress Press may mark an important shift in Bonhoeffer scholarship from a generation that understood its task as establishing the text of Bonhoeffer's writings in a reliable form and in chronological sequence to a generation that wants responsibly to bring the theology within these texts to bear upon the most pressing issues facing the Church today. If I am right about this shift then Moberly's book shows how this transition can best be made. On the basis of the exemplary scholarship of the 1992 German critical edition of Bonhoeffer's *Ethik* she has worked with and through Bonhoeffer's twentieth century moral theology creatively to engage an issue in twenty-first century moral theology, namely how to live the Christian life—in Alasdair MacIntyre's cleverly ambivalent phrase—after virtue.

I have read this book twice—once in its original form as a dissertation, and now in its significantly revised form for publication. It is a mark of quality that I have learned from it just as much on a second reading as on the first.

Stephen Plant
Trinity Hall, Cambridge
Whitsunday, 2012

Preface

It is surprising, even to me, to note that this book is the product of eleven years of thought. It began with a puzzling question as I was reading Alasdair MacIntyre's *After Virtue* for an essay I was writing on virtue ethics in the context of my training for ordained ministry. As I read MacIntyre, quotes from Bonhoeffer's *Ethics* came unbidden to my mind. I had read Bonhoeffer's volume several years earlier, and had found it enigmatic in a variety of ways. However, it was infinitely more baffling to me that certain passages of his *Ethics* seemed to fit so well with what MacIntyre had to say about virtue ethics. What on earth should a German Lutheran theologian writing in the first half of the twentieth century have to do with virtue ethics? In the context of that essay there was no chance of trying to discover the answer to my question, but to my surprise I discovered that I was able to locate the passages I was remembering, and that my memory wasn't playing tricks on me. And so began the research that lies behind this book. I hope there may be something of the same joy of discovery for the reader as there has been for the author.

Jennifer Moberly
Durham

Trinity Sunday, 2012

Acknowledgments

My thanks go first, both chronologically and substantively to my parents, Karl and Bonnie McClure. It was my father who introduced me to the works of Dietrich Bonhoeffer and who gave me my first copy of his *Ethics*. He had most of Bonhoeffer's works on his shelves after having been introduced to them by Franz Hildebrandt, Bonhoeffer's close friend and one of the professors at the seminary where my father trained as a Methodist minister. Additionally, my parents read my doctoral thesis and have encouraged me throughout the time of study (and all my life long).

Additionally, it is not only a matter of justice to acknowledge my indebtedness to a number of other people who have given me assistance in completing this work, but also a great joy to note their help and kindness. To Dr. Philip Ziegler I owe thanks for his generosity in giving me time for discussion, helpful suggestions for further reading, and encouragement regarding the nature of my study. I am grateful also to Dr. Sibylle Rolf for reading an earlier draft of two of the chapters, sharing her knowledge of German Lutheranism and Christian ethics, and providing a sounding board within the goods of friendship.

Unending thanks go to my family, Walter, John-Paul and Rachel, who have given me their loving and patient support through the years of this research. Walter generously read early essays that were part of my preparation for my doctoral dissertation, which is the origin of this book, and proof-read this manuscript. More importantly, he gave me encouragement when I most needed it.

However, without the support of my doctoral supervisor, Dr. Robert Song, I could not have completed my research. He was unfailingly generous with his time, gracious in seeing the best in my efforts, patient as I learned, and both kind and wise in offering criticisms and suggestions. One could not ask for a more virtuous Doktorvater.

Jennifer Moberly
Durham
Trinity Sunday, 2012

Abbreviations

DBW 1:	*Dietrich Bonhoeffer Werke 1: Sanctorum Communio*
DBW 2:	*Dietrich Bonhoeffer Werke 2: Akt und Sein*
DBW 3:	*Dietrich Bonhoeffer Werke 3: Schöpfung und Fall*
DBW 4:	*Dietrich Bonhoeffer Werke 4: Nachfolge*
DBW 5:	*Dietrich Bonhoeffer Werke 5: Gemeinsames Leben/ Das Gebetbuch der Bibel*
DBW 6:	*Dietrich Bonhoeffer Werke 6: Ethik*
DBW 7:	*Dietrich Bonhoeffer Werke 7: Fragmente aus Tegel*
DBW 8:	*Dietrich Bonhoeffer Werke 8: Widerstand und Ergebung*
DBW 10:	*Dietrich Bonhoeffer Werke 10: Barcelona, Berlin, America 1928–1931*
DBW 11:	*Dietrich Bonhoeffer Werke 11: Ökumene, Universität, Pfarramt 1931–1932*
DBW 12:	*Dietrich Bonhoeffer Werke 12: Berlin 1932–1933*
DBW 14:	*Dietrich Bonhoeffer Werke 14: Illegale Theologenausbildung: Finkenwalde 1935–37*
DBW 15:	*Dietrich Bonhoeffer Werke 15: Illegale Theologenausbildung: Sammelvikariate 1937–1940*
DBW 16:	*Dietrich Bonhoeffer Werke 16: Konspiration und Haft 1940–1945*
DBWE 6:	*Dietrich Bonhoeffer Works 6: Ethics*
CD II/2:	Karl Barth, *Church Dogmatics: The Doctrine of God, Part 2*

Abbreviations

CD III/1:	Karl Barth, *Church Dogmatics: The Doctrine of Creation*.
CD III/4:	Karl Barth, *Church Dogmatics: The Doctrine of Creation*.
CD IV/2:	Karl Barth, *Church Dogmatics: The Doctrine of Reconciliation*.
KD II/2:	Karl Barth, *Die kirchliche Dogmatik: Die Lehre von Gott*.
KD IV/2:	Karl Barth, *Die kirchliche Dogmatik: Die Lehre von der Versöhnung*
NE	Aristotle, *Nicomachean Ethics*
ST	Thomas Aquinas, *Summa Theologiae*
WA	Martin Luther, *Kritische Ausgabe*, Weimar

1

Introduction

THE TITLE OF THIS BOOK, "THE VIRTUE OF BONHOEFFER'S ETHICS," is meant to suggest the inherent strengths of his work, one of which, I will claim, is the presence of both virtue ethical and divine command modes of ethical discourse. As the subtitle makes clear, however, the central question of this study is how Bonhoeffer's *Ethics* is related to virtue ethics. Of course, the question presupposes the possibility of a variety of answers: that the two are utterly unrelated; that there was no intended relationship, even if a reader now may make correlations through her own perspectives that she brings to the reading; that there is an intentional relationship, even if the *Ethics* is not simply an example of virtue ethics; that Bonhoeffer was unwittingly so influenced by others that his account is one of virtue ethics; or that Bonhoeffer quite purposefully set out to offer a Protestant construal of virtue ethics. In the following book I shall endeavor to discover which of these possibilities accords best with the evidence, and to see what "virtue" this might entail for the current situation in theological ethics.

1.1: Rationale for Study—Introduction

A study such as this must necessarily face difficult questions at the outset: Why should it be undertaken? and, Why should it be read? Given that the aim of this book is to examine the relation of Bonhoeffer's *Ethics* to what is now called "virtue ethics," one might fairly consider that there are already more than enough books on both Bonhoeffer and virtue ethics. Yet although some scholars have seen the possibility of interpreting Bonhoeffer's *Ethics* with reference to virtue ethics or have at least identified "conformation" as one of the leitmotifs of the work (and have seen it as in some sense related to virtue ethics), no sustained attention has hitherto been given to the question of how Bonhoeffer's *Ethics* as a whole might be related to virtue ethics. Since the existence of this lacuna is not necessarily sufficient justification either to undertake or read such a study, what reason might there be?

One reason, paradoxically, may be the reason mentioned already *not* to engage in such a project: the sheer number of studies already available about virtue ethics. The impact of Alasdair MacIntyre's (and others') work has been such that the central concerns articulated in virtue ethics (the character of the ethical agent, her continuity and development over time, her motives for acting, etc.) have been widely recognized to be of real significance, even by those who do not include them in their primary account of the nature of ethics. To appreciate the impact the resurgence of virtue ethics has had, and the questions emerging from this development (and thereby the potential significance of this study), it may be helpful to consider more generally the theological background of this development.

1.2: A Theological Backdrop

The two actors taking the centre stage of this study will be Bonhoeffer's *Ethics* and virtue ethics, but before the reader's attention is focused solely on these two, it is good to observe the theological backdrop, which provides important clues as to the meaning of the action taking place, as well as parameters and perhaps even constraints for the play as a whole. As with any stage scenery, this is necessarily painted with broad brushstrokes, and should be taken as a general view of the landscape rather than a surveyor's map.[1]

1.2.1: *Justification by Faith*

On one side of the stage, a key doctrine of the Reformation is represented, for the article of faith on which Martin Luther said the church stands or falls—namely justification only by faith, only by grace, and not by works—was to be one of the determining factors for how Christian ethics may be conceived.[2] The early Luther followed the Augustinian and Thomist

---

1. Among the myriad of offerings in this area, for a more detailed look at the theology of major figures of the Reformation, see Reardon, *Religious Thought*. For a good overview to some of the issues here, see Gustafson, *Protestant and Roman Catholic*.

2. I concentrate here on Luther and Lutheran positions because Bonhoeffer was a Lutheran. Of course there are differences within the Lutheran tradition, and between the Lutheran and Reformed traditions. I will, however, try to show in general terms where there are agreements or divergences.

traditions in expecting that God truly *makes* the believer righteous, but from late 1518 he began to speak of her having an "alien" righteousness through being in Christ.[3] She is righteous because God has declared her to be so and has imputed to her the righteousness that belongs to Christ. This came to be called a "forensic" notion of justification because of the courtroom language typically deployed of God as Judge, acquitting the believer. Moreover, the Christian was said to be simultaneously a sinner and righteous, and Luther was unwilling to consider any of her actions as having "merit." Although Luther did speak of good works as a necessary consequence of faith, these were said to have nothing to do with a sinner being declared righteous, justification.[4]

Turning to view the backdrop of the other side of the stage, the Roman Catholic understanding of justification as articulated in the Council of Trent was that it consists both of the remission of sins and sanctification. God's prevenient grace works in a person to dispose her towards conversion, and although she, of course, could not become righteous before God apart from God's grace, her will is nonetheless to be active so that she cooperates with that grace. Thus the council stated that justification is not by faith *only*, but faith accompanied by hope and love. Moreover, the believer was expected to grow in holiness (described both in terms of justification and sanctification), and eternal life is both a gift of grace and a reward for her life-long merit. Similarly, although Christ infuses virtue, that virtue can be said to be the believer's, as can the works (and their merit) that are thus enabled.[5] A distinction was made between merit that is appropriate, *de congruo*, to a human, and merit that is genuinely "worthy," *de condigno*, which can only be granted by God's gracious act.[6] Thus a Christian may be said not only to grow in holiness, but also in "merit" (even if merit that is appropriate to a human is limited), and to become by degrees less sinful as she exercises the virtues. In this conception, then, Luther's language of receiving an "alien" righteousness was all but incomprehensible, and seemed to suggest that God, who is all truth, was party to some pretence or even deceit. Luther was thus seen to impugn God's character by suggesting that God was involved in some fiction by declaring the believer righteous when she was really a sinner. God, it was insisted, does not declare a person righteous without making her so. Grace is given by God, but must be used

---

3. Reardon, *Religious Thought*, 53–55.
4. *Freedom of a Christian*, 1520.
5. Drewery, "Council of Trent," 406–7.
6. Drewery, "Martin Luther," 327.

aright to do "meritorious" works, which would prove the believer worthy of the grace given.[7] The contrast between this position and that espoused by Luther was such that many thought of him as being "antinomian" or allowing for moral anarchy, and indeed the council's decree on justification concluded with 29 anathemas related to Protestant teachings.[8]

Yet, returning to the first side of the scenery, Luther was horrified by being labeled an antinomian. In his preaching and teaching he emphasized the change of life that being in Christ certainly must make in the believer. He described faith as being "a divine work in us which changes us and makes us to be born anew of God, John 1. It kills the old Adam and makes us altogether different men, in heart and spirit and mind and powers; and it brings with it the Holy Spirit. O, it is a living, busy, active, mighty thing, this faith. It is impossible for it not to be doing good works incessantly."[9]

Yet talk of a supposed growth in holiness or merit in any form made him all the more polemical in his insistence that the believer remains a sinner, and that her only righteousness or merit is what is given her in Christ. Although a careful distinction was made by Roman Catholic theologians between virtue that may be called salvific (which must be given, or "infused" by God) and such virtue that a person may achieve through her own practice and habit, such accounts accorded more place to human effort (and less to God's sovereign act) than Luther and other Protestants would accept. It was asserted that Roman Catholics in fact believed in "justification by works," and that Roman moral theology did not take seriously enough the consequences of the Fall, both in terms of its damage to the believer's ability to choose the good and her capacity to do it.

Naturally enough, on the Catholic side it was felt that Protestants emphasized too little the need for the believer's will to be aligned with God's and thus for her to participate by choosing to act well. Furthermore, Roman Catholic moral theology considered at least part of God's will to be accessible to anyone by rational thought through what is called the natural law.

Against this, the Protestant front upheld not only Augustine's belief that as a result of the Fall the human will is not free to choose the good, but also that human reason itself is vitiated and incapable of discerning God's will apart from God's revelation.

---

7. Reardon, *Religious Thought*, 56.

8. Not all of these anathemas related to Luther's teachings, but most did.

9. Luther, "Preface to the Commentary on Romans," 370. See also 371, where he says "it is impossible to separate works from faith, quite as impossible as to separate heat and light from fire."

Introduction

Unsurprisingly, the mutual misreadings, polemical discourse, and a papal bull excommunicating Luther did nothing to bring these two sides together to hear and appreciate how much they had in common.[10] Instead a seemingly widening gulf opened between them, creating a sharp division between the two halves of the stage.

1.2.2: *The Basis for Ethical Discourse*

Yet even this sharp division in all its garish colors does not paint the full picture required for the backdrop. For these theological disagreements had important consequences for ethical discussion. The Roman Catholic perspective on justification, including both the remission of sins and sanctification, meant that moral theology in that context emphasized the role of acting well with the recognition that the Christian must grow in holiness. This process continued to be related in terms of her developing virtues and eradicating (or at least doing penance for) vices.

Meanwhile, Luther and the other Reformers were clearly convinced that the Christian will do good works because they are the fruit of her being a new creation, and Christ in her will enable her to act well. Nonetheless, this was not anchored in the aspect of theology that is most central to Lutheran self-understanding, justification by faith alone. Moreover, the concern that there should be no hint of "works salvation" meant that justification and sanctification were treated separately. For these reasons ethical discourse seemed to become an optional extra.[11]

In this context (and for centuries to come) Protestants asked what abiding significance ethics might have, which, under the influence of nominalism, was often discussed in terms of "the law."[12] For Lutherans there were two clear uses for the law: the first being to prevent sinful hu-

---

10. The papal bull was *Decet Romanum Pontificem* of January 3, 1521; an earlier bull, *Exsurge Domine* in 1520, had given him sixty days to recant. An attempt was made to mediate, and a group of three representatives each from the Catholic and Protestant sides reached an accord and produced an agreed document covering the disputed issues, *Epistola de justificatione*, May 25, 1541. Luther himself was not satisfied by the compromises made, and Rome repudiated the document, Reardon, *Religious Thought*, 326 n. 4.

11. It is interesting to note that this division led both to Kant's version of ethics without theology, and to others offering theology without ethics. Ritschl and other liberal theologians of the nineteenth century often seem, like Kant, more concerned with ethics than theology.

12. See Grabill's account of this development, *Rediscovering the Natural Law*, 57–62.

man beings from utterly destroying themselves and others. This had a civic function, in that enforcing such commands as "you shall not steal" or "you shall not commit murder" enabled a decent ordering for society. Thus for her own (as well as others') good, and though she may not know it, the sinner is preserved by the first use of the law from even more heinous sin than might otherwise have been the case.

The second (spiritual or theological) use of the law pertains to Luther's reading of Paul[13]: because a person cannot possibly keep every part of the law perfectly, she realizes her own sinfulness and therefore becomes aware of her need of God's grace and mercy. She cannot be justified by keeping the law, but through this very realization the law leads her to discover the true means of her salvation: the grace of God.

Melanchthon even spoke of a third (didactic) use of the law, namely in developing holiness (sanctification) in those who have been declared righteous through God's grace. Through the work of the Holy Spirit, the law of love is fulfilled by the believer in spontaneous self-giving.[14] Despite the contentiousness of this notion, and the emphasis of subsequent Lutheranism being firmly on the second use of the law, some have noted that Luther himself insisted that God makes the believer righteous.[15] The function of the law then becomes "to order that sort of new life which those who have become saints and new men ought to enter upon" and a "pattern for doing good works."[16] Against later Lutheran orthodoxy, Bonhoeffer's own teacher on Luther, Karl Holl, interprets Luther's position as, "To declare righteous and to make righteous are inwardly connected as means and end," suggesting that for Luther the sinner is justified precisely to make her holy.[17]

For Roman Catholics, the theoretical understanding of virtue ethics, as early as the twelfth century, became a matter for theologians; the

---

13. Regarding Luther's reading of Paul, see e.g. Sanders *Paul and Palestinian Judaism*, especially his claim that justification by faith alone is not central to Paul, 434; and Dunn, ed., *Cambridge Companion*, especially Stanton, "Paul's Gospel"; and Morgan, "Paul's Enduring Legacy."

14. Calvin, among others, also acknowledged this third use of the law, *Institutes*, 2.7.12.

15. See Althaus, *Theology*, 226.

16. WA 39 I, 542; WA 39 II, 274.

17. Holl, *Luther*, 102. I have not seen any convincing evidence that Luther himself thought in terms of means and end. I am indebted to Dr. Sibylle Rolf, who suggests that Holl is closer to Kant than Luther in speaking of means and end in this context. See also Harnack, *Lehrbuch der Dogmengeschichte*, 825, 845. Both quoted in Stayer, *Martin Luther*, 23, 5.

Introduction

believer's awareness of her continuing viciousness and her growth in virtue, however, was focused on the confessional.[18] In this context, the grille between priest and penitent creates the possibility for anonymity, and if every communicant is required to go to confession, the sheer numbers mean that the confessor can hardly hope to know—even without the grille—all the personal factors of each penitent that are significant according to virtue ethics. In such a context, the particularities of the agent that are so important for our current understanding of virtue ethics become invisible. Instead, the contours of the particular case came to the fore and provided the basis on which the priest was to offer godly counsel and require particular penance for offences. This focus on the given case is what is known as casuistry, and, taken together with the classification of certain sins as venal and others as mortal, was part of a codification that Protestants considered to be legalistic.

Thus typically for Lutherans, ethical discourse occurred in the context of discussion of the law, and was treated separately from the doctrine of justification by faith alone, by grace alone.[19] Meanwhile Roman Catholic moral theology handled justification and sanctification together, and ethical discourse relied to some extent on notions of receiving, acquiring and practicing the virtues, but increasingly on the pastoral work of the confessional, with casuistry to offer the confessor guidelines for how to respond to specific issues. So it was that the Lutheran position was perceived by Catholics as having nothing to do with ethics, and that Roman Catholic teaching was thought by Protestants to advocate "salvation by works."

1.2.3: *The Suspension of Disbelief*

The backdrop is in place, but now a word needs to be said about the suspension of disbelief. In a theater, the audience is meant to forget the surroundings of the theater (suspend the awareness that what is viewed is a play and not reality) and become engaged in what unfolds on stage. In the context of this book, there is a similar issue. While noting the

---

18. See Pinckaers's account of how the effects of nominalism led to dependence on "manuals" which gave priests guidance for the confessional, *Sources of Christian Ethics*, chapters 10 and 11.

19. Melanchthon, despite his notion of the third use of the law, discussed this separation in temporal terms as a second, distinct phase in salvation, Reardon, *Religious Thought*, 133. John Calvin also made a distinction between the two, but insisted that they are inseparable—as Lane nicely puts it, like trousers rather than socks, *Justification by Faith*, 18.

gulf opening up between the two halves of the stage, the reader will no doubt be aware that the landscape the backdrop purports to depict has changed in remarkable ways since the time Bonhoeffer was writing. Although many of the old prejudices and caricatures have not yet passed from existence, it is significant that a process of theological dialogue continuing over several decades resulted in 1999 in the "Joint Declaration on the Doctrine of Justification" between the Roman Catholic Church and the member churches of the Lutheran World Federation.[20] In this agreed statement both churches recognized the misunderstandings involved in their division, and acknowledged that neither had intended to interpret justification in the ways their mutual distorted misreadings had suggested. Further, each church removed the existing condemnations that had continued to be in effect regarding the (false perceptions of the) other's teaching.[21] This fact, taken together with lively interest in virtue ethics among many Protestants, means that the boundaries and contrasts are no longer as sharp as they were at the time Bonhoeffer was working.

However, rather than suspending disbelief as such, it is important in this case to maintain awareness simultaneously of two levels. The first is the theological, social, and political world in which Bonhoeffer lived and worked, which influences the action on stage; the second is our current context. Although I shall only return to the discussion of how this study impinges on a contemporary understanding and articulation of ethics in the final chapter, this consideration figures significantly in my rationale for this book.

1.3: Rationale for Study—Conclusion

Apart from wider theological agreement noted above about the nature of justification (and sanctification) between Protestants and Catholics, the other significant change is the widespread interest in virtue ethics, not least among Protestants. Despite the attention paid to this form of ethical

20. The Lutheran World Federation and the Roman Catholic Church, *Joint Declaration*, especially 4.7. That some Lutheran churches refused to sign the document, and that many have expressed dissent from it, is proof that the gulf has not been eradicated, even if a bridge has been built.

21. However, the agreed statement was based on the Lutheran Church's stance of forensic justification. It is somewhat ironic that parallel with this agreement, many Lutheran scholars (especially of the Finnish School) have been saying that Luther himself did not advocate (simply) that position. See e.g., Cavanaugh, "A Joint Declaration?"; Braaten and Jenson, eds., *Union with Christ*; Marshall, "Justification as Deification and Declaration"; Kärkkäinen, *One with God*; and Yeago, "Martin Luther."

thought, sharp questions as to how virtue ethics may be articulated while emphasizing that justification is by faith in Jesus Christ and not through human works must still be asked, and satisfying answers sought.

Just to speak of the work of contemporary Protestant ethicists, it is useful to contrast the positions of Oliver O'Donovan and David Cunningham. Each represents an Anglican tradition, and each has seemingly felt the force of the claims made in favor of virtue ethics. O'Donovan appears in many ways to be concerned about possible dangers of adopting virtue ethics as the main way of conceiving of ethics, and makes a case that it can be of use only in a secondary capacity related to the retrospective evaluation of an act, rather than in the process of deliberation.[22] On the opposite end of the spectrum, Cunningham espouses virtue ethics almost to the exclusion of any other frame of reference for moral thought.[23]

In the current context, then, there is a real need for discovering how Protestant ethics may give due attention to issues pertaining to the agent and her character without losing its emphasis on the primacy of grace. If the results of this study are at all correct, Bonhoeffer's *Ethics* may, despite its fragmentary nature and the necessity of interpreting such unfinished writings with caution, offer an example of attending to the concerns of virtue within a Protestant account of ethics. If so this could have implications both for how Protestant ethics can incorporate the insights of virtue ethics, and for how virtue ethics may be articulated in relation to an understanding of justification by faith.

Nonetheless, I wish to make no exaggerated claims. In my study I shall not attempt to give a detailed exegesis and interpretation of the manuscripts of Bonhoeffer's *Ethics*, nor will I seek to demonstrate my interpretation by appeals to his biography. There is too little space here for the former, and the latter must rely on a degree of speculation that is dangerous, if not unwarranted.[24] My understanding of the manuscripts,

22. This is stated and argued in ongoing discussion, but for a succinct statement, see O'Donovan, *Resurrection*, 224–45.

23. *Christian Ethics*, especially chapter 1.

24. Many, of course, have insisted on the essential unity of Bonhoeffer's life and thought, and so have considered it necessary to offer evidence from his own decisions and actions. See Burtness, *Shaping the Future*, 7–8; Ebeling, *Word and Faith*, 282; Feil, *Theology of Dietrich Bonhoeffer*; Gremmels and Pfeifer, *Theologie und Biographie*; Hauerwas, *Performing the Faith*, 34, 40; Haynes, *Bonhoeffer Phenomenon*, ch. 1 (see especially 6 n. 22 and 9 n. 38 for further references); McClendon, *Ethics*, ch. 7; Ott, *Reality and Faith*, 269; Tödt, "Conscience," 46–58; Wendl, *Studien zur Homiletik*, 3; Wüstenberg, *Theology of Life*. See also Bethke Elshtain's interesting inversion: "'the life' cannot be separated from . . . 'the work,'" "Freedom and Responsibility," 273. See also

however, should become apparent as various issues arise thematically. Similarly, although I do not treat separately any other of his works, I shall draw on them as they pertain to various points of discussion. Also for reasons of space I do not give a survey of the literature available either on Bonhoeffer or on virtue ethics; although this will be implicit, I shall endeavor to make my own position clear as regards various debates.

Before I give a short overview of what I will be attempting to do, it may be helpful to make a few general remarks about how I have approached this work.

1.4: Guide for the Reader

One aspect of this study to which I must draw the reader's attention is the translation of Bonhoeffer's works. Many others have commented over the years that Bonhoeffer is not always best served by his translators.[25] In my estimation this remains so, despite the invaluable work of translating the *Dietrich Bonhoeffer Werke* into English. Fluency and beauty of English often seem to take precedence over strict adherence to Bonhoeffer's usage, and at times even to his meaning.[26] For this reason I use my own translation of all his works throughout, which I keep as literal as possible while still providing intelligible English. This results in a somewhat angular translation, and often lengthy sentences, but I hope the effort required in reading will be repaid by a faithful rendering of Bonhoeffer's meaning.

In translating Bonhoeffer I have chosen to retain also his gender usage. This is a vexing matter, since German is at all events a "gendered" language, which changes the nature of how it may be "inclusive" or "exclusive." For instance, it is the case that Bonhoeffer normally speaks of the "human" (*der Mensch*) rather than "man" (*der Mann*) or "person" (*die*

Ford's elegant and nuanced treatment, *Self and Salvation*, ch. 10. Despite the high quality of some of these treatments, and the level of cohesion of Bonhoeffer's life and work, it seems to me that theological arguments based on elements of his biography are often necessarily speculative about his thoughts and motivations, and require interpretive moves that I am unprepared to make.

25. See Lehmann, "Bonhoeffer: Real and Counterfeit"; Rumscheidt's preface to Feil, *Theology*, xiii; and Godsey, "Reading Bonhoeffer in English Translation."

26. In my article on the translation of the *Ethics* for the critical edition, I cite many examples which demonstrate weaknesses in understanding German idiom, faulty translation which gives rise to possible misinterpretation of theological and philosophical issues, and problematic editorial decisions. As a result of these considerations, I conclude that, although many passages are translated impeccably, the whole is rendered unreliable for detailed study, Moberly, "'Felicity to the Original Text'?."

Person) or "individual" (*das Individuum*). In meaning, then, Bonhoeffer uses a neutral term, yet it is grammatically masculine. Thus a case could be made for rendering "human" inclusively, as was done in the *Dietrich Bonhoeffer Works* series. I have, however, chosen to keep his masculine referents because I would not like to imply that Bonhoeffer shared our concern for gender inclusive language, which would at the very least be anachronistic.[27] As a counterweight to this, when I speak in my own voice I shall use only feminine referents. This will, I hope, provide a balance in the overall book as well as marking a contrast between my citations of Bonhoeffer and my own commentary.

Similarly, I have retained in translation Bonhoeffer's gendered language for God, not assuming that he imagined God to be anthropomorphically male, but realizing that this is not one of his concerns. When writing in my own voice, I shall use non-gendered language for God.

Finally, to provide some orientation to the study as a whole, I turn to an overview that notes the questions that will be asked in the following chapters, and the materials consulted in seeking their answers.

1.5: Overview

Chapter 2: Bonhoeffer and "Virtue Ethics"

The prime question of the second chapter is whether Bonhoeffer himself would have seen himself as what we might now call a "virtue ethicist." My reason for starting with this question is the fact, as noted at the outset, that there are stronger and weaker forms of relationship that might be suggested between Bonhoeffer's account of ethics and virtue ethics, the strongest of which would be the claim that Bonhoeffer was engaged in virtue ethics and saw himself as an exponent of this form of moral theology. I do not wish to anticipate the answers that more careful examination within the chapter will find, but it is right to say that there are *prima facie* reasons for assuming that Bonhoeffer neither saw himself as a virtue ethicist nor was engaged in expounding an account of ethics based on virtue. One such reason is the fact that Bonhoeffer uses the word "virtue" in ambivalent and even negative ways; furthermore, Thomas Aquinas was almost the

---

27. Moreover, many have been concerned that Bonhoeffer was, if anything, patriarchal. See *DBW* 8:213–14, where Bonhoeffer hopes that his fiancée will be guided by his taste in literature. On Bonhoeffer and the role of women, see Renate Bethge, "Bonhoeffer's Picture of Women"; and her "Bonhoeffer and the Role of Women"; and Haynes, *Bonhoeffer Phenomenon*, 56–58.

only exponent of virtue ethics who was well known in the early twentieth century, and Bonhoeffer's references to him are also largely negative; and finally, though Bonhoeffer makes frequent allusions to a variety of classical sources, which might have offered a virtue-ethical slant to his thought, these refer mostly to figures from legends or plays rather than to philosophical forms of virtue ethics. Taken together, these facts would seem to suggest that not only must the chapter's main question be answered in the negative, but that the question of the whole thesis may be misguided.

To ascertain whether these apparent reasons for such assumptions are valid or not, I shall attend carefully to the evidence internal to the *Ethics* manuscripts, as well as the opinions of those who have commented on the mode(s) of ethical thought in which Bonhoeffer worked. This evidence will enable me to refute some of the assumptions, while others will require further examination (either of the nature of virtue ethics or of particular issues within Bonhoeffer's thought) to be able to discover how valid they may be.

Chapter 3: Virtue Ethics in the Christian Tradition

To explore the strength of certain possible objections that are raised in chapter 2 to seeing Bonhoeffer's *Ethics* as related to virtue ethics, it will be necessary to be more precise about what it might mean to speak of "virtue ethics" in the context of Christian moral theology. To address this question I shall look closely at the work of three influential thinkers from different eras: Augustine of Hippo, Thomas Aquinas, and Alasdair MacIntyre. Augustine and Thomas have been widely influential on the shape of Christian thinking and have become classics, as it were. It is much too soon to make such claims for MacIntyre, though his work has certainly changed the nature of ethical debate in the English-speaking world in the last twenty years or so. Focusing on Augustine's account of the cardinal virtues as forms of love, Thomas's Christian appropriation of Aristotle's understanding and his own addition of the theological virtues, and MacIntyre's emphasis on the communities and practices that enable the development of virtues should offer a broad perspective on how virtue ethics may be understood in a Christian context. The variation between their accounts will make it clear that to make definitive claims about what constitutes virtue ethics even simply in the context of Christian moral theology would be contentious. Instead of attempting this, I shall try to describe the kinds of concerns that seem to typify or underlie these various versions of virtue ethics. With this basic description of features necessary for any account to be considered virtue-ethical, I shall return to a number of issues left unresolved in the second chapter.

Chapter 4: Bonhoeffer's Ethics as Virtue Ethical

Having thus addressed reasons one might not think of Bonhoeffer's *Ethics* as being virtue ethical, I shall turn to the evidence that is suggestive that such a construal may be possible. One theological reason for considering this possibility is Bonhoeffer's treatment of sanctification. This is important, since in theological terms becoming virtuous is in some ways analogous with being sanctified, and his handling of this doctrine may give clues as to how close his thought is to virtue ethics. For this I shall attend not only to sections of the ethics manuscripts that deal with sanctification, but also to other works as they refer to this topic. Then I shall look at Bonhoeffer's overall concerns in the *Ethics* (providing a Christian foundation for ethics; offering a concrete ethic; taking seriously the historical context; attending to the relation of the Church to the world; and articulating structures of ethical life) to see how they accord with virtue ethics. With this understanding of how the overarching concerns relate to virtue ethics, I shall look at how two more specific themes might be related, namely his (implicit) anthropology, and his holistic conception of human life.

Having thus laid the groundwork for considering how Bonhoeffer's *Ethics* as a whole might be seen as related to virtue ethics, I shall turn my attention to particular themes that bear some resemblance: conformation, and "virtues" in Bonhoeffer's account.

Chapter 5: Mode of Ethical Discourse

If my analysis is correct (and if Bonhoeffer's own work is relatively consistent and coherent), I would expect there to be further evidence of some virtue-ethical aspects in Bonhoeffer's method of arguing when he addresses concrete issues. Therefore in chapter 5 I shall look at some examples of his treatment of specific topics to discover whether his way of engaging with them is indicative of a relation to virtue ethics.

Chapter 6: Divine Command and/or Virtue Ethics

If in the preceding chapters I have explored how Bonhoeffer's *Ethics* may be related to virtue ethics, in this chapter I am interested in how this strand relates to the other major (and more widely recognized) aspect within his *Ethics*, namely Barthian divine command ethics. First I shall trace the language and motif of divine command in the manuscripts to see both how pervasive this theme is, and what its connections are with Bonhoeffer's principal concerns. Then I shall look at two recognized commentators who have discussed (not "virtue ethics" but) conformation and command as the two major ethical motifs in Bonhoeffer's *Ethics*, Larry Rasmussen and Stephen Plant. My view here is both to assess their understandings of the relationship between these themes, and to articulate my own. As I attempt this, I shall look particularly at the issues that Bonhoeffer treats both in virtue-ethical and command language to see what difference the mode in which he was working made to the handling of his concerns. An appreciation of how the virtue-ethical and command-based elements of Bonhoeffer's thought are related should make it possible to speak more definitively (or at least less tentatively) about the place of virtue ethics in Bonhoeffer's *Ethics*.

Chapter 7: Conclusion

In this final chapter I shall first summarize the discoveries from the whole thesis, and then ask about the relevance for moral theology today. In thinking about this I shall consider briefly some of the characteristics of our current context, and suggest ways in which my understanding of virtue (and command) in Bonhoeffer's *Ethics* might be helpful.

2

Bonhoeffer and "Virtue Ethics"

2.1: Introduction

IN THE FIRST CHAPTER, I NOTED THAT IN LOOKING AT HOW BONHOEFfer's *Ethics* may be seen to be related to virtue ethics there are stronger and weaker claims that could be made. One strong positive claim would be to assert that Bonhoeffer was essentially engaged in what we now call virtue ethics, and that was his intention. At the other end of the spectrum of positive claims would be to suggest that, although one could not state that he intended to give a virtue-ethical account, there are elements that bear some resemblance to virtue ethics. Of course, it would also be possible to make a strong but negative claim, namely that Bonhoeffer did not see himself as a virtue ethicist, and that his *Ethics* does not contain any material that could be said to be related to virtue ethics.

My starting point in attempting to discover which claim is best substantiated is to ask whether the strong positive claim might be seen to have merits, in other words, "Did Bonhoeffer see himself as a virtue ethicist?" In seeking an answer to this, I shall first look at one suggestion that there is a case to be made for seeing the connection between "formation" (*Gestaltung*) and virtue ethics (2.2). However, as relating virtue ethics only to the theme of formation is not fully satisfying, I shall examine evidence from the manuscripts regarding his usage of the word "virtue" (*Tugend*) (2.3.1), his attitude to Thomas Aquinas and other Roman Catholic sources (2.3.2), his use of themes from classical philosophy (2.3.3), and his own statements regarding modes of ethical thinking (2.3.4). Finally, I shall look at how other commentators have approached the question of what form Bonhoeffer's *Ethics* take (2.4).

2.2: A Case for Connection

At least one theologian has suggested the possibility of linking Bonhoeffer's *Ethics* with virtue ethics. Nicholas Sagovsky said:

> Bonhoeffer discusses not only the theological ground for such [sc. responsible] action (focusing very much on Christology) but also such action as the outcome of the process of formation (*Gestaltung*). Bonhoeffer talks more in terms of character (cf Hauerwas) but his thought could be linked with the "virtue" ethics of MacIntyre and others at this point. "Responsible action" does not come out of nowhere. It comes from being "conformed to the image of Christ" through membership of the Church, reading Scriptures, meditation and committed action. It comes through formation of a Christian "conscience" (a knowledge and awareness of both God and reality). It is this which Bonhoeffer was seeking to teach and develop at Finkenwalde.[1]

There is only a hint at how Sagovsky sees a possible link between Bonhoeffer and virtue ethics being made: through the emphasis in the *Ethics* on formation and conformation. Undoubtedly, Bonhoeffer's work on this theme shows the central hallmark of virtue ethics: an emphasis on the nature of the ethical agent. Thus it would seem to be a fruitful avenue to explore, and one that has been suggested by at least one other commentator, Frederick Carney.[2]

Yet there are major drawbacks to a proposal for claiming a relationship to virtue ethics based on conformation: first, it would leave at least half of the manuscripts underrepresented; and secondly, it would be open to the possible charge that Bonhoeffer might have changed his mind about those concepts, since the later manuscripts feature ethics as formation less prominently.[3] Some who knew Bonhoeffer have said that

---

1. Sagovsky, "Bonhoeffer, Responsibility and Justice," point 11.

2. Carney, "Deciding in the Situation," 5. But note also his claim that Bonhoeffer's notion of formation in Christ shapes the character to make the agent "inwardly disposed to right decision in each situation," 4–5. This statement would seem to involve quite a variety of forms of ethical thought, and not just virtue.

3. There has been major debate on the relative disjuncture or continuity of Bonhoeffer's thought from his student days to his death. Advocates of distinct working periods include Müller, *Kirche zur Welt*; Godsey, *Theology*; and Dumas, *Reality*, 70. Those suggesting a higher degree of continuity include Burtness, *Shaping the Future*, 11–14; Hauerwas, *Performing the Faith*, 34; Ott, *Reality and Faith*, 65–66; Pfeifer, "Rechtfertigung," 178; and Plant, *Bonhoeffer*, 9, 36 n. 12. However, see also Nickson's view that such discussion assumes "a lineal view of development" that offers "unnuanced

he was an "impulsive thinker," taking ideas up only to discard them after a time.[4] Thus if one were to make a case for a correlation of the predominant orientation of Bonhoeffer's ethics to virtue ethics on this basis, it might be difficult to defend, even if the theme of formation and conformation might be seen as related to character.

2.3: The Evidence from Bonhoeffer

A more important starting point is to ask how Bonhoeffer himself might have seen his ethics and virtue ethics. At all events it seems apparent that Bonhoeffer did not see himself as a virtue ethicist. At one level, this statement is patently obvious, so much so that it ought not even be made, since in Bonhoeffer's time one could hardly have spoken meaningfully of "virtue ethics" or a "virtue ethicist." Of course anyone acquainted with classical philosophy would have encountered a variety of forms of ethics that include an understanding of virtues and their centrality to the moral or good life. Nonetheless, the term would not have been used; it is anachronistic and as such it may seem improper for use in the context of this study. However, it is meaningful to anyone writing about this subject in the wake of Alasdair MacIntyre's *After Virtue*, and since it would be cumbersome and perhaps inaccurate (as one would need to make reference to classical philosophy as well as Roman Catholic moral theology if not specifically Thomism) to try to formulate this in ways Bonhoeffer and his contemporaries might have spoken, it is a convenient shorthand that I shall use without quotation marks.

2.3.1: Bonhoeffer and Virtue (Tugend)

Given that Bonhoeffer did not write (and could hardly have written) about virtue ethics, to discover his attitude towards an ethic that sees virtue(s) as having a large role to play, it is necessary to look at his usage of the concept of virtue (*Tugend*). In the first manuscript he wrote, "Christ, Reality and

---

categorisation," and her assertion that "Bonhoeffer's thought is too complex and rich" to admit of such treatment, *Freedom*, 6. My own view is that there are of course developments in his life and thought which result in changes in emphasis. However, there is a high degree of continuity in terms of themes which interest him and basic theological convictions.

4. See for example the excerpts of Barth's letter to P. W. Herrenbrück, reprinted in *World Come of Age*, 89–90; and Gerhard Jacobi's comments in *I Knew Dietrich Bonhoeffer*, 72.

the Good: Christ, Church and World," Bonhoeffer refers only obliquely to virtue, but in such a way as to make it seem worthy almost of ridicule: "Wanting to be good, so to speak, as an end in itself, a life-calling, succumbs to the irony of unreality; out of the genuine striving towards the good comes the pushiness of the paragon of virtue [*Tugendbold*]. The good in itself is no independent theme of life; as such that would be the maddest Don Quixotry."[5] It is clear from Bonhoeffer's letters as well as the number of references in the *Ethics* to *Don Quixote* that Bonhoeffer does not think of the title character as a figure of fun.[6] Yet his speaking of the "irony of unreality" and "pushiness" (*Streberei*) in relation to a paragon of virtue makes clear that he cannot take seriously an ethic that has as its starting point the desire to be good. Indeed, the opening words of the first manuscript he wrote demand a rethinking of the very questions that might lead one to consider Christian ethics: neither the question of being good nor of doing good will suffices, but only the question concerning the will of God (31). Or again, "Not that I should become good, nor that the condition of the world should be improved through me is of final importance, rather that the reality of God proves itself everywhere to be the ultimate reality" (32).

A little further in this first manuscript Bonhoeffer states, "All questioning about my own being good or the goodness of the world becomes impossible without first asking the question of the goodness of God. For what meaning could being good have for human or world without God? But since God as the ultimate reality is none other than the One who testifies, bears witness to himself and reveals himself as God in Jesus Christ, the question about the good can only find its answer in Christ" (33).

Thus, once again the starting point to be assumed for virtue ethics is discounted and we are directed towards the person of Christ. Moreover, since all of reality is also given a Christological definition, the desire to be good must become "a longing for that which is real in God" (35). In these passages it is clear that Bonhoeffer rejects what one might naturally assume to be foundational for virtue ethics, the questions of what the good is for humans, and of how a human can be or become good. This is no doubt part and parcel of his agreement with Karl Barth's rejection of "religion" as being a human method of trying to reach God, and his insistence on discussing the Christian faith instead in terms of God's initiative towards

---

5. *DBW* 6:35. In the following, the page references in brackets will refer to this edition.

6. See *DBW* 10:122; Bethge, *Biography*, 101, 716, 720, and 845.

humanity through revelation in Christ.[7] In the case of ethics, Bonhoeffer insists that the good is discovered by looking to Christ and seeing all reality in him.

In the manuscript "Ethics as Formation," Bonhoeffer states, "The most shining virtues of the apostate are night-black compared to the darkest weaknesses of the faithful" (63).[8] It is notable that in this example "virtues" are not necessarily positive (and they are not contrasted with "vices" but rather "weaknesses"). They obviously relate to things that would in other contexts be viewed positively, but when possessed by "the apostate" they are "night-black." That is to say, for Bonhoeffer it would seem that character traits are not in themselves meritorious (or worthy of censure) but can only be assessed in relation to Christ, since both "faithful" and "apostate" relate to the response of faith (or lack thereof), rather than moral character as such.

Likewise, in the manuscript "The Love of God and the Decay of the World," written about two and a half years later, Bonhoeffer states, "The Pharisee himself can recognize himself only in his virtues and vices, but not in his being, his falling away from the Source" (318). Again in this passage, character traits are not seen as positive or negative in themselves, rather the focus on them is treated as symptomatic of a falling away from Christ, since Bonhoeffer considered the knowledge of good and evil to be a product of the Fall and part of the division of humans from our Creator. In a sense it would seem that for Bonhoeffer virtues and vices are superficial, merely human characteristics; the depth and reality of a person's being cannot be discussed in those terms, but only in her relationship to Christ.

In a more oblique reference to the classical virtue of temperance, Bonhoeffer states, "Whoever undertakes in his *utterly own freedom* to stand in the world, whoever values the necessary deed as greater than the purity of his own conscience and reputation, whoever is prepared to sacrifice an unfruitful principle to a fruitful compromise or an unfruitful wisdom of moderation to a fruitful radicalism, he should take care that precisely his presumed freedom does not finally cause his downfall" (65,

---

7. See e.g., Karl Barth, *On Religion*, especially the translator's comments 6–7, and 9-10.

8. Intriguingly, Bonhoeffer uses "apostate" in the singular but "faithful" in the plural, leaving open the possibility that the singular was an intended reference to Hitler. See also *DBW* 6:125, where Bonhoeffer speaks of repentance as being necessary not simply for occasional mistakes and transgressions, but for "falling away," a cognate of the word used in his discussion of apostasy above and also in my next paragraph.

his emphasis). Bonhoeffer's concern here is obviously to address a mode of ethical thinking—namely, acting responsibly in one's own freedom, not relying on any form of justification or assurance of handling correctly, i.e., the position closest to what seems to be Bonhoeffer's own—so it may be wise not to make too much of his treatment of "moderation," or temperance. (It is noteworthy that not even this understanding of how one might act ethically was deemed by Bonhoeffer to be able to stand the strains of the times.) Yet it is also worth noticing that, like the purity of one's conscience or reputation and an unfruitful principle, moderation is something that the person acting in utter freedom (and responsibility) may have to abandon. It may be called "wisdom," but it could yet be "unfruitful"—an understanding of moderation that is at some remove from Thomas's, for example.

In a more direct example from this manuscript, Bonhoeffer asserts, "One or another will reach a refuge from the public debate by escaping into a *private virtuosity*. He doesn't steal, doesn't murder, doesn't commit adultery, he does good according to his ability. But in his voluntary renunciation of public life he knows how to keep precisely within the permissible boundaries which protect him from conflict. Thus he must close his eyes and ears to the injustice around him. Only at the cost of self-deception can he keep his private blamelessness pure from the defilement of responsible action in the world" (66, his emphasis).[9] Like the previous citation, this comes within a long passage that describes a variety of ethical positions and how they failed to meet the challenges posed by the extreme situation in Nazi Germany. Only "private virtuosity" follows the responsible act in freedom, and it, like all that preceded it, is weighed and found wanting in the balance. For all the good things that can be said about private virtuosity, the "sins of omission" outweigh such that the one whose focus is on this cannot come to peace; she will be destroyed by the restlessness caused by what she has failed to do, or she will become the most hypocritical of all Pharisees (66). Thus it would seem that, again, Bonhoeffer utterly rejects an ethic based on the focus on the character of the agent, this time stating the concern that it allows, so to speak, a veneer of good to cover a refusal to address or prevent evil.

In a similar vein, in the manuscript "History and the Good," written some two years later, Bonhoeffer states, "The world remains the world *because* it is the world which in Christ is loved, judged and reconciled. No one has the commission to bypass [*überspringen*, literally 'to leap over,'

---

9. See also *DBW* 7:142, where he speaks of virtuosity (*Tugendhaftigkeit*) pejoratively.

meaning to omit] the world and to make of it the kingdom of God. Nonetheless, pious indolence is not thereby supported, which leaves the wicked world to its fate and saves only its own virtue" (266, his emphasis). Once again, "virtue" is used to denote something that seems to be good, but allows a multitude of evils to go unchecked.

In one of the last manuscripts to be written, "The 'Ethical' and the 'Christian' as a Theme," written in early 1943 just before his arrest, Bonhoeffer mentions the Greek myth of Hercules at the crossroads, saying that before God's command the person is not like this, constantly wrestling with the decision about what is right (388).[10] According to the editorial footnote, the legend by Prodicos, a contemporary of Socrates, actually concerns the decision for "virtue" and against "vice."[11] Clearly what is most at stake in this passage is Bonhoeffer's rejection of any notion of permanent ethical conflict. Yet it is at least worth pondering that he is happy to exchange the concept of choosing the path of virtue with that of the right decision. It could be argued that the terms are synonymous for him; but equally it could be that he so rejects the language of virtue and vice that he reformulates the fable in the more acceptable term of decision.

Thus it can be seen in these examples that Bonhoeffer first of all rejects the standard starting points of virtue ethics, the question of the human good or of how one might be/become good. However, it is important to note that it is precisely the element of founding ethics on what is human rather than on God's revelation in Christ that Bonhoeffer rejects.[12] Moreover, he does not use the word "virtue" positively, rather at times even pejoratively, such as when he speaks of private virtuosity. Yet virtue is mostly seen simply as irrelevant, since what matters is Christian faithfulness. It remains, however, a question whether Bonhoeffer's negative associations with "virtue" necessarily correspond to virtue ethics. For instance,

---

10. For a contemporary echo of this, see Pincoffs, "Quandary Ethics."

11. Note 70. Barth made reference to this fable in *KD* II/2, 573–74. Barth also does not speak of "virtue and vice" but of "good and evil." For literature regarding Barth's influence on Bonhoeffer, see Godsey, "Barth and Bonhoeffer"; de Lange, *Waiting for the Word*, ch. 4; Marsh, *Reclaiming Dietrich Bonhoeffer*, ch. 1; Pangritz, *Karl Barth*; Pfeifer, "Rechtfertigung," especially 187–88; Plant, *Bonhoeffer*, 71, 181; Rasmussen, *Significance*, especially 96–102; Torrance, *God and Rationality*, 56; Webster, *Word and Church*, ch. 3; Tödt, "Glauben in einer religionslosen Welt"; and Wüstenberg, "Theology and Philosophy."

12. See also "Gibt es eine christliche Ethik?," *DBW* 11:303–13, where he also rejects any attempt to base ethics "in the closed human sphere," and apparently wants to start rather with the forgiveness of sins, 308 n. 20. This remains a controversial issue; see Honecker, "Theologische Ethik."

is a virtue-based ethic necessarily a private one? Or, how do virtues and vices relate to the hypocrisy that he calls "Phariseeism"? Or, is virtue ethics necessarily an example of humans trying to reach God? These are questions that must be explored in the next chapter.

Another avenue internal to Bonhoeffer's thought for exploring the possibility that his ethics may be close to what is now called virtue ethics, is to consider how he responded to the form of virtue ethics that was propagated in his time, at least in some quarters: Thomism.

2.3.2: *Thomas Aquinas and other Roman Catholic Sources*

As is common in Bonhoeffer's writing, in the *Ethics* he only rarely mentions the names of his "dialogue partners," those thinkers whose ideas he wishes to discuss, challenge, refine or even refute. Thus to gain a picture of how Bonhoeffer viewed Thomas Aquinas it will not suffice to look for his name in the text.[13] In the first manuscript Bonhoeffer wrote, "Christ, Reality and the Good," he states, "In high scholasticism the realm of the natural is subordinated to the realm of grace; in Pseudo-Lutheranism the autonomy of the orders of this world are proclaimed over against the law of Christ; in 'enthusiasm,' the church of the elect goes into battle against the enmity of the world for the establishment of God's kingdom on earth" (41–42). Although the editorial footnote points to Thomas Aquinas as the foremost representative of high scholasticism, Bonhoeffer's comment at the start of this sentence may or may not be directed against him.[14] If it was, it is plain that Bonhoeffer found Aquinas's thought inadequate to correct a fallacious understanding of the relationship of the Church to the world. However, it is also clear that he finds fault also in "Pseudo-Lutheranism" and in "enthusiasm," traditions with which he was more closely connected.

Another oblique reference, also from this earliest period of Bonhoeffer's work on the *Ethics*, is in "Inheritance and Decay," where he writes, "Luther's great discovery of the freedom of the Christian and the Catholic false doctrine of the essential goodness of the person both end in the divinization of humans" (114).[15] Again, this may well be an indirect reference

---

13. The editors of the *Werke* helpfully give information where they see a conversation with Aquinas. See also Harvey, "Augustine and Thomas Aquinas."

14. *DBW* 6:41 n. 33. If Bonhoeffer does refer here to Thomas, Bonhoeffer's interpretation of Thomas's understanding of the relation of nature and grace is questionable: grace "perfects" nature, but that need not be seen in a hierarchical way. Cf. *ST* I/1, 8 ad 2. See also the editorial comments *ST* I, p. 220.

15. Bonhoeffer is making a historical point here rather than a philosophical one.

to Thomas Aquinas and his view of humans after the Fall.[16] As before, the question at hand is not whether Bonhoeffer is right in this characterization of Roman Catholic teaching, but whether the view he expresses gives any clue as to his attitude to Thomist virtue ethics. The answer would seem to be that if virtue ethics depends on an apparently optimistic view of anthropology, Bonhoeffer would reject it.

Even where one might assume Bonhoeffer would be more in accord with Thomas (in his discussion of "The Natural," written in the winter of 1940–41), he does not endorse Aquinas's views. At the outset of this manuscript, he states, "The concept of the natural has fallen into disrepute in Protestant ethics. Among some it was utterly lost in the darkness of general sinfulness; among others it received conversely the shine of primeval creatureliness. Both were an evil abuse, which had the result that the concept of the natural departed completely out of Protestant thinking and was left to Catholic ethics" (163). In this example Bonhoeffer is not addressing Roman Catholic moral theology, but trends within Protestant theology. Nonetheless, it seems fair, given Bonhoeffer's comments above regarding the more optimistic view of human nature he found in Roman Catholic teaching, to suggest that he would hold that Aquinas was like those "others," for whom the natural was confused to some degree with the original created state. Furthermore, as the editors suggest, if he had discussed the position commonly held in Roman Catholic teaching, he is most likely to have disliked the pairing of natural with supernatural, and the lack of explicit Christology in the treatment (163 n. 4).

In another reference to Roman Catholic teaching Bonhoeffer writes, "Reason perceives the general in what is given, thus also the given natural, as reason perceives it, is a general one. It encompasses the whole of human nature. Reason recognizes the natural as of a general law, independent of the possibility for empirical testing" (167). Here Bonhoeffer inserts one of his rare footnotes: "What has been said differs from the Catholic theory in that in our view 1) reason is seen as involved in its entire compass with the Fall, whereas in Catholic dogmatics it has retained an essential integrity, 2) that reason according to Catholic teaching is also able to grasp the formal determination of the natural, which relates again to the first point." This point might be seen as a subset of the point above, and at the very least it

---

He considered that Christians of the Protestant churches as well as the Roman Catholic had for different reasons developed wrong understandings of humanity.

16. See *ST* I–II 17, 9 ad 3, which refers to nature being left to itself after the sin of our first forebears.

must be seen as related to the fact that Bonhoeffer sees the Roman Catholic view of human nature as less affected by the Fall than is the case in his own estimation. Yet how one perceives the human capacity for reasoning will affect to a large degree how one approaches any form of thinking, and it would seem that Bonhoeffer disagrees fundamentally with Aquinas on this point.

One area where he does agree, even explicitly, with Aquinas is to be found in dealing with one of the issues treated as part of the natural life, namely slavery. Bonhoeffer notes that Thomas considered not the name of slavery but the reality as to be condemned, saying, "There are historical forms of slavery which better protected the essential freedom of humanity than certain social institutions in which the term 'slavery' is disdained but in reality the total enslavement of so-called free persons exists" (213).[17]

The final example of a positive view of Thomas is to be found only in the brief introduction to a section Bonhoeffer began to write, "The natural rights of intellectual life." Here he states, "There are three fundamental forms of relationship of intellectual life to reality: judging, acting, and enjoying. In these the person comes before reality, to which he himself belongs, in freedom, and proves thereby his humanity" (216-17). This tantalizing fragment would suggest that Bonhoeffer may well have been following Josef Pieper's treatment of temperance, in which he set out a Thomist notion of this cardinal virtue. Bonhoeffer possessed this volume and the relevant passage shows both underlining and an exclamation mark in the margin.[18] If so, it is instructive that he intended to draw on a Thomist thinker for this planned section, the theme of which clearly remained important for him in prison when he wrote that only a Christian could enjoy music in such times.[19]

This fact leads directly to Bonhoeffer's wide range of reading generally and, of specific interest here, within the domain of Roman Catholic theology, both traditional and contemporary sources.[20] These include Jacques Maritain, Romano Guardini as well as Pieper, which, as the editors

---

17. *ST* II–II 57, 3 ad 2; II–II 104, 5 and 6 ad 2.

18. *DBW* 6:476. Pieper, *Four Cardinal Virtues*, 166. *ST* II–II 141, 4 ad 3. The passage in question occurs in Pieper's chapter on chastity and states, "That Christian teaching does not exclude sensual enjoyment from the realm of the morally good (as against the merely 'permissible') does not need to be specifically stated."

19. *DBW* 8:291

20. See Plant, *Bonhoeffer*, 39–40, where he notes that Bonhoeffer read others' theology "less for its own sake than for the contribution it might make to thinking through the problems he faced."

say, "might have encouraged Bonhoeffer towards that 'brave, powerful grasp of the old and new Catholic wisdom,' which in the Protestant theology of those days was uncommon" (424).[21] The editors go on to speak of Bonhoeffer's "critical honoring" of Roman Catholic moral theology in taking up the concept of the natural. Rightly they note that his work in this manuscript was "topically urgent," for example his comments regarding euthanasia.

It is known from Bonhoeffer's letters that he was not only working in the Benedictine monastery at Ettal for the second period of his writing (November 17, 1940–February 1941), but that he had access to their library, and had regular conversations with the abbot and others there.[22] Notably, Bonhoeffer wrote to Bethge on January 20, 1941, "I find Catholic ethics in many ways very instructive and more practical than ours. Until now one always chalked it up against them as 'casuistry.' Today one is thankful for much, especially concerning my current topic [sc. euthanasia]" (460).[23] Just a few weeks later he wrote to Bethge again, "now I'm working on the question of marriage [the choice of spouse, sterilization, contraception]—here the Catholic ethic is indeed almost unbearably legalistic" (460).[24]

Comparing the comments from these two letters it is quite clear that Bonhoeffer was evaluating carefully whatever sources he consulted. Yet precisely because one cannot know which volumes in the monastic library he read, nor the content of his conversations with the brothers and abbot, the full extent of his familiarity with Roman Catholic sources will probably never be ascertained. What is quite clear is that Bonhoeffer had a broader familiarity with and respect for Roman Catholicism in general and moral theology in particular than most Protestants of his time.[25] In places he disagrees strongly with what he perceives to be Thomas's teachings (optimism regarding human nature); and in other places he borrows

21. The internal quote comes from one of Bonhoeffer's preparatory notes for his work on ethics, *Zettelnotiz 76*.

22. See the Timetable in *DBW* 6:459. See also Lovin's comments regarding Roman Catholic influence, "Biographical Context," 45; and Bethge's account, *Biography*, 59–62, 237, 721, and especially 724–25 but also more negatively, 101–2.

23. *DBW* 16:114.

24. *DBW* 16:138–39.

25. Cf his wanting "together with Luther, to know that the sound core [of Roman Catholic theology] which is in danger of being lost to us, is preserved in Protestant dogmatics," *DBW* 1:121. See also his approving claim that the right understanding of the mandates would create a connection to the Middle Ages, *DBW* 8:291. See further Feil, *Theology*, 25–26.

freely (euthanasia, intellectual life). Thus one could not demonstrate any clear link between Bonhoeffer's *Ethics* and virtue ethics on the basis of Roman Catholic influence.

Yet before summarily dismissing the possibility of Bonhoeffer's *Ethics* being seen in relation to virtue ethics, some questions must be explored: does a virtue ethic demand a view of human nature in general and human reason in particular which Bonhoeffer would perceive as giving too little account of the Fall? and is virtue ethics actually legalistic?

2.3.3: *Classical Philosophy*

However, as noted above, Roman Catholic moral theology is not the only source from which Bonhoeffer would have had contact with virtue ethics. Given his upbringing he will of course have had familiarity with Greek and Roman classics. Indeed, Bonhoeffer shows such familiarity in writing about suicide in his treatment of "the natural life," where he notes that Aristotle considered its attempt to be a punishable offence (195).[26] Yet in the same sentence Bonhoeffer suggests that the one who would take her own life is hardly likely to be persuaded by that fact or by the arguments Aristotle offers. Thus it would appear that although Bonhoeffer is aware of Aristotle's views, he is not greatly swayed by them.

Bonhoeffer quotes Aeschylus with more affirmation in his treatment of responsibility in "History and the Good": "The action of a responsible person takes place in the bond (which alone is completely liberating) to God and neighbors as they encounter me in Jesus Christ; it takes place thereby wholly in the region of relativities, wholly in the twilight which is spread by the historical situation over good and evil; it takes place amid the innumerable perspectives in which every given appears. It [responsible action] does not have simply to choose between right and wrong, good and evil, but between right and right, wrong and wrong. 'Right wrestles with right,' said Aeschylus" (284).[27] Here it is interesting that Bonhoeffer is developing a theme that some consider to be most central and original to his ethics, responsible action, and almost as a throw-away offers a supporting quote from classical literature.[28] Yet it is not clear that this represents an

---

26. Cf *NE*, III.viii.2. Regarding suicide, see 5.1.5 (151–53).

27. Aeschylus *Libation Bearers* 109, line 461, referenced in *DBW* 6:284, note 123.

28. See for example Godsey and Kelly, eds., *Ethical Responsibility*; Elshtain, "Freedom and Responsibility"; and Sagovsky, "Responsibility and Justice."

influence on his thinking so much as a classical adornment to thoughts already formulated.

Likewise, the theme of *"suum cuique"* in "The Natural Life" is a concept that comes from classical philosophy, to be found in Plato and Cicero, among others.[29] Here his treatment of the classical material is more positive, finding a "relative correctness" in the notion, seeing a particular importance in the fact that "to each his own" not only gives rights to one but insists that rights are given to all, to the collective and to the individual (175–76). The consideration of the rights of the individual and the rights of society was of particular importance in Bonhoeffer's context because the National Socialist ideology recognized only those of the collective, whether the state or the German "race." From the time of the enactment of the emergency laws of 1933 individuals were no longer accorded any rights.

So in all of these examples Bonhoeffer shows awareness of classical themes, but is not obviously influenced by them. Instead he critiques them all using biblical evidence and systematic theology.[30]

Yet it must be noted that classical themes appear not only in the form of teachings but in the form of myths and plays. In a passage about whether it is appropriate to see human life in terms of tragedy, Bonhoeffer refers to the characters of Greek tragedy: Creon, Antigone, Jason, Medea, Agamemnon and Clytemnestra. Their lives, he claims, are tragic in the sense that they are subject to differing, irreconcilable laws and so will necessarily suffer for breaking the one or the other. This is a view of human life that he stoutly rejects, upholding rather the notions of simplicity and reconciliation rather than tragic conflict, and the teaching of election to become children of God rather than the notion of the demise of humans under the triumph of gods (265).

In another reference to figures from classical mythology mentioned briefly above in discussing virtue (2.3.1), Bonhoeffer states, "Before God's command, the human is not permanently Hercules at the crossroads, not the one eternally wrestling to reach the right decision, the one tearing himself apart in the conflict of duties, repeatedly failing and beginning anew; and God's command itself does not always appear only in those great, moving crisis moments of life, experienced in heightened awareness"

---

29. *DBWE* 6:181 n. 39 directs the reader to *Institutes of Justinian* 1.1; Plato's *Republic* 1.331e; and Cicero's *De Officiis* 1.5.15 and *De Finibus* 5.23.67.

30. For further examples of classical writings and themes to which Bonhoeffer alludes, see *DBWE* 6:201 n. 107; *DBW* 6:192 n. 88; and *DBW* 6:197 n. 101, which focuses on Augustine more than on the Roman legend of Lucretia, which he mentions.

(388–89). This is another example that he uses negatively, to say that this picture does not convey accurately what he believes to be human life (including the ethical) before God.

Thus it can be said that Bonhoeffer draws frequently on classical thinking, myths and dramas, but not in such a way as to suggest that they are formative or even especially influential in his conception of ethics. Such sources are scrutinized in the light of Christ and at least as often as not found wanting. Indeed, it is probably fair to suggest of the figures from legends or tragedies that they occur no more frequently than Don Quixote, or characters from Goethe or Shakespeare—well known, evocative figures who can represent a variety of ethical situations or outlooks useful for illustrating Bonhoeffer's thought.[31] At all events, they hardly represent a cryptic form of virtue ethics. What then, one must ask, was the form of ethics Bonhoeffer was expounding?

2.3.4: Bonhoeffer and Modes of Ethical Thinking

Bonhoeffer does not set out a methodology for doing ethics, nor does he situate his account within any particular mode of envisaging theological ethics. In fact, he seems to reject any set form of conceiving the ethical life. The opening of the manuscript "Ethics as Formation," written sometime between summer and November 1940, thus one of the first manuscripts written, sets out a variety of types of ethical figures, some of which were noted above (2.3.1). One after another, they are all seen to be unable to cope with the complex and startling ethical demands of Nazi Germany. Neither the rational person, nor the one holding fanatically to principles, nor the person of conscience, nor of duty, not even the one acting in free responsibility, nor the one trying to rescue a private virtuosity is able to stand (64–66). Yet at the end of this passage he writes, "Who could want to calumniate such failure and breakdown? Who wouldn't recognize himself here or there as complicit? Rationality, ethical fanaticism, conscience, duty, free responsibility, quiet virtue are goods and attitudes of high humanity. It is the best who are sunk with all that they can do and all that they are" (66). It is clear that Bonhoeffer does not reject these modes of ethical thought and behavior lightly, nor with a desire to set up some model of his own. He is doing nothing short of claiming that any system must be inadequate when tested in such an extreme situation. Thus one might not only say that

---

31. See Wendl, *Homiletik*, 199–204 on the influence on Bonhoeffer of various novels.

Bonhoeffer did not see himself as a virtue ethicist, but that he also did not see himself as representing any other strand of ethical thinking. Nonetheless, it is important to consider such things as he did write about ethical theory before reaching any firm conclusions.

2.3.4.A: ABSTRACT ETHICS

The first thing to note is that Bonhoeffer is insistent throughout the various manuscripts that ethics needs to be concrete, not abstract, or a matter of principle. Thus in the first manuscript he wrote, "Christ, Reality and the Good," he sees God in Christ as the ultimate reality such that, "[A]ll seeing and recognizing of things and laws without Him becomes an abstraction, a tearing away from the source and goal" (33, his capitalization).[32]

In the next manuscript he wrote, "Ethics as Formation," he takes up this theme again:

> Not that which could be good once for all can and should be said, but rather *how Christ can win form among us today and here*. The attempt to say what may be good once for all has always failed in itself. Either the statements became so general and formal that they no longer held any substantive meaning, or else, through the undertaking to consider and treat the breadth of all imaginable meanings, and thus to say in advance what might be good in every conceivable case, one slipped into such an unmanageable casuistry that neither the general nor the concrete receive their due. A concrete Christian ethic is beyond formalism and casuistry; for while formalism and casuistry proceed from the battle of the good with the real, the Christian ethic can take as its starting point the accomplished reconciliation of the world with God in the person Jesus Christ, the acceptance of the real humanity by God. (86–87, Bonhoeffer's emphasis)

Thus in these early manuscripts, Bonhoeffer consistently and repeatedly rejects abstract ethics and insists on concrete, and it is apparent that when he speaks of the abstract he means that not only in conceptual terms but theological as well: the abstract is not merely whatever is general or notional, but anything that is not understood in its relation to Jesus Christ.

The issue of abstraction or concretion appears again in the following manuscript, "Guilt, Justification, Renewal," written in 1941: "Since [the

---

32. This is the tenor of much of this manuscript. See also *DBW* 6:35; 39; and 54, and 61, where he treats the same theme christologically. On his insistence on concretion, see Feil, "Gottes Wort is konkret."

time] God became human in Christ, all thinking about humanity without Christ is unfruitful abstraction" (125). While Bonhoeffer is clearly more interested in the Christological dimension of anthropology than the notion of abstraction or concretion, this is nevertheless of interest in considering how he believed one should engage in ethical thinking. For ethical thinking must have some sort of anthropology at its foundation, whether elucidated or implicit, and according to Bonhoeffer, humanity is to be understood with reference to Christ, the model of what humanity is intended to be. Other forms of anthropology would be abstract rather than concrete.

More complex is his treatment of how the general might be distinguished from the abstract in the section on "*suum cuique*" in "The Natural Life": "His 'own,' that which belongs to each, is at the same time always different, unequal (but precisely not arbitrary!) and nevertheless objectively grounded in the naturally given and therefore general (but precisely not abstract/formal)" (175). Again, Bonhoeffer's direct concern is not to deal with the issue of the particular mode of ethical thought, but to show how his treatment of "to each his own," while general, does not violate his stated concern that ethics must be concrete rather than abstract, and he does this by distinguishing between the general and the abstract.

He does treat the question of methodological presuppositions more explicitly in "History and the Good":

> We have left behind us (with all that has been said already) the abstraction, largely dominating ethical thinking, of an isolated single person who has continually and exclusively to choose according to an absolute measuring rod of an in-and-of-itself good between this clearly recognized good and the equally clearly recognized evil. There is neither such an isolated individual, nor is that absolute measuring rod of an in-and-of-itself good available to us, nor do the good and the evil in history present themselves in their pure form. Moreover, the basic scheme of this abstraction misses in each of its parts precisely the specifically ethical problem. Whether an isolated individual, separated from his historical situation and his historical ties, can even been seen as ethically relevant is at the least very questionable, and in view of his lack of reality he is at all events an uninteresting theoretical borderline case; the absolute measuring rod of an in-and-of-itself good—assuming that such a thing even could be thought without contradiction—makes of the good a dead law, a Moloch, to whom all life and all freedom is sacrificed and which itself loses the obligation of a genuine "should" precisely

because it is a metaphysical in-and-of-itself-being construction which is without any essential relationship to life; the decision between the clearly recognized good and the clearly recognized evil excludes human perception itself from the decision, transplants the ethical into the battle between perception which is already oriented toward the good and the rebellious will, and it misses thereby that genuine decision in which the whole person, with perception and will, seeks and finds, only in the risk of action itself, the good in the ambiguity of an historical situation. The ethical is in this abstraction from life reduced to a static basic formula which tears the person out of historicity of his existence so as to place him in the vacuum of the purely private and the purely ideal. (246–47)

I quote this passage at length because it seems to represent a programmatic statement about the dangers of abstraction and the necessity of concrete thinking for ethics. It is telling that Bonhoeffer does not merely claim that an isolated individual does not exist; he questions whether such a person, if she did exist, could be seen as ethically relevant, with the implicit message that the person's "historical ties and situation" are important in any consideration of ethics. Another note of interest is his claim that, not only do good and evil not normally appear in their pure form, but also that there lies behind ethics that presume such to be the case an assumption that the ethical agent's perception is already focused on the good and that the ethical battle is then between her perception and her will. This division of the person he rejects, saying it is the whole person who must seek the good, though it will be ambiguous, and though she might only discover the good in acting. This account has some affinity with a Thomist understanding that a person requires prudence to perceive reality aright and to recognize what the salient features of any context are. Moreover, Bonhoeffer says that this abstraction leads either to a retreat into the private sphere (as expressed by his notion of "private virtuosity") or a kind of radical fanaticism of ideologies, both of which must finally and utterly fail because they are unreal. Thus he sees abstraction as ultimately in conflict with life, which the abstraction reduces to a negligible quantity (247–48).[33]

Furthermore, in "The 'Ethical' and the 'Christian' as a Theme," Bonhoeffer asserts that, "A timeless and placeless ethical discussion is lacking the concrete *authorization* which every genuine ethical discussion requires" (373, his emphasis). No one may claim such authorization for

---

33. See also *DBW* 6:250–52, 261, and 268 for christological emphasis and concretion.

The Virtue of Bonhoeffer's Ethics

herself; it must be received through her objective place in the world: "Thus it is the old and not the young, the father and not the child, the lord and not the knave, the teacher and not the pupil, the judge and not the accused, the governor and not the subject, the preacher and not the member of the congregation to whom the authorization for ethical discussion is given" (375).[34]

A few pages later he adds that when the ethical is understood as timeless and placeless, life falls apart into "an infinite number of unconnected time-atoms, just as human community dissolves into single reason-atoms." In this he asserts that both the formal/universal and existential approach to ethics are similar—both destroy connections and the concrete determinations of the ethical (376).[35]

In summary, it is clear that in rejecting abstraction Bonhoeffer was both affirming the centrality of Jesus Christ in moral theology, and insisting on the importance of the specific, the contingent, the particular, the historical in discussing ethics. It would seem that it was his intention to write an ethic that would be appropriate for Germany in the Nazi era, and in the time he hoped would come after, rather than an abstract account of the good, of human nature, of how humans are to choose the good, etc. Most of his arguments are essentially philosophical (broadly understood) in nature, though time and again he shows through biblical passages or systematic theology that this is a Christian viewpoint.[36] It is another question altogether as to how far he was able to write such an ethic, a question that is not uninteresting, but is also not germane to this exploration.[37] It is,

---

34. See also *DBW* 7:32, and 112, where he insists on the above/below in a play and a novel. See however Barth's critique of Bonhoeffer's patriarchalism, which surely refers to this insistence on above/below, *CD* III/4:23. Bonhoeffer himself struggled with the fact that as a young man he was unable to convince his elders in the church of the dangers he saw regarding Nazism. Nonetheless, he upholds the principle. See Bethge's account, *Biography*, 325–26. See also Bonhoeffer's letter to Barth explaining his hesitance to believe that Bonhoeffer was right in opposing the views of his elders, *DBW* 13:13–14.

35. See also *DBW* 6:381, relating to concretion and the command of God. See 116 n. 44, and 179–80 regarding concretion and authorization for ethical speech.

36. For literature regarding Bonhoeffer and philosophy, see Feil, *Theology*, 17; Feil, "Die Zukunft der philosophischen Theologie"; Frick, *Bonhoeffer's Intellectual Formation*; Wüstenberg, "Philosophy"; Marsh, *Reclaiming*, ch. 3; and Köster, "Nietzsche als verborgener Antipode."

37. There is indeed some irony in the frequency with which he states the need for concrete ethics, given the relatively brief passages which address concrete issues. Here the fragmentary nature requires circumspection, though I am surprised that this is not discussed more in the literature. See, for instance, Hauerwas, *Performing the Faith*,

Bonhoeffer and "Virtue Ethics"

however, important to look carefully at what Bonhoeffer wrote about abstract, theoretical ethics and his own insistence on the concrete for at least two reasons. First, given the number of times he deals with the subject, it is clearly deeply important to him, and if one is to understand his ethics it is necessary attend to his concerns. Secondly, the question must be explored, whether Bonhoeffer's arguments against abstract ethics should be seen as a reason to reject the possibility that there might be a close link between his ethics and virtue ethics. This is a question to which I shall return in the next chapter.

2.3.4.B: SYSTEMS

Another issue regarding modes of envisaging ethics, and not perhaps unrelated to the concern for concrete ethics, is Bonhoeffer's stated dislike of systems: "The academic question of an ethical system appears to be the most superfluous of all questions" (62). Indeed in the various manuscripts, one of the leitmotifs is that the concern of Christian ethics is to ask, "what is the will of God?," and this, he says, "is no system of rules firmly established in advance, but is always new and different in different life situations" (323).[38] The fact that Bonhoeffer is quite determined and consistent in rejecting any system for ethics may be used to suggest that it is wrong to see Bonhoeffer's conception of ethics as belonging to any "form" or "system" of ethics, whether virtue ethics, deontology or some other. Certainly his critique would make it implausible to link his ethics with the most systematic versions of any form of ethics, but as above, the question must be asked whether indeed virtue ethics need necessarily be construed as a type of system, another question to which I shall need to return in the next chapter.

2.3.4.C: NATURAL LAW

And finally, in terms of modes of ethical thinking, Bonhoeffer mentions natural law a few times, a subject to which he had been giving some thought in early 1940, when he wrote that the "doctrine of the lex natura

---

67, who assumes that abstraction (in the sense of theoretical discussion) was no real temptation for Bonhoeffer, rather than seeing his frequent reference to the need for concretion (and the dangers of abstraction) as being a warning to himself as much as a criticism of other accounts.

38. See also *DBW* 6:44, 85, and 374 for further examples of his rejection of a "system" of ethics.

33

which forms a basis for Catholicism presupposes several constructions of rights sui generis (family, economy, etc.), which all have their source in the Creator of the world."[39] This he contrasts with Barth's conception in which "all orders of the created world are related strictly to Christ."

Bonhoeffer only rarely mentions natural law in the ethics manuscripts, but where he does, he rejects it firmly: "God's relationship to the world is determined in Jesus Christ; a different relationship of God to the world except through Jesus Christ is unknown to us. Therefore there is also for the church no other relationship to the world but through Jesus Christ; that means the right relationship of the church to the world does not arise by proceeding from a natural law, rational law, universal human right, but *only* from the gospel of Jesus Christ" (358, Bonhoeffer's emphasis). In the following passage he concludes, "Therefore it is denied that the church could speak to the world on the basis of any perceptions shared with the world through rational or natural law, and thus temporarily excluding the gospel. The church of the Reformation, in distinction to the Catholic Church, can *not* do that" (359, Bonhoeffer's emphasis). These quotes come from notes that Bonhoeffer was preparing, "Regarding the possibility of a word of the church to the world," which were probably not intended for the book he was writing.[40] Yet it seems clear enough that they represent his thinking about natural law: the insights thus derived may be correct, but this is not the basis on which he believes the Protestant church should try to speak to the world.[41] Therefore, it will be necessary to explore whether virtue ethics must be dependent on natural law, which I shall address in the next chapter. However, before I turn to the many questions that have been raised here, it is important to examine what others have made of the mode of Bonhoeffer's ethical thinking.

2.4: An Analysis of Bonhoeffer's Commentators[42]

Perhaps it is well in keeping with Bonhoeffer's skepticism about the role of forms of ethics, but at all events it is the case that many of his commentators

39. Letter to Gerhard Leibholz, March 7, 1940, *DBW* 15:297–98.

40. See for instance Plant, "Sacrament," 82 n. 39. See also Feil, Nickson, and Godsey.

41. It will be interesting to bear this in mind in chapter 5, when I examine how Bonhoeffer argues when he does address concrete issues, to see if there is any discrepancy.

42. To attempt to speak of "Bonhoeffer's commentators" is somewhat daunting, given the vast amount written about him and his theology, both at the popular level and the more academic. For an overview of secondary literature until 1996, see Feil, ed. *Internationale Bibliographie*. For more recent literature, the Dietrich Bonhoeffer

do not discuss this question of his mode of ethical thought explicitly.[43] However, many do discuss the form Bonhoeffer's ethical thought takes, and I turn now to four different positions of such commentators: that he does not expound virtue ethics (2.4.1); that his stance approximates that of situation ethics (2.4.2); that he formulated a kind of "kingdom of God" ethics (2.4.3); and finally that conformation and command are the two modes of his ethical thought (2.4.4).

2.4.1: *Not Virtue*

2.4.1.A: HANS VAN HOOGSTRATEN

Few commentators have spoken directly about virtue ethics in relation to Bonhoeffer, which makes the comments of Hans van Hoogstraten interesting for this study. In an article about ethics and metaphysics, he looks at Bonhoeffer's poem written in prison, "Who am I?" and claims that, "[A]ccording to Bonhoeffer, we have to get rid of metaphysical ideas, including abstract catalogues of virtues. For even morality, coming to light in a doctrine of virtues, can be used as means to power. In Bonhoeffer's thought, justice is the most central biblical virtue, but it can only be practiced by representing Christ's powerlessness, not by the representation of his heavenly power! If we don't engage ourselves in the messianic movement, we play roles—like those indicated in the poem *Who Am I?* These kinds of roles are supported by a moral and metaphysical approach to reality."[44]

Here van Hoogstraten makes use of MacIntyre's "types" from *After Virtue*, the rich aesthete, manager and therapist, to show examples of roles to correspond with Bonhoeffer's musings in the poem, in which

---

Society publishes its *Jahrbuch* with annual updates. An interesting guide to interpretations of Bonhoeffer's theology is Haynes, *Bonhoeffer Phenomenon*.

43. What I intend with this somewhat cumbersome formulation is the kind of classification usual in ethics, such as virtue ethics, deontology, utilitarianism, etc. Some commentators (especially Rasmussen) refer to this as "methodology," which is less awkward than "mode of ethical thought," or strand, form, or style, or perhaps "ways of envisaging ethics" or "moral vision." However, "methodology" is not appropriate, because the question is about classification of thought pattern rather than the "method" for engaging in ethics. Hence I shall continue to use the more unwieldy formulations, and use them interchangeably. For examples of some commentators who do not explore this, see Feil, *Theology*, 84–89; Godsey, *Theology*, 171–72, 205, 267–68, 280; Nickson, *Bonhoeffer on Freedom*, 145;

44. Van Hoogstraten, "Metaphysics," 228.

Bonhoeffer contemplates the images of himself noted by others and contrasts these with his own impressions of himself.[45] Van Hoogstraten states, "Ultimately, MacIntyre pleads for a return to virtue. What he has in mind are principles like honesty and justice.... Here we encounter a problem: in order to perform virtues and to make them acceptable, we need a *concept of community*."[46] In this van Hoogstraten sees MacIntyre as pretending to make the world come of age, arguing for "a dominating structure, which neglects the development of modern time."[47] Against this, van Hoogstraten finds it more promising to accept a concept of the autonomous subject that *"is decentered inasmuch as there no longer exists metaphysical foundations,"* and if we do accept this premise, *"then we have to give up the claim of (all kinds of metaphysical) representation,"* such as truth, justice and God.[48] Here he notes that Hitler made claims to represent the German people, the nation, even God. So instead of allowing for any metaphysical representation, van Hoogstraten advocates the political practice of following Christ in being there for others, thus not speaking of Christ as heavenly King, Son of God, etc. "Existing for others, however, still contains a certain kind of representation—but in a different sense from the above criticized one. It means the representation of those people who are the victims of the system, speaking in the context of their narrative. This might be the most profound understanding of Bonhoeffer's decentering himself as a subject. I'm thine, O God."[49]

This article potentially raises serious objections to the intention of reading Bonhoeffer's *Ethics* as related in some way to virtue ethics. Are the virtues "metaphysical" constructs, dependent on highly problematic philosophical notions? If so, the whole enterprise would be dubious.

Yet there are important questions that need to be asked of van Hoogstraten. It seems doubtful that Bonhoeffer had MacIntyre-like types in mind in writing his poem, in which he is attributed with such characteristics as cheerfulness and calm, or restlessness and fearfulness, rather than any types, such as a manager or therapist. It may be that van Hoogstraten sees the reference to Bonhoeffer seeming like a squire stepping out of his

---

45. MacIntyre, *After Virtue*, ch. 3. That van Hoogstraten seems to use MacIntrye's "types" differently from MacIntyre is not of concern to this discussion, but it is a category mistake to see the iconic types MacIntyre believes modernity has brought forth as "roles" that one might "play."

46. Van Hoogstraten, "Metaphysics," 229, his emphasis.

47. Ibid., 229.

48. Ibid., 234, his emphasis.

49. Ibid., 235.

country home as a kind of "character," in MacIntyre's terms, though this would be misreading both MacIntrye and Bonhoeffer. Yet he does not argue this, and Bonhoeffer himself makes nothing further of the notion that he seems to have the power to command. The contrast drawn is between the attributes of cheerfulness and anger, freedom and being caged, calm and fearfulness.[50] Thus, it is surely mistaken to use the notion of roles, let alone "playing roles" in looking at Bonhoeffer's poem. Although Bonhoeffer wonders whether there is something hypocritical about the discrepancy he discerns between how others perceive him and how he sees himself, there is no suggestion that he accuses himself of "playing a role."[51]

Likewise, it is not clear that Bonhoeffer is actually saying anything here about "metaphysical ideas, including abstract catalogues of virtues." We have already seen that Bonhoeffer was concerned about abstraction and any attempt to construct a theoretical system of ethics valid for all times and places (2.3.4.a). Yet that is hardly the same thing as rejecting all "metaphysical ideas." We have also seen that he rejected theoretical definitions of the good that were metaphysical constructs of things in and of themselves (246–47, cited in 2.3.4.a), yet it is highly questionable to see the virtues as such constructs. Surely, for all his emphasis on the concrete, Bonhoeffer's theology and ethics would be impossible without any "metaphysical ideas" if these are understood to be things presumed to exist, albeit not tangibly. Indeed, there is no suggestion within the poem that Bonhoeffer sees the cheerfulness and calm that others saw in him, or the restlessness and fearfulness he found in himself to be invalid because of being "metaphysical ideas." It would seem, to the contrary, that although van Hoogstraten would like to rid us of such notions as truth, justice or God, Bonhoeffer plainly expects that there is a "truth" about him, whether one thing or the other, or perhaps some complex of "both," and he equally believes that there is "God," who knows that truth and to whom he belongs. It can be argued that Bonhoeffer would reject a "metaphysical" definition of any of these terms, if "metaphysical" means abstracted from Jesus Christ. Yet, can any definition be given to these terms that is not "metaphysical" if that is understood in terms of non-physical existence? For if not, it seems clear that Bonhoeffer was not saying that we had to get rid of them, and indeed, he seems happy enough to use many of them in his *Ethics*.

50. *DBW* 8:513–14.
51. *DBW* 8:513–14.

Another question that must be posed to van Hoogstraten is how he distinguishes between the "metaphysical representation" he obviously found dangerous in Hitler, and the representation (*Stellvertretung*) he recognizes as important in Bonhoeffer. He tells us that the latter "contains a certain kind of representation – but in a different sense," yet the difference he observes seems to have to do not with metaphysics, the thing he says he is criticizing, but with the intent behind the representation, i.e. whether the representation is used for one's own benefit or for others'. Thus it would seem that it is not metaphysical representation as such that he really critiques, but the unjust uses to which it might be (and has been) put.

A more trivial question, perhaps, is how van Hoogstraten can assert both that Bonhoeffer demands that we get rid of abstract catalogues of virtues, and that justice is for Bonhoeffer the most central biblical virtue. This could be an indication that van Hoogstraten himself would not necessarily conceive of virtues as abstract or metaphysical constructs.

Finally, it is important to ask the question how valid any of van Hoogstraten's comments can be for Bonhoeffer's thought more generally, given that they are premised on his reading of a single poem. If his reading of the poem were defective, all that follows would have no basis.[52] If Bonhoeffer's poem itself were unrepresentative of his thought in general—and it may be that this poem, while it is clearly a profound reflection on his prison experiences, should not be taken to be definitive for his perceptions on his own identity let alone ethical thought—it would again make any claims made on the basis of that poem insubstantial. Indeed, I have queried his reading of Bonhoeffer's poem, on the grounds that I cannot see that Bonhoeffer is dealing with types or playing roles. I have queried it too, since he suggests that Bonhoeffer wants to do away with metaphysical constructs such as truth, justice or God, and this does not accord either with the poem or the evidence we have seen in the *Ethics*.

Yet even if van Hoogstraten's method of argument is weak or flawed, it is worth asking whether he might not yet be right about Bonhoeffer's rejection of an "abstract catalogue of virtues." From what we have seen of Bonhoeffer's thoughts on abstract ethics, it seems plain that his critique would apply to any form, including abstract catalogues of virtues, if by this were meant one list of what is good for all times and places, or of attributes lacking any reference to Christ. It may well be that he would have seen Thomist virtues as expounded in his own times as being just that. Yet it

---

52. Indeed there are far better readings of this poem. See, e.g., Williams, "Suspicion of Suspicion"; and Ford, *Self*, 261. See also Northcott, "Who am I?".

remains to ask, in the next chapter, whether virtue ethics must necessarily mean abstract catalogues of virtues. For if not, van Hoogstraten's statements will not hold.

2.4.1.B: LARRY RASMUSSEN—EARLY

Another commentator who rejects the notion that Bonhoeffer's ethics may in some way be connected with virtue ethics is Larry Rasmussen, at least in an early article. He insists that for Bonhoeffer as well as for Luther, ethics begins and ends with justification by faith; it is not a way from vice to virtue, but from vices and virtues to grace.[53] In no way could one, or would I wish to, dispute Rasmussen's claim about the centrality of grace and justification by faith in Bonhoeffer's theology and ethics. Yet his statement begs the question: is virtue ethics opposed in some way to grace such that one must categorize Bonhoeffer's thought as not one but the other? If this were the case, then older Protestant notions of Roman Catholic theology (and ethics) as being based on "works righteousness" would be upheld, and no argument could possibly be made for seeing Bonhoeffer's ethics as being related in some way to virtue ethics. This is a question that must be explored in the next chapter.

2.4.2: *Situation Ethics*

2.4.2.A: HEINRICH OTT

Unlike those discussed thus far, Heinrich Ott sees Bonhoeffer as a kind of situation ethicist: "What happens to ethics at the collapse of 'natural law' or 'natural morality,' as a system of pronouncements to be applied to each case as it arises? . . . Instead, then of what is called a casuistic one, do we reach what is called a 'pure situation ethic'?"[54] Yet it is not a "pure" situation ethic that he perceives in Bonhoeffer, but one "that is non-casuistic but not formal, that has a concrete, namely a Christological, content," and one that he believes has "a strong biographical determination," to wit,

---

53. Rasmussen, "Ethik des Kreuzes," 141. Rasmussen also sees *Gestaltung* in terms of *imitatio Christi*, *Significance*, 147. For Luther's influence on Bonhoeffer, see also Gremmels, "Rechtfertigung," 81–99; Plant, "Sacrament," 50–51, 85; Plant, "Uses of the Bible," 334–36; Ford, *Self*, 248; Green, *Sociality*, 141–42, and 277; and Prenter, "Bonhoeffer and the Young Luther," 161–81.

54. Ott, *Reality and Faith*, 257–58. Regarding situation ethics, see Fletcher, *Situation Ethics*; and Cunningham, *Situationism*.

Bonhoeffer's participation in the assassination plot against Hitler, which put him beyond every norm or rule.[55] In short, he sees here a situation ethic with content, thus preventing an amorphous arrangement in which anything could be seen as ethically justified.[56] Moreover, it is a Christological content: "From the concrete situations of his life man receives the light of Jesus Christ the real. When he sees him he knows what he should do, and, on the other side, it is in activity that he sees him. Seeing and action become one."[57]

The question arises whether what Ott perceives is simply that Bonhoeffer's ethics cannot be classed either as deontology or as utilitarianism, the major types of ethical thought under discussion at the time. It would be thinkable to explore, for instance, how the unity of vision and action to which Ott refers might relate to themes in virtue ethics, and I shall want to do so in chapter four. Yet, perhaps because of the conjuncture of an almost invisibility of virtue ethics, and the rise at this time of situation ethics (which, it was hoped, would transcend the perceived limitations of each of the other types), Ott sees in Bonhoeffer a situation ethicist with Christological content. It may therefore be that Ott was classing Bonhoeffer with situation ethics simply because his proposals do not fit neatly with deontology or utilitarianism.[58]

2.4.2.B: Harold Lockley

Harold Lockley sees Bonhoeffer as engaged in a "search for a concrete ethic which is capable of incorporating the advantages of a situationist ethic on the one hand and a normative ethic on the other."[59] Lockley

---

55. Ott, *Reality and Faith*, 269. For literature about Bonhoeffer's life, see E. Bethge, *Biography*; Renate Bethge, "Bonhoeffer's Family"; Renate Bethge, "Memory of a Child"; *Love Letters*; Karl Bonhoeffer, "*Lebenserinnerungen*"; Gremmels and Pfeifer, *Theologie und Biographie*; Leibholz-Bonhoeffer, *Portrait of a Family*, and *Weihnachten*; Pangritz, "Theological Motives"; Stahlberg, "Dietrich Bonhoeffer," 102–4; and Wind, *A Spoke in the Wheel*.

56. Ott, *Reality and Faith*, 276–77. See also 274, where he refers to the mandates as "collective" situations.

57. Ibid., 442.

58. Of course, I may be faced with a similar charge: of trying to understand Bonhoeffer's ethics according to the most popular type of ethics of our era. It remains to be seen whether my analysis will prove more persuasive. See Glazener *The Cup of Wrath*, ch. 26 and 33 for an interesting example of an imagination seemingly incapable of envisaging an ethic which is neither strictly deontological nor relativistic. For other literary treatments, see, e.g., Berryhill, "Cup of Trembling"; and Auden, "Friday's Child."

59. Lockley, *Ethics*, 27.

also contends that "Bonhoeffer was looking for a middle way between the catholic treatment of the natural, which required the supernatural to perfect it, and the protestant attitude which tended to deprecate the natural when confronted with supernatural grace. The catholic way seemed to lead inevitably to naturalism, and the protestant to pietism – both of which Bonhoeffer rejected – so another way had to be found."[60]

The distinctive features of Bonhoeffer's ethics, so Lockley, include "occupying the middle ground between opposing positions" using a dialectical method and arriving at often paradoxical conclusions.[61] Indeed, following Ott, he considers it one of the strengths of Bonhoeffer's ethics that he gave content and the concretion of human experience and responsibility to situation ethics.[62] Sadly, Lockley does not argue the case for seeing Bonhoeffer's ethics as being a form of situation(ist) ethics, but merely asserts this.

2.4.2.c: Karsten Lehmkühler

Yet Ott and Lockley are not alone in perceiving Bonhoeffer's ethics in this way. Karsten Lehmkühler points to the extremity of Bonhoeffer's situation, where necessity might demand breaking commandments in the form of participating in the murder of a tyrant: "Bonhoeffer votes here most clearly for a situation ethic in the sense that the good is not established in advance, but rather proves itself only in concrete action."[63] This is, of course, a broad definition of situation ethics, and one obviously not dependent on Joseph Fletcher's conception, but on the basic foundation that the good, or right action is to be found only at the moment of action. Lehmkühler describes the process in this way: "the concrete judgment about one's action is laid in the hand of God because the responsible person lives 'through God's grace and judgment'. The foundation here is always the participation in Christ, such that one can well say: Christ himself shows the Christian in a concrete situation the good action."[64] Yet whether it is more helpful to call this a "situation ethic," or to call it by the more Barthian designation of "divine command ethics" is at least debatable, since Bonhoeffer insists not

60. Ibid., 29.
61. Ibid., 126.
62. Ibid., 133–34.
63. Lehmkühler, "Einwohnung," 329–30, citing *DBW* 6:267, all citations my translation. For other such accounts, see also Klassen, cited in McClendon, *Ethics*, 200; and Robinson's use of Bonhoeffer to support the "new morality," *Honest to God*, 106, 121.
64. Lehmkühler, "Einwohnung," 330, citing *DBW* 6:268.

on the primacy of one's reading of the situation, nor on a principle decided (such as love, in Fletcher's situation ethics) in advance, but on the question of the will of God.

Moreover, Lehmkühler's discussion of how God's will might become known does not ring true to Bonhoeffer's thought when he states that in every situation of ethical decision one may rely on the Holy Spirit to show what must be done, just as Jesus taught in Matthew 10:19–20 that at the time needed it will be given to one what one should say. Lehmkühler does not show how Jesus' words about testimony when under the threat of persecution might relate to "every situation of ethical decision"; nor does he show how this passage relates to Bonhoeffer's own conception of discovering the will of God, since Bonhoeffer himself does not cite this passage. All this makes unpersuasive his suggestion that Bonhoeffer's ethics is situationist.

2.4.2.D: JAMES BURTNESS

Against this construal of Bonhoeffer's ethics, James Burtness sees it not only as situationist, but also as consequentialist because of his repeated emphasis on taking responsibility for the future: "The emphasis upon the future places Bonhoeffer with those ethicists who concentrate on the consequences of actions rather than the motives out of which the actions are done. It is not the rightness of an action but the result of an action which commends it."[65] Nickson rightly criticizes this assessment by noting that Bonhoeffer quite clearly does not equate "success" with the will of God.[66] In fact, the first mention of "success" (or indeed, "result," since "*Erfolg*" could be translated with either word, and consequentialist ethics may be called *Erfolgsethik*), is when Bonhoeffer states: "The old conflict of whether only the will, (respectively the intellectual act, or the person) could be good, or whether also the accomplishment, the work, the result, the condition could be called good, and which of them precedes the other, and to which should be accorded the greater importance—this conflict, which has also penetrated theology and which has brought about grave confusion here and elsewhere, proceeds from a fundamentally reversed way of questioning. It tears apart what is originally and essentially one, namely the good and the real, the person and his work" (35).

---

65. Burtness, *Shaping the Future*, 16. See also 15.
66. Nickson, *Freedom*, 137.

Bonhoeffer and "Virtue Ethics"

Later in the same passage he says, "The question of the good must not be narrowed to the examination of actions in terms of motives or consequences through the application of an already prepared ethical measuring rod. An ethic of intentions remains as much on the surface as an ethic of consequences" (36–37).

Moreover, Bonhoeffer also warns against an idolization of success in a thinly veiled reference to Hitler and the Nazi regime (76–78). "Success," like all of human life, stands under the 'Yes' and 'No' of God's judgment" (251).[67] Bonhoeffer's concern here was surely to counter the stance of many theologians in Germany who supposed that Hitler's success must be seen as proof that the course of events being played out was God's will. Against this Bonhoeffer is clear that success is neither proof of the validity of an ethical act, nor can its validity be demonstrated through what the agent intends, nor through the outcome of her act. Thus it must be seen as impossible to speak of a "consequentialist ethic" in the sense of an emphasis on the outcome of one's action. Nor would it be possible to make a case for Bonhoeffer's thought to be seen as consequentialist on the basis of his treatment of the ultimate and the penultimate because Bonhoeffer is clear that the penultimate can in no way be seen as a precondition or cause of the ultimate.[68]

Burtness, however, does not treat Bonhoeffer consistently as a consequentialist, but speaks also of situation ethics: "He often sounds like a pure situationist. But his own position becomes increasingly interesting as one notices the persistent drive towards some way of acknowledging and even creating structures."[69] It is Bonhoeffer's willingness to work with or create structures that prevents Burtness from classing him simply as a situation ethicist. "Like other ethicists on the situationist side of the ethics spectrum, Bonhoeffer's position may seem elusive, but it is neither contentless nor arbitrary. He is constantly working at the intersection of situations and structures ... The structures that Bonhoeffer constructs are built on his commitment to time and history as ethical constituents, and to the shaping of the future as the heart of the ethical task."[70] Later he adds,

---

67. See also *DBW* 6:221, 239, 241, and 244.

68. See *DBW* 6:140–45; 151–52; 155–56, and 160–61. Although an attempt could be made to describe Bonhoeffer's participation in the assassination plot as having a consequentialist rationale, this is not a case that he makes. In his talk of wresting the wheel away from the mad driver running down pedestrians on the pavement, his own description involves what he calls "the necessary deed."

69. Burtness, *Shaping the Future*, 63. See also 42.

70. Ibid., 67.

"Bonhoeffer is certainly an ethical 'situationist' in that he opposes ethical absolutes of all kinds and emphasizes concrete times and places. Yet to label him a situationist without qualifying that term is to misconstrue him completely. The Jesus Christ of time and history is also the one in whom the reality of God and the reality of the world come together. Reality, always on the move, is structured by Jesus Christ . . . Bonhoeffer was as interested in structures as he was in situations, and worked his entire life at the intersection of the two."[71]

It would seem from all this that Burtness sees Bonhoeffer as a situation ethicist, insofar as he develops a position that is not based on the timeless absolutes of deontology, and insofar as he insists that the particularities of life are ethically relevant. Yet Burtness himself is aware that simply to call Bonhoeffer a situation ethicist would be a misconstrual of his thought because it is apparent that Bonhoeffer works both with structures and content that would be foreign to the formulations of Joseph Fletcher or John Robinson. It is undoubted that Bonhoeffer insisted on the necessity of considering the contingencies of historical and geographical placement seriously. Yet that on its own is hardly enough to deem his ethics to be situation ethics. Thus, neither Burtness's comments about consequentialism nor situation ethics are ultimately persuasive.

Despite the fact that so many commentators have placed Bonhoeffer's *Ethics* in the realm of situation ethics, this is not adequate for at least two reasons. First, Bonhoeffer does not speak about the situation as such, nor about the salient features of the situation. Secondly, he does not offer a guiding principle such as Fletcher does with love; indeed, he rejects such proposals.[72] Therefore I shall turn to other possible construals offered by commentators.

2.4.3: Kingdom of God Ethics: Hans Pfeifer

Unlike the commentators seen thus far, who either dismissed the possibility of seeing Bonhoeffer's *Ethics* as related to virtue ethics, or who saw him as a sort of situation ethicist, Hans Pfeifer is of the opinion that Bonhoeffer's ethics "aims ultimately beyond the question of command, of [creation] orders, of natural theology, and also beyond the possibilities of

---

71. Burtness, *Shaping the Future*, 69–70. Though see also 66–67, where he likens Bonhoeffer to Hauerwas and states that Bonhoeffer takes "seriously not only the moral agent but also the communal character of decision making." Nonetheless, it is as a situationist and consequentialist that Burtness identifies him.

72. E.g., *DBW* 6:324.

a situation ethic. Formally he is approaching the kingdom-of-God ethics of Albrecht Ritschl; in content he differs fundamentally because he sees the real future of Christ as valid and virtually makes it the foundation of his ethic."[73] That the kingdom of God is not the most prominent theme in Bonhoeffer's *Ethics* does not invalidate this view, Pfeifer believes, because he sees "reality" as taking the place of the kingdom of God in Albrecht Ritschl's ethics.[74] The major categories in Bonhoeffer's ethical thought, according to Pfeifer are: "first, discipleship, then conformation with the acting Christ, and then above all representative action."[75] All these themes he sees as being determined by their relationship to another person, namely Christ, and foundational to them all is the concept of obedience, not to a law but to Christ.[76]

One problem in this account is that, like others writing in this era, Pfeifer relies on the *Ansatz* theory, assuming that Bonhoeffer "had the theme [sc. Christian ethics] in his sights time and again with new approaches without reaching a definitive clarity for himself."[77] He sees some parts as being virtually situation ethics, and others as relating to given structures, the mandates; "the final higher unity is not achieved."[78] This is patently true, if he means simply that Bonhoeffer's *Ethics* was never completed, and that we cannot extrapolate how he might have sought to bring his various themes into a unity. Yet it is perhaps claiming too much to say that he never achieved clarity for himself, even as he continued to read and

---

73. Pfeifer, "Rechtfertigung," 179, all citations my translation.

74. For references to the kingdom of God, see *DBW* 6:38, 42, 117, 223–24, 266, and 359. The term is used with some ambivalence which no doubt arises from its misuse by others.

75. Pfeifer, "Rechtfertigung," 194.

76. Ibid., 194–99.

77. Ibid., 199. The *Ansatz* (approach) theory assumed that each of the manuscripts represents a different "approach" to Bonhoeffer's work on ethics. According to this theory, later manuscripts were presumed to supersede earlier ones, and the dating of the manuscripts was based on the assumption that Bonhoeffer progressed from an ecclesiastical to a worldly outlook and focus. See Bethge, *Biography*, 622; and especially the preface to *DBW* 6:11–12; and in a different preface, *DBWE* 6:2, 27–28. That Bonhoeffer's work progressed in this way was advocated in Müller's early and influential study of Bonhoeffer's theology, *Kirche zur Welt*. He describes a "logical" (*folgerichtig*) way from interest in the structures determining religion to the word of forgiveness, from a bourgeois indebtedness to tradition to a free view into a new time, 9. However, the work on dating the manuscripts which has been incorporated in *DBW* 6 has shown that Bonhoeffer's writings did not follow the assumed progression of "church to world," and this theory has now largely been abandoned.

78. Pfeifer, "Rechtfertigung," 199.

work in prison. Certainly one or two letters to Bethge would suggest that he felt he had communicated the major outlines of his thought to him.[79] It seems questionable to assume that because the work was unfinished that Bonhoeffer had not reached a high degree of, or perhaps even definitive, clarity for himself.

However, the more important question is whether Pfeifer might be justified in describing the structure (the formal aspects) of Bonhoeffer's *Ethics* as being like Ritschl's, though centering on reality rather than the kingdom of God. There can be no doubt that reality is an extremely important concept in Bonhoeffer's ethics; the question is whether it acts in the same way as the "kingdom of God" in Ritschl's. For the nineteenth century theologian the most important aspects of Christianity were salvation (of the individual) and ethics (in the community), and ethics was understood in terms of the realization (through work in the world, prayer, and submission to the will of God) of the kingdom of God. Moreover, the goal of salvation is that the Christian should work in and for the kingdom of God.[80]

Pfeifer's claim is not ultimately persuasive. I say this for three reasons. First, Ritschl's understanding is built on the notion of something that is to be realized; Bonhoeffer is insistent that what is at stake is not an idea that must be realized, but the reality that the world has been reconciled to God in Christ, and that the reality of God and the reality of the world are both known in Christ (34–35; 60–61).

Secondly, in Ritschl's view the Christian is to work for (the coming of) the kingdom and in the kingdom of God. In Bonhoeffer's understanding, the Christian participates in reality by grace,[81] and though she is attentive to and obeys the will of God, this is not seen as a form of realization:

---

79. See his letter to Bethge, November 18, 1943, where he speaks of reproaching himself for not finishing his *Ethics*, but "it comforted me somewhat that I had told you the essentials," even if his ideas were incomplete, *DBW* 8:188.

80. Ritschl, *Justification and Reconciliation*, 11. See also Stayer, *Martin Luther, German Saviour*, 5. There is some similarity between Ritschl's conception of work, prayer, and submission, and Bonhoeffer's "Thoughts for the Day of Baptism of D.W.R." of May 1944, where he writes, "our being a Christian today consists of only two things: prayer and doing what is righteous among the people," *DBW* 8:435. Nonetheless, this is not sufficient warrant to suggest the same form or content in Ritschl and Bonhoeffer.

81. Bonhoeffer frequently uses words for "participation" which include an element of grace, rather than the more usual form, "*teilnehmen*," which literally means to "take part." Instead he often speaks of "*teilbekommen*," literally to "receive a part" (*DBW* 6:40, and 61), or "*teilhaben*," literally to "have a part" (35, 38, and 43).

> The will of God, however, is nothing other than the becoming real of the reality of Christ among us and in our world. The will of God is thus neither an idea which demands first to be realized; it is much more itself already reality in the self-revelation of God in Jesus Christ. The will of God is, however, also not simply identical with what exists, such that submission to that which exists would be its fulfillment; it is much more a reality which wants to become real ever anew, in what exists and contrary to what exists. The will of God is already fulfilled by God himself in that he reconciled the world with himself in Christ . . . Following the appearance of Christ, ethics can only be concerned with one thing, namely receiving a part of the reality of the fulfilled will of God. (60–61)

Thirdly, there is a problem with Pfeifer's notion that Bonhoeffer is speaking about some future reality of Christ. The above quote should make it clear that even if in some sense the reality of Christ is still "becoming real," it is quite wrong to speak of it therefore as a "future reality"; it is "already fulfilled." Bonhoeffer may have been able to give greater clarity to this aspect had he discussed the relation of time and eternity, but it is clear that the reality of reconciliation is not something he considered to belong (simply) to the future.

For these reasons it seems to me a mistake to categorize Bonhoeffer's *Ethics* as having the same form as Ritschl's though with a focus on reality instead of the kingdom of God. However, other commentators have pointed to two themes as being the most important in Bonhoeffer's *Ethics*, and have discussed them in terms of his mode of ethical thought. I turn now to these accounts.

2.4.4: *Conformation and Command*

2.4.4.A: Hanfried Müller

Hanfried Müller was one of the earlier commentators (writing before Bethge reordered the manuscripts in the sixth edition of the German text according to the *Ansatz* theory) on Bonhoeffer's theology, and, as mentioned above, he helped to shape the view that dominated interpretations of Bonhoeffer's work for several decades, namely that Bonhoeffer's concerns shifted from the church to the world.[82]

---

82. See note 81.

The Virtue of Bonhoeffer's Ethics

In speaking specifically of the *Ethics*, Müller refers to two introductions (*Einführungen*) to ethics, form (*Gestalt*) and command (*Gebot*).[83] Müller identifies a number of similarities in these two introductions: both approach ethics from praxis (as concrete ethics addressing the problems of his time); both assume not an individualistic ethic but a "social" ethic; both attempt an historical ethic rather than a timeless one; and "[B]oth approaches, the first [sc. *Gestalt*] more obviously, the second [sc. *Gebot*] more subtly, come to grief precisely over this difficulty which Bonhoeffer himself raises practically to a theme in another of the fragments through the thesis 'that it is questionable whether it is meaningful to speak at all about a Christian ethic.'"[84] The differences Müller identifies in these two "introductions" are that ethics as formation "shows in context a not inconsiderable affinity to Catholicism," while command is more Protestant.[85]

The two "introductions" to ethics are complemented, in Müller's view, by considerations of the theological foundation of ethics (defining the good, and drawing on justification, incarnation and resurrection) and the content of Bonhoeffer's ethics (the mandates, responsible living, and the natural).[86]

While this analysis has much to commend it, there are questionable aspects.[87] One small query I have is what Müller means by "introduction." Given that the other categories in which he analyses the material are "theological foundation" and "content," I am inclined to think that he sees *Gestalt* and *Gebot* as the prime metaphors through which Bonhoeffer envisages ethics, much as I have hitherto spoken of "modes" or "forms" of ethical thought.

If I am correct in interpreting Müller thus, he identifies the most important of Bonhoeffer's ways of conceiving ethics. I am concerned, however, that in comparing them, there seems to be much more emphasis placed on the ways in which they are similar than on the distinctive character each of them may be said to have. I don't believe it will suffice merely to speak in terms of their affinity respectively with Roman Catholic or Protestant moral theology, even if this assertion is correct. Surely it makes some difference to a Christian's ethics as a whole if she conceives of ethics

---

83. Müller, *Kirche zur Welt*, 273–93.

84. Ibid., 288–93, quote 293, my translation.

85. Ibid., 289, 291.

86. Ibid., 295–353.

87. I set to one side the issues related to the political or ideological nature of much of Müller's critique.

in terms of her being formed to become like Christ, or if she considers the dominant metaphor to be responding to God's command. I shall examine this more fully in chapter 6, but Müller's assessment may prove to be too facile or reductive for understanding these aspects of Bonhoeffer's thought.

2.4.4.B: LARRY RASMUSSEN—LATER

Müller is not alone in identifying form (or "formation") and command as the most important ways in which Bonhoeffer envisaged ethics, nor in looking for their similarities. Larry Rasmussen raised "A Question of Method" at the Fifth International Bonhoeffer Society Conference in Amsterdam in 1988, where he, like Müller, recognized these two themes in Bonhoeffer's ethics.[88] Rasmussen traces each motif through Bonhoeffer's overall work, showing that each is important in his thought.[89]

In comparing the two, like Müller, he finds a number of similarities and identifies only one difference, the Roman Catholic or Protestant "tone."[90] Although Rasmussen states that it remains "an open question" whether formation and command are really two "methods" or just one: "'ethics as formation' is both the more original and the more enduring theme."[91] Thus he treats command ethics as a subordinate motif, even if it is also "genuine."[92]

As with Müller, I have misgivings about Rasmussen's reducing the differences to proximity of thought to Roman Catholic or Protestant ethics. Again, I shall return to this in chapter 6.

---

88. Rasmussen, "Question of Method." This was written up more fully and in a more nuanced way in his *Significance*.

89. Rasmussen, *Significance*, 92–108.

90. He however disagrees marginally with Müller as to how precisely this should be understood. Müller is happy to speak of *Gestalt* as offering a Lutheran form of grace as perfecting nature (rather than replacing it), *Kirche zur Welt*, 289–92. Rasmussen suggests that this "underestimates the *dialectic* of the natural and the unnatural, . . . the ultimate and the penultimate, and the yes and no to the world," *Significance*, 110. Rasmussen's claim is correct, but it does require real nuance to avoid the risk of falling into a dualism which Bonhoeffer rejects, even when he employs these notions.

91. Rasmussen, *Significance*, 110.

92. Ibid.

2.4.4.c: Stephen Plant

Stephen Plant, meanwhile, sees Bonhoeffer as working on ethics in two, as it were, grammatical moods: the subjunctive of ethics as formation, and the imperative of command ethics.[93] Only in the manuscripts "Ethics as Formation" and "The 'Ethical' and the 'Christian' as a Theme" does Plant see "what can be called an explicit method."[94] "Setting Bonhoeffer's command based ethics alongside his ethics as formation, enables us to see these ethical 'methods' as two sides of a dialectic: the one concerned with being in Christ (conformation to the Gestalt of Jesus), the other concerned to emphasize God's freedom to command particular things to particular people (God's freedom to act)."[95]

With such a view, it is unsurprising that Plant insists that the two "moods" must not be in any way conflated, or either one subsumed under the other.[96] This understanding seems both robust and more faithful to what is actually present in the manuscripts than Müller's or Rasmussen's, though I shall return to the whole question of how the two ways of conceiving of ethics may be related in chapter 6. Particularly, it will be important to ask whether if the two modes are conceived as forming a dialectic, one could still imagine Bonhoeffer's ethics as related to virtue ethics.

2.4.5: Summary of Commentary on Bonhoeffer's Mode of Ethical Thought

We have seen that some commentators have rejected the possibility that Bonhoeffer's ethics might be related to virtue ethics, though their grounds for arguing this seem less than convincing. More commentators have placed his ethics within the realm of situation ethics, a move that seems to be more suggestive of the time of their writing, given the popularity of situation ethics at that time, than of any real engagement with the structures of Bonhoeffer's thought, since he does not emphasize the specifics of situations nor suggest any principle (such as love) that is to guide. One commentator even suggested his ethics was (in part) consequentialist,

---

93. Plant, *Bonhoeffer*, 118–24. Plant helpfully clarified this metaphor in a conversation in December 2009, saying his concern is to note that any language will need both ways of speaking to be adequate, and so it is too with the ethical "language."

94. Ibid., 119.

95. Ibid., 122.

96. Ibid., 118–19.

though it is hard to make a case for that. One has put forward the notion that the structure is a Ritschlian "kingdom of God" ethic in which reality is substituted for the kingdom of God. None of these ways of analyzing the form of Bonhoeffer's ethics is convincing.

Some, however, have noted two different forms of ethical thinking, but are not agreed as to how they may be related to one another, whether one strand might be seen as somehow subordinate to the other, or whether they are irreducibly plural. Either way, addressing both the themes of conformation and command shows greater faithfulness to Bonhoeffer's work than the other construals mentioned above, and it is worthy of more prolonged attention to discover how the two themes might be related to one another. I shall return to this in chapter 6.

2.5: Conclusions

To return to the question of this chapter, it is possible to say with some certainty that Bonhoeffer did not see himself as a virtue ethicist. Moreover, his use of the term "virtue," his references to the Thomist tradition, and his allusions to classical philosophy and myths are all such as to preclude an easy assumption that Bonhoeffer should be seen as advocating a form of virtue ethics. Such evidence internal to his *Ethics* as seen above (2.3), however, is also not sufficient to rule out the possibility of the reality of some correlation. Therefore, it will be necessary to consider both the nature of Christian virtue ethics (in chapter 3) and the substance of Bonhoeffer's thought (in chapter 4) before attempting to articulate what relationship there may be between Bonhoeffer's *Ethics* and virtue ethics.

Moreover, the interpretations offered by other commentators have been widely divergent and can offer no definitive guide. Among those who have treated the issue of how Bonhoeffer envisages ethical thought there is no widespread agreement. Of all these construals, however, those that take seriously the themes of ethics as formation and ethics as command seem most faithful to Bonhoeffer's thought. Thus on the basis of the analyses of other commentators no case could be made for Bonhoeffer's ethics to be seen as related to virtue ethics, but neither could such a case be conclusively refuted.

To discover what relationship Bonhoeffer's *Ethics* may bear to virtue ethics, a number of questions need to be addressed regarding how Christian virtue ethics should be conceived. These I shall take in groups of related issues:

- Is a virtue-based ethic necessarily a private one? Is virtue ethics actually legalistic? How do virtues and vices relate to the hypocrisy that he calls "Phariseeism"?
- Is virtue ethics necessarily an example of humans trying to reach God?
- Is virtue ethics necessarily based on natural law?
- How might virtue ethics relate to the question of how Christ takes form among us here and today? Is virtue ethics necessarily abstract? Is virtue ethics necessarily a form of system? Is virtue ethics necessarily based on an abstract catalogue of virtues?
- Does a virtue ethic demand a view of human nature in general and human reason in particular that Bonhoeffer would perceive to give too little account of the Fall? Is virtue ethics opposed to grace such that one must categorize Bonhoeffer's thought as not one but the other?

These are questions that I shall address in the next chapter once I have looked in more detail at some accounts of Christian virtue ethics and have considered the features that seem to be necessary for an ethic to be considered virtue ethics.

Finally, there are questions arising that will only be appropriate to consider after taking a closer look at the nature of virtue ethics: If command and formation are the two modes in which Bonhoeffer does ethics, how might these relate to virtue ethics? This will require a more concentrated consideration of both of these themes and how they might be related to one another. I shall return to this in chapter 6.

3

Virtue Ethics in the Christian Tradition

To answer questions raised in the previous chapter, it is necessary to explore what might be meant, at least in Christian theology, by virtue ethics. This is not a question with only one possible answer, since various conceptions of ethics based on virtues have been offered in the almost two thousand years of Christian history.[1] While it would be possible to sketch the various versions of virtue-based ethics proposed by Christian thinkers through the ages, it is my hope that by looking in greater depth at the thought of Augustine of Hippo and Thomas Aquinas, as two of the most influential Christian theologians in the area, and then at more contemporary developments focusing on the work of Alasdair MacIntyre, a clearer view of the commonalities and differences of the major strands of Christian virtue ethics will begin to emerge.[2] Then, with this picture in mind, it should be possible to consider what elements may be necessary for an ethic to be rightly called "virtue ethics" or "virtue-based ethics."[3] Finally, in the light of these considerations, I shall attend to the questions raised in chapter 2.

---

1. I will focus on the accounts of theologians rather than basing an account on the Bible for two reasons. First, historically Christian virtue ethics grew up in contexts where philosophical accounts of virtue were influential. Secondly, although I consider virtue ethics to be (at least in some construals) consonant with the biblical witness, it does not arise, strictly speaking, out of exegesis. However, see Cessario's account of the biblical underpinnings of virtue ethics, *Moral Virtues*; and Pinckaers's rooting of virtue ethics in scripture, *Sources of Christian Ethics*, xvii, xxi, and ch. 5 and 6. See also Kotva, *Christian Case*, especially ch. 5; and Davis, "Preserving Virtues."

2. Though I emphasize here the conceptions of these thinkers, I shall offer some comments as to how others have agreed or disagreed.

3. Although I recognize the anachronism in many instances of speaking of "virtue ethics," the phrase will occur often enough to make the continued use of scare quotes each time cumbersome.

3.1: Augustine and Virtue Ethics

Christian (re-)formulations of the strand of ethical thinking now called virtue ethics exist from as early as the patristic period and there were many such examples, but it seems appropriate to start with Augustine because of his stature in the Western church, his influence on the Lutheran tradition, and because of his important redefinitions of key aspects of virtue ethics in the light of Christian doctrine, especially that of grace.[4] As John Rist put it, "Augustine was the most radical and the most influential" of those who sought to transform Greco-Roman thought in Christian terms.[5] It is important to notice at the outset, however, that Augustine did not treat ethics in the way that has since become standard: a systematic treatment of the rather narrow subject of morality. There are at least two reasons for this: first, the ethical framework in common use at this time was broader by nature, considering what makes for a good life in total, rather than the more limited questions we might ask regarding good and bad behaviors, choices, character traits, or outcomes;[6] secondly, Augustine's mode of discourse and writing was not what is now called systematic, but "occasional" or "discursive"[7] and so Augustine's writings that address ethical concerns comprise a variety of genres including letters, commentaries on the Bible, teachings on doctrine to combat current heresies, and even an autobiography.

3.1.1: *De moribus ecclesiae catholicae*

The closest Augustine comes to a systematic treatment of ethics is in his *De moribus ecclesiae catholicae*, written in AD388, and so it seems appropriate to look at this work in some detail. As he states at the opening, his methodology includes both argument from reason, and appeals to authority in the form of New Testament texts, which were regarded by his intended readers, the Manicheans, uncontroversially as scripture,[8] and thus it could

---

[4]. See Porter, "Virtue Ethics," 100.

[5]. Rist, *Ancient Thought Baptized*, 1. Cf. Porter's comments that Augustine was the most influential of patristic theologians in the long run, but others held more sway in the later patristic period, "Virtue Ethics," 100.

[6]. Burnaby, *Amor Dei*, 46–47; Kent, "Augustine's Ethics," 205.

[7]. Rist, *Ancient Thought Baptized*, offers as a possible reason for Augustine's mode of writing the various demands on his time because of his roles as bishop, priest, and correspondent, 10.

[8]. *De moribus ecclesiae catholicae*, 2.3. All further references to *De moribus ecclesiae* in this section will be included in brackets in the main text.

be claimed that Augustine's use of philosophy is determined in part by his attempt to argue from grounds that they could accept.

Augustine's starting point in this early work is a consideration of how humans ought to live, assuming that everyone wishes to be happy or blessed or to flourish (*beata vita*) and that this good life can be found when the highest good is both loved and possessed (which also means enjoyed) (3.4). This eudaemonist way of construing ethics, based on what makes for human flourishing, clearly has its roots in the philosophical way of life that Augustine had embraced before he became a Christian. Indeed, John Burnaby in writing about Augustine's theology said, "No understanding of his religion is possible without regard to the Platonist foundation upon which all his thinking is built."[9] Carol Harrison gives some insight into why that might be when she states, "What matters now [at the time of his conversion in 386] is his faith, for it is only through that faith, through the authority of Christ, that he realizes that transcendent truth can be fully and ultimately grasped. The philosophers are useful—and he uses them in a general way—to articulate this, but the details and the framework are now irrevocably Christian, for it is the *true* philosophy, the rest are simply tributaries which derive from, and if rightly directed, flow into the stream of Christian faith."[10] Certainly, this early work shows not only a general reliance on Greco-Roman philosophy, but more specifically on a form of eudaemonism that had its origins in that philosophy, though Augustine had less familiarity especially with Plato, Aristotle, and Plotinus than scholars are able to enjoy now.[11] Augustine's starting point and framework are borrowed from philosophy: the assumption that everyone seeks "happiness," and the supreme good is that which is sought not as a means to an end, but for its own sake.[12]

The supreme good for humans he defines as something greater than humanity that cannot be lost against a person's will, though in what sense or to what degree that happiness is obtainable in this life is less clear (3.5).[13]

---

9. Burnaby, *Amor Dei*, 25. See also Rist, *Ancient Thought Baptized*, 2, 6–8.

10. Harrison, *Rethinking*, 38, her emphasis.

11. Rist, *Ancient Thought Baptized*, 1. See also Wetzel, *Limits of Virtue*, 10–11, for his view on Augustine's dependence on Stoic philosophy for his ethics.

12. Burnaby, *Amor Dei*, 46. Nor was Augustine alone in thus borrowing from philosophy: Origen urged his disciples to pursue a "philosophical life" of seeking to live virtuously, striving for truly good things and shunning evil (*Panegyric* 6.75, 78), cited in Wilken, *Early Christian Thought*, 267. John Cassian and Pope Gregory the Great also wrote in terms of virtues as corrective tools for eliminating vices, Porter, "Virtue Ethics," 101.

13. He felt the need to clarify this in his *Retractiones*: a person's love of God, and

It would not be unfair to state that Augustine sometimes relies on (pagan) philosophy, even to the detriment of a fully Christian understanding, especially as regards human bodily nature.[14] Whether he was consciously using such arguments as would hold the most sway with his intended audience, or perhaps his own thinking was not fully developed in terms of Christian theology, this is one area in which Augustine later changed his stance as his Christian faith and awareness of scriptures deepened.[15]

Having set out this framework, he begins to give it more content via revelation through scripture ("authority") instead of philosophy ("reason"), though his thoughts are almost always framed in relationship to philosophical concerns. Thus he states that human happiness is to be found in seeking God. Moreover, to follow God authoritative teachings are needed, which he takes to include the Old Testament patriarchs, law and prophets as well as the teachings of the New Testament concerning Christ's incarnation and the witness of the apostles and martyrs (6.10-7.12). Having given this general list of what counts as authoritative, he is more specific: the good that Jesus prescribes is that we should "love God with all our heart, all our soul and all our mind."[16] Augustine complements this with a quote from Paul: nothing can separate us from the love of God in Christ Jesus.[17]

Augustine's choice of scriptures to use in *De moribus ecclesiae* is of interest in itself. While most Christians would accept Jesus' use of the Shema along with the second greatest command, "which is like it," as being central to Christian faith (and of course the Shema itself is central to Judaism), Augustine's use of the verse from Romans is more surprising. However, it is congruent with classical philosophy at least in its Stoic form, with its concern that happiness must be something internal, such that outside forces and changes of fortune cannot determine one's happiness.[18]

If human happiness is found in God as our supreme good, it makes sense that Augustine turns his attention to addressing who he believes God is. "We do not worship a God who repents, or is jealous, or needy, or

---

therefore happiness, will be greater when she sees God face to face, 1.7.4. See also *City of God* 19.20, where he speaks of the present hope of happiness in the afterlife; a person may be "called" happy if she has this hope, Kent, "Augustine's Ethics," 211.

14. Augustine has a dualistic conception of the relationship of the soul and body, 4.6; 5.7; 12.20; 27.52.

15. Rist, *Ancient Thought Baptized*, 20–21.

16. Matt 22:37; Deut 6:5.

17. Rom 8:36.

18. See 11.18–19 for another surprising choice.

Virtue Ethics in the Christian Tradition

cruel, or who seeks pleasure in the blood of men and beasts, or is pleased with depravity and crime, or whose possession of the earth is limited to some small part," he says (10.16). Catholic teaching is that God is not contained in any space, nor does God change, a teaching that Augustine states requires true maturity and wisdom to understand (10.17). Although Augustine relies here on the church's doctrine, his use of philosophy is apparent in the concerns he chooses to address, and the mode of defining his concepts. For he asserts, without any exegetical or theological exposition of the Old Testament texts that claim or suggest that God repents, is jealous or wrathful, etc., that these things are not true of God. Paul Kuntz in speaking about similar concerns within the *Confessions* asks, "Is it that passion is too particular, or too possessive, or too sensual to be ascribed to God? Probably all three."[19] Kuntz misses the mark in these conjectures: Augustine's chief aim is to uphold the philosophical notion of immutability, that God's nature must not be subject to any changes, and emotions were understood (whether rightly or not) as mutability. Thus it would seem that even his choice of scripture ("authority") is to some degree dependent on, or in service of, philosophy or "reason." Certainly in this discussion of the nature of God, Augustine's purpose would seem to be to show that Christian teaching is reconcilable with philosophical understanding: God is not contained within the boundaries of any place; God's nature never changes (10.17).

Having made clear how he understands God, who must be sought for true human happiness, he then states that reaching God does not mean becoming altogether what God is, but coming close to God, being pervaded by divine truth and holiness, precisely through loving God wholly, as Jesus taught. Here Augustine warns of the dangers of presumption and pride (for example, imagining oneself to have become like God), insisting on the necessity of submission to God to receive enlightenment, a submission that paradoxically leads not only to happiness but also to freedom (12.20–21). This is a notable departure from classical philosophy, which assumes not only that a truly wise person becomes god-like through her own effort, but also that such a sage would be aware of the greatness thus attained.[20]

19. Kuntz, "I-Thou Relation," 110.

20. E.g., *NE*, IV.iii–iv, vii, which I again cite, though Augustine had no direct awareness of Aristotle, only to underscore the widespread agreement among philosophers concerning this point. Contrast Augustine's stance with Clement of Alexandria, who accepts the notion of perfection as likeness to God, but redefines that in terms of imitation of Christ (*The Tutor* 1.14; 1.2.1, cited in Wilken, *Early Christian Thought*, 276).

Because Paul calls Christ the virtue and wisdom of God and Jesus says he is truth, Augustine states that living rightly (striving for happiness) must mean loving virtue, wisdom and truth.[21] Thus, just as Augustine seems to speak of God's nature in philosophy's terms, in discussing Christ's nature, he does not draw on the narratives of the gospels to speak of Jesus, but on teachings that relate to the concerns of philosophy—virtue, wisdom and truth (13.22). It is this love of Christ as virtue, wisdom and truth that allows the Christian to see the Father, and through sanctification by the Holy Spirit she can cling to this love and be conformed to God rather than the world (13.22–23). This discussion, so heavily informed by and dependent on philosophy, is Augustine's means of introducing the doctrine of the Trinity (14.24).

Unsurprisingly in this framework, Augustine now turns to define the cardinal virtues, but in a new way, namely as forms of love.[22] Thus temperance he defines as giving oneself whole-heartedly to the beloved and preserving oneself unblemished for God, fortitude as enduring all things for the sake of the beloved, justice as serving God alone, and prudence as choosing wisely between those things that are helpful in reaching God and those things that are harmful in this endeavor (15.25, 19.35). Prudence he considers to be required in the operation of the other virtues (24.45).

Intriguingly, although Augustine states that prudence is the virtue needed for the operation of the other virtues, it is in fact *love*, not a "cardinal virtue" from classic philosophy at all, which is actually pivotal.[23] Augustine's change is an important departure from anything in philosophy. In this sense Burnaby is right in noting that Augustine is moving away from the assumption that knowledge and reason are of primary importance such that to know the good is to do it: love takes that place in his thinking.[24] Even so, Augustine's very conception of what love is and its power to inspire action are dependent on Platonic thought and changed little as his thought developed.[25] It might even be said that he no longer speaks of cardinal virtues but cardinal loves, so central is the theme in his thinking, even at this early stage.

21. 1 Cor 1:24; John 14:6. Note also Ambrose's view: "When we speak about virtue, we speak about Christ," *Explanatio psalmi* xxxvi, cited in Cessario, *Moral Virtues*, 150.

22. Ambrose considered the cardinal virtues to be a suitable starting point for Christian ethics, Cessario, *Moral Virtues*, 19.

23. Rist suggests this is borrowing from Stoicism, where "right reason" occupies this position, *Ancient Thought Baptized*, 161.

24. Burnaby, *Amor Dei*, 52.

25. Rist, *Ancient Thought Baptized*, 156–57, also 173.

Virtue Ethics in the Christian Tradition

Even if there are questions regarding Augustine's integration of philosophy and scripture, this is an attempt to reformulate what constitutes a good life in the light of his new Christian faith, and it is remarkable that Augustine, even at this early stage in his Christian understanding, was able to redefine much of the philosophy that had fascinated him for some years, offering a new construal of the supreme good, and new definitions of the cardinal virtues.[26] Kuntz sees his reformulations of these virtues as "at the very least, a remarkable formula of reconciliation between pagan and Biblical cultures."[27] Burnaby is surely right in asserting that such strongly Neo-Platonist emphases in this work are not nearly so surprising as is Augustine's use of scripture, which he considers "anticipates the future Augustine."[28]

Augustine also considers some of the things that could hinder a person from reaching God: covetousness, which he sees as Adam's first sin (19.36); being deceived through false philosophies (though the love of wisdom itself is excellent) (21.38); being conformed to the world in deception and vanity (21.39); and fear of physical hardship, pain, and death (22.40). In these discussions, which might be seen as analogous to the consideration of vices in more philosophical treatments, he shows the cardinal virtues as overcoming such hindrances: temperance averts covetousness, deception and vanity; and fortitude will preserve a person from fear and help her not only to disdain death but to desire it. As a kind of summary, he later states that human love and God's revelation so work that "such ardent charity is engendered, and such a flame of divine love bursts forth that all vices are burned away and man is purged and sanctified" (30.64).[29] Such awareness of sanctification and grace is another area in which Augustine makes substantial changes to the virtue ethics of the philosophers. The fact that he could speak of submission to God and sanc-

---

26. It may be, as Markus claims, that in his redefinition (collapsing them all into love) Augustine shows little interest in the cardinal virtues themselves and how they might be distinctive, "Will and Virtue," 393–94. However, it may rather be that in terms of his understanding of the unity or at least interrelatedness of the virtues that he does not wish to speak of them separately. See also Langan, "Unity and Interconnection"; and Kuntz, "I-Thou Relation," 111.

27. Kuntz, "I-Thou Relation," 114, where, intriguingly, he notes that this enables both "the humanist" and "the theist" to find confirmation of their ways of seeking a happy life!

28. Burnaby, *Amor Dei*, 88.

29. In his *Retractiones* (1.7.5) of AD 426 he makes clear that he regrets any suggestion that perfection might be possible in this life. At this later stage he is much more overtly speaking of an eschatological hope.

tification by the work of the Holy Spirit rather than ascent through human effort to become like God shows that he had already moved some distance from the views of Plotinus at the time of writing *De moribus ecclesiae*.[30]

After all this he comes to the second commandment, which Jesus says is like the first, to love our neighbors as ourselves, which Augustine sees as the duties we have to human society: to cause no harm, and to do good (26.48-50). It is startling that Augustine can speak for some twenty-five chapters about the supreme good and loving God before finally turning to the commandment that Jesus gives in tandem with loving God. This seems no less—and perhaps all the more—puzzling, given that he states that love of God and love of neighbor must go together (26.51). This delay may be caused, as Rist suggests, by Augustine's dependence on Platonic concepts—that pure love is for God alone.[31] If so, this prolonged attention to the love of God before turning to its parallel commandment would be in keeping with his philosophical emphases. Moreover, when he finally does address love of neighbor, this too has resonances with Platonism—for love of neighbor is a participation in God's love for her.[32]

Loving neighbor (and self is included) he defines as caring both for physical needs and the health of the soul via instruction (27.52; 28.55–56). He discusses here the role played by human kindness or compassion or mercy in motivating a person to help her neighbors, though this he describes as being impelled by duty rather than any painful feeling, so that she does not suffer any "anguish of the soul" (27.53). In this discussion he attempts to show the possibility of being compassionate without losing the serenity and tranquility that, according to philosophy, a wise person possesses (27.53–54).[33] Yet it must be conceded that these concerns adopted from philosophy are not in full accord with those of the biblical witness. A fully Christian anthropology should have Jesus as exemplar of

---

30. Such dependence on sanctification and grace has also been seen earlier (13.22–23). Burnaby speaks of Plotinus's views in terms of "self-realisation and enfranchisement of the divine element in humanity," *Amor Dei*, 28. It is, however noteworthy that Augustine had continued to use the language of ascent to God in the *Confessions* when speaking about the memorable experience he and Monnica had (ibid., 29–32, citing Book 7 of *Confessions*, written in AD 401). Other Christians who emphasized the work of the Holy Spirit in acquiring and practising the virtues include Origen (*On First Principles* 1.3.8), and Gregory of Nyssa (*On the Holy Spirit against the Macedonians* 23, both cited in Wilken, *Early Christian Thought*, 276, 278–79).

31. Rist, *Ancient Thought Baptized*, 166.

32. Ibid., 168.

33. See also Kent, "Augustine's Ethics," 208, regarding freedom from trouble and anxiety.

true humanity and faithful living, and that would include the expression of a wide variety of emotions, including some that must be seen as "losing serenity and tranquility," not least in the Garden of Gethsemane.[34]

In this early work, Augustine speaks of love of self as the rational prerequisite of love of neighbor (26.48) (if a person is to love her neighbor *as* herself), which is expressed not least in the fact, as he saw it, that everyone seeks happiness. However, love of God in his view necessarily entails not only self-love, but love of others; and love of others is here depicted in terms of duty, and is shown in benevolence: doing no malice, neglecting no good (26.49–50).[35] In all, his manner of approaching the love of others seems to be the fulfilling of an obligation. Nowhere does he speak of others as created in God's image, or as worthy of love (perhaps a lesser love, in his scheme of ordering love) in their own right.

Thus we have seen that in *De moribus ecclesiae catholicae* Augustine spoke of the moral life in terms of eudaemonism, what happiness is for human beings, and in the language of virtues, which he substantially redefined. He clearly relied in this early work on Greco-Roman philosophy not only for this framework, but also in relation to the concerns he chose to address. At times his emphasis on philosophical themes came at the expense of faithfulness to biblical and doctrinal concerns. Now, however, it must be asked whether this early work can be taken to be representative of Augustine's thought as a whole. For the fact that it is his only full treatment of virtue ethics could seem suggestive that in his mature thought it played little role, or even that he may have changed his views.

3.1.2: *Later Developments*

One thing that changed only marginally, if at all, is his dependence on philosophy. Burnaby, for instance, considers that there is great continuity in his thought, which remains shaped by Neo-Platonism.[36] Augustine

---

34. Especially if reading the account from Matthew or Mark rather than Luke.

35. It should be noted that his understanding of neighbourly love changed quite markedly in later works. See Harrison, *Christian Truth*, 97–99; Rist, *Ancient Thought Baptized*, 148, 153, 156–58; Markus, "Will and Virtue," 390–91; and Burnaby, *Amor Dei*, 255. Much is made of whether others are to be loved for their sake, or as a "means to an end." I don't think Augustine ever quite meant the latter, but his manner of speaking (*uti* and *frui*) left him open to that construal. In his later works he speaks of loving others in God, so loving them as ends in relationship to God. See O'Donovan, *Self-Love*, and "Usus and Fruitio."

36. Burnaby, *Amor Dei*, 27. See e.g. *Confessions* 7.9; *City of God* 8.8–10, cited in Kent, "Augustine's Ethics," 209.

famously claimed that Plato thought that to be a philosopher necessarily entailed being a lover of God. It may well be, as Bonnie Kent claims, that the "affinities between Neo-Platonism and Christianity were especially striking [in terms of metaphysics], so that Augustine's praise of 'the Platonists' would not have been surprising at the time."[37] However that may be, as time went on Augustine redefined certain aspects of philosophy, kept others and struggled sometimes to articulate his new thoughts within the old framework, yet many of the themes most important to this discussion of ethics remain of fundamental importance, such as aspects of love, knowledge, and human happiness. This is a far cry from Kent's suggestion that philosophy became for the later Augustine merely an influence and a willingness "to meet [pagan thinkers] on their own ground."[38]

One of the areas of moral thought with which Augustine is most famously associated is his notion of the will. Perhaps his departure from other accounts is related to his own experience related in the *Confessions* of not being able to will (and therefore to do) what he knew was good,[39] though it may rather be that he framed his previous experience in the light of the theories he had by now formulated. At all events his discussion of the will is striking in its differences both from classical philosophy[40] and from popular usage of *voluntas*: because of the Fall of Adam, human nature has been distorted such that human desires do not simply point to the way of happiness.[41] Even if a person rightly perceives what her supreme good is (and how lesser goods relate to this), she is not capable of willing (and doing) what is right. The human will is now "blinded, fettered and hampered."[42] Rist likens this perception to Aristotle's *acrasia* in the *Nicomachean Ethics*, except that the "incontinence" is suffered by all people always.[43] As a consequence, human actions cannot properly be described as free, but as subject to the wrong desires and loves that after the Fall prevail. James Wetzel states, "Not to know the good, or to refuse

---

37. Kent, "Augustine's Ethics," 206. See also Harrison, *Christian Truth*, 80. Cf Markus's suggestion that Augustine was reading back into Plato his own interpretation of love and wisdom, "Will and Virtue," 380, citing *City of God* 8.8.

38. Kent, "Augustine's Ethics," 209.

39. See Wills, *St Augustine*, 46–47, citing *Confessions* 8.20.

40. Rist identifies close links to Seneca's use of *voluntas* as moral character related to sets of desires, but denies that this could account for Augustine's link of will with love, *Ancient Thought Baptized*, 188.

41. Markus, "Will and Virtue," 382.

42. Harrison, *Christian Truth*, 86.

43. Rist, *Ancient Thought Baptized*, 184. See Aristotle, *NE* 1146a4–119b24.

Virtue Ethics in the Christian Tradition

to acknowledge the good we know, is to compromise our autonomy by having to act, by default or by perversity, on the wrong sorts of desires."[44]

Yet just as Augustine had earlier redefined the virtues in terms of love, so here he gives new meaning to the notion of willing. Markus states, "Augustine refers collectively to the driving forces of human nature, the inclinations, desires and drives behind human action, by the name 'love' or 'loves.'"[45] He likens them to physical weights that pull a person in various directions in activity, whether towards good (usually *caritas*) or towards evil (usually *cupiditas*).[46] Moreover, Augustine now sees the emotions as related to the will, such that if "the will is wrongly directed, the emotions will be wrong; if the will is right, the emotions will be not only blameless but praiseworthy."[47] He has changed from his earlier notion that the ideal of virtue is a Stoic *apatheia*, and adopted a more Christian understanding, namely that this "ideal" is neither desirable nor attainable in this life or in the life to come, and emotions may even be called praiseworthy.[48]

If then the will is to be seen as crippled because of original sin, and to will something is to be motivated by love to act, how can a person ever hope to love the good and will it? Wetzel claims that from the time Augustine wrote his second reply to Simplicius, he never again defined human freedom over against grace.[49] Freedom is now precisely that which is restored and given by grace—namely the freedom to act in accordance with the good. As noted above, Augustine spoke even in his early work *De moribus ecclesiae catholicae* of grace and the necessity of receiving infused virtues if one is to attain the supreme good. Even when he wrote *De beata vita* in AD 386 he already spoke explicitly about dependence on grace, the need for the gift of God for a person to have a happy life.[50] In his later works, with his much more severe stress on human inability to will and do the good, his emphasis on grace becomes ever more central. A person needs grace to be enabled to love what is truly good, to order her loves

---

44. Wetzel, *Limits of Virtue*, 12.

45. Markus, "Will and Virtue," 382.

46. Ibid., 383, citing *Confessions* 13.9.10; 7.17.23. See also Harrison, *Christian Truth*, 95; and Rist, *Ancient Thought Baptized*, 174.

47. Harrison, *Christian Truth*, 93–94.

48. Ibid., 94, citing *City of God* 14.9.

49. Wetzel, *Limits of Virtue*, 164.

50. Burnaby, *Amor Dei*, 46, citing *De beata vita* 5. There are some mentions of grace in *De moribus ecclesiae*, such as the work of the Holy Spirit in sanctification mentioned above. See also 26.51, where he speaks of the understanding and prudence required to love our neighbour which one can only have if they are given by God.

aright, and for her will to be prepared to obey God's commands.⁵¹ As Harrison says, "There is no room for merit, for antecedent efforts or the choice of faith; all is of grace."⁵²

This being the case, Augustine's famous maxim, "love and do as you will" is hardly surprising, for the love here envisaged is the (infused) love that moves a person towards God. What one might "will" when grace enables right love can only be in accordance with God's will, with the good. Thus here too Augustine's focus is on God's grace as enabling right action.

With such effects of the Fall, the question arises whether the mature Augustine still could speak of ethics in terms of eudaemonism and virtues, or whether some discrepancy had arisen between his understanding of human nature and virtue ethics. In fact, Augustine continued to speak of the virtues and eudaemonism in his mature thought. In the context of his argument against Pelagius, for example, Augustine speaks of the virtues and how "human beings are able to turn to God and hold fast to the good."⁵³

Another example of his continuing use of the virtues appears in John Langan's study of Augustine's views on the unity of the virtues as discussed in a letter to Jerome in 415 AD. In a careful reading of that letter he shows that Augustine uses his assumptions regarding the unity of the virtues in considering how to expound James 2:10—"whoever keeps the whole law but fails in one point has become accountable for all of it." The problem Augustine is trying to avoid is the suggestion that all sins are equal in their evil, a belief of the Stoics.⁵⁴ Throughout this discussion, Augustine seems to equate sin with vicious habit (rather than a vicious act). However, he disagrees with the Stoics about the virtues and vices: while the Stoics would argue that one does not possess any virtue unless one possesses them all, and that one only possesses the virtues if they are fully and perfectly developed,⁵⁵ Augustine allows that gradual progress can be made from vice to virtue, allowing for the presence of some things contrary to virtue while still possessing the virtue, albeit imperfectly.⁵⁶ Augustine assumes his earlier position seen in *De moribus ecclesiae* re-

51. Rist, *Ancient Thought Baptized*, 180–81, citing *On Romans* 44.3; *83 Questions* 66; *Against Two Letters of the Pelagians* 4.5.11.

52. Harrison, *Christian Truth*, 113, citing *On the Predestination of the Saints* and *On the Gift of Perseverance*.

53. Wilken, *Early Christian Thought*, 286.

54. Langan, "Unity and Interconnection," 85.

55. Ibid., 90.

56. Langan, "Unity and Interconnection," 90–92, citing *Letter* 167, ch. 13–14.

garding the definition of virtue as love as expressed in love of God and love of neighbor.[57] He then uses this reasoning to explain the verse from James: the love of God and neighbor fulfils all the law; any sin offends against love and therefore against all the law, though sins are not all equal in their evil.[58] Thus Augustine even at this late date continues to use his eudaemonist framework and definition of virtue, even in the interpretation of scripture, as well as his emphasis on the dual commands of love of God and neighbor. In addition, in his mature thought Augustine had, as Wetzel puts is, a "dual aspect of virtue," which includes "virtue as vision," which "transforms human desires to align them with the object of vision, the good," and human autonomy, which means being conformed to the good. Thus what would in classical philosophy have been described as problems of knowing the good are seen as problems related to the will, or difficulties appropriating knowledge of the good.[59] Whatever has changed in Augustine's moral thought, it is not at the basic level of eudaemonism and virtues as the categories for his ethical thought.

3.1.3: Habits and Intentions

However, there are related areas that must also be examined before claiming that Augustine continued to work with something like virtue ethics in his mature writings, such as habit and intentions. Markus quotes from another letter that "what we are bidden is to take away from the weight of unlawful desire (*cupiditatis*) and to add to the weight of charity (*caritatis*), until the former vanish and the latter be perfected."[60] Here again Augustine is using the language of weight, as we have already seen, to describe the pull of loves, whether "unlawful desires" or the pure love called "charity." It is interesting that he speaks of gradual growth in right love (right willing) towards perfection. Likewise, in another mature work, he speaks of the need to be "progressively . . . formed from his eternity, truth and charity." In speaking of this passage, Robert Innes writes that "the form of spiritual progress demonstrated in a central work such as *de Trinitate* is one in which understanding, piety and virtue are positively related to

---

57. Similarly, in *City of God* he says "the briefest and truest definition of virtue is that it is an order of love" (15.22), cited in Harrison, *Christian Truth*, 97. He also continued to use his redefinition of God as the supreme good, Harrison, *Christian Truth*, 79, citing *City of God* 19.1.

58. Langan, "Unity and Interconnection," 92–93, citing *Letter* 167, ch. 16–17.

59. Wetzel, *Limits of Virtue*, 13–14, citing *Soliloquies* 1.6.13.

60. Markus, "Will and Virtue," 385, citing *Letter* 157.2.9.

one another."[61] In *The City of God* he also speaks about transformation in Christ as a continual process of "daily advances whereby the soul is made anew."[62]

However, it must also be noted that in speaking more directly of habits, Augustine states that because of fallen nature a person's habits are more likely to be vicious than virtuous. A Christian needs grace to have the right will (love) to move away from sinful habits.[63]

Just as the forming of right habits is usually a part of virtue ethics, so is a consideration of the agent's motives when assessing any action. In the companion work to *De moribus ecclesiae catholicae*, called *De moribus manichaeorum* (also of AD 388), Augustine states that the praise- or blame-worthiness of any action is determined by the end or intention.[64] This is again a position that Augustine maintained throughout his writing. Thus in rebutting Julian of Eclanum he defines virtue in terms not only of performing the right action, but also acting for the right reason.[65]

Given that in his mature works Augustine still spoke of seeking the supreme good, still used his redefinition of virtues as forms of love (though latterly speaking more often of "order of love"), still addressed the moral life in terms of graced progress in unlearning vicious habits and acquiring virtuous habits, and still stressed the importance of intentions in judging an action, his moral thought can surely best be described as a form of virtue ethics, even if it is one that has been notably changed from its Neo-Platonist origins.[66]

3.1.4: What kind of ethics?

Nonetheless, there is some nervousness about speaking of Augustine and virtue ethics. Oliver O'Donovan describes his ethics as a eudemonistic and teleological ethic, which, he says, "serves to give intelligibility to ethics that are in substance command-based."[67] Harrison notes that he uses

61. Innes, "Integrating the Self," 99, citing *De Trinitate* 12.21.
62. *City of God*, Book 14, cited in Innes, "Integrating the Self," 103.
63. Rist, *Ancient Thought Baptized*, 175–77; 182–83.
64. *De moribus manichaeorum*, 13.27.
65. *Contra Julianum Eclanum* 4.21, cited in Langan, "Unity and Interconnection," 94.
66. For an extended argument for the continuity of Augustine's thought, see Harrison, *Rethinking*.
67. O'Donovan *Self-Love*, 46; see also 154.

Virtue Ethics in the Christian Tradition

the "language of obligation, of responsibility, of social duties, of love of authority, expressed in the Decalogue, the teaching of the New Testament, and most especially the commandment of love of God and neighbour. Conformity to God is therefore not only described by Scripture as man's good, but, in order to attain it, as his duty or moral obligation."[68] Rist goes further, asserting, on the basis on God's unchanging nature and Augustine's understanding that the eternal law is based on that nature, that he held absolute moral rules.[69] Kuntz meanwhile sees Augustine's ethics as "aretaic" (virtuous) but also based on divine command.[70] Such notions of deontology, divine command, obligation, and absolute moral rules centre on the fact that Augustine placed the "greatest commandment" and the "second which is like it" at the heart of his ethical thinking, which gives focus and content to his eudaemonism. Yet, as already mentioned, Augustine is quite clear that what matters is not only the right action (whether or not this is discovered through rules, commands, etc.), but acting with the right intentions. He is happy to speak of good deeds done apart from love as vicious rather than virtuous.[71] Furthermore, Rist's talk of absolute moral rules is not borne out by the passages he quotes,[72] let alone when compared with passages about the necessity of right motives. Indeed, Augustine used the language of "obligation" more in the early *De moribus ecclesiae* in relation to love of neighbor than he does in the mature works, where he most often speaks of love in terms of enjoyment. So however one weights Augustine's use of command, it is not his determining framework, nor is it used in an absolute sense, and it may even be that he used it less in later years. More problematic for those who want to claim Augustine as a deontologist is the fact that, as Burnaby notes, there is a paradox about the commandment to love God and neighbor: "if it is obeyed because it is commanded, it is not obeyed."[73]

---

68. Harrison, *Christian Truth*, 84. See also 91 regarding his use of "natural law," the "light of reason" and eternal law.

69. Rist, *Ancient Thought Baptized*, 191, citing *De libero. arbitrio* 2.15.31ff.

70. Kuntz, "I-Thou Relation," 108.

71. E.g. in *Retractiones* 1.1.4; 1.2; and *City of God* 19.25.

72. In *On Lying*, for example, while Augustine upholds that it is wrong to lie, he makes distinctions between contexts where the lie might be a greater or lesser sin, though this is determined not by the lie itself but by the consequences lying has on the soul of the agent, which Rist calls, "agent-relative consequentialism," *Ancient Thought Baptized*, 194, citing *On Lying* 9.14.

73. Burnaby, *Amor Dei*, 234, citing *Commentary on John's Gospel* 41.10

Thus the question remains: how should we categorize a formulation of ethics that has as its starting point a teleology of human flourishing or happiness, and a discussion of virtues, but the double commandment of loving God and neighbor in a central place? To call his ethics command-based seems inappropriate, given that it is an ethic that rarely speaks of any commandment other than love and regards the fulfillment of that commandment as dependent on grace. Kent comments that in respect of his treatment of the supreme good that provides human happiness, "his moral thought comes closer to the eudemonistic virtue ethics of the classical Western tradition than to the ethics of duty and law associated with Christianity in the modern period."[74] She suggests that Augustine holds a middle way regarding virtue, namely that it is neither a means to an end nor is it something to be valued for it own sake, because only God is to be loved purely for his own sake, everything else is to be loved in relationship to God.[75] Burnaby identifies a similar tension as a result of the biblical and the philosophical elements in Augustine's ethics: "it was not possible to make an honest attempt to set forth an ethic based on the two great commandments, without introducing confusion into the Neo-Platonist pattern."[76]

Another tension Burnaby notes is between grace and ethics: "In fact, it was not easy for the doctrine of grace to find accommodation in a frame of ethical thought which persistently assumed that man's destiny hereafter will depend upon his deserts."[77] In classical virtue ethics happiness is defined as the end and virtue as the means of attaining or as constitutive of that end. However, when that end is defined as "the enjoyment of God," which is almost coterminous with "salvation," speaking of virtue as constituting or as the means to obtain this end becomes problematic. There may be moments when Augustine seems to speak of "blessedness in heaven" as the reward for a virtuous life,[78] but his emphasis on the need for the virtues thus rewarded to be given by God makes clear that he does not mean what philosophers might mean when using the same words. Even if, as Burnaby says, Augustine's emphasis on grace "was far from being a disguised equivalent of the Lutheran denial of all human merit,"[79] he is

---

74. Kent, "Augustine's Ethics," 205.
75. Ibid., 215, citing *De Trinitate* 9.8.13.
76. Burnaby, *Amor Dei*, 89.
77. Ibid., 226–27.
78. E.g. *City of God* 14.25; 19.20; 19.4.
79. Burnaby, *Amor Dei*, 238.

not advocating virtue as achieved by human effort as the means to the supreme end. His view of a human's ability to will and do the good should make that abundantly clear. Later, Augustine resolved a similar tension by attributing the act of will both to God's calling and to human response, at least until he was embroiled in the Pelagian controversy; against the backdrop of that debate, however, he began to emphasize grace further in the famous formulation *extra nos*, without us.[80] Yet in Burnaby's view, Augustine saw life as a pilgrimage to become fit for the enjoyment of God, and on this pilgrimage the person needs to grow in grace and in merit, though these will only be perfected in heaven.[81]

The fact that so many commentators speak of such tensions within Augustine's ethics reflects, I believe, the unique contribution he made to Christian ethics. His framework is indeed teleological, both in the sense that there is a goal to the moral life, happiness in loving God, and in the sense that it is, at least in his mature thought, an eschatological goal—human fulfillment is only complete or perfect in the face-to-face vision of God. Strictly speaking, Augustine's ethics is not only eudemonistic but based on virtues, though these are redefined in terms of love. To call his ethics "command-based" is surely mistaken, since commandment and obedience are not the prime categories of his thought. Yet within his form of virtue ethics, Augustine takes with utter seriousness the effects of the Fall, and the Christian's absolute dependence on grace for her will to be freed to recognize, will, and do the good, which, as we shall see, makes his form of virtue ethics interesting in relation to Bonhoeffer's concerns (3.5.5).

3.2: Thomas Aquinas's Virtue Ethics

In the sense that they both sought to integrate Christian theology and classical philosophy, Augustine and Thomas Aquinas had much in common. Yet, as divergent Christian traditions attest, their thought is different in many ways. If in Augustine there are difficulties collating his thought on ethics from various genres of writing, there is little difficulty doing so in Thomas's works. His writing, it would seem, is nothing if not systematic, at least in his *Summa Theologiae*, where his greatest sustained exposition of virtue ethics is found.

---

80. Ibid., 229, citing *De diversis quaestionibus ad Simplicainum* 1.2.10, and *De gratia et libero arbitrio*.

81. Ibid., 240.

3.2.1: *Setting*

The setting for Thomas Aquinas's most extensive discussion of ethics is in his great work of systematic theology, which may seem both an obvious and an insignificant statement.[82] Yet the importance of the context for his discussion is a subject of some contention. Thus such a noted scholar as Anthony Kenny could state, "Take it out of its context and this treatise on *habitus* is a work of philosophy, not of theology."[83] Of course, as Kenny points out, in the questions Thomas addresses in this section, Aristotle is quoted on every page, while the Bible is quoted only three times. These bare facts, however, will not settle the debate as to whether Aquinas's virtue ethics is really a philosophical construct (with a superficial Christian gloss) or whether it is an integral part of his theology, and if so, if Christian theology is a necessary part of his ethics. If there are some who would read him apart from Christian theology,[84] others contend that this cannot do justice to Thomas's own treatment.[85] Of course it is possible to extract his discussion of dispositions and the cardinal virtues as acquired dispositions in a non-theological treatment. However, this is tantamount to borrowing elements of his work, but using them apart from his meaning. Outside of the context of his theology, any construal of his ethics must become significantly different. My first reason for claiming this is that his ethics stands in a careful and systematic treatment of Christian faith. Secondly, and more importantly, his understanding of God dictates his understanding of human life, both in what it means to be human (chiefly, being created in God's own image) and in the meaning, goal and purpose of human life (to know God now and enjoy the face-to-face vision of God after this life, which constitutes beatitude).[86] Thus to use his ethics non-theologically would demand the alteration of the meaning of key concepts, such that even if his words were quoted verbatim, they would, so interpreted, no longer express his meaning. Thirdly and finally, it seems from his comments in the prologue to the *Summa Theologiae* that Aquinas was writing for students of theology and that he presupposes a high level of theological

---

82. See Boyle, "Setting—Revisited."

83. Introduction, Thomas Aquinas, *ST* vol 22, xix.

84. Kerr cites as one example Anthony J. Lisska, *Aquinas' Theory of Natural Law: An Analytic Reconstruction* (Oxford: Clarendon, 1996), *After Aquinas*, 107. See also Pinckaers, *Sources*, ch. 7.

85. See e.g., Kerr, *After Aquinas*, 65, and especially his discussion of virtue ethics, 115-19. See also Pinckaers, *Sources*, ch. 7.

86. See e.g., Pope, "Overview," 30; and Boyle, "Setting—Revisited," 7.

Virtue Ethics in the Christian Tradition

acumen (even if he calls it an introductory work!). Thus I believe his virtue ethics is theological both in its setting and in its content.[87]

It is important also to consider Thomas's historical setting, which predates a modern approach that seeks to derive moral norms from first principles.[88] Yet beyond this, it is salient that he embraced both the mendicant movement (as a Dominican) and natural philosophy at a time when these were seen to be opposing forces, and that to such an extent that shortly after his death there was a papal condemnation of teachings that prefer philosophy to theology.[89]

Another significant aspect of Thomas's historical setting is that the heresy that was most common (and which he therefore is most often addressing) is not Pelagianism or Manichaeism (as with Augustine), but the dualism of the Cathars.[90] His insistence on the intrinsic goodness of all created things (everything that *is*) must be seen in this context rather than as an argument with later Protestants.

3.2.2: *Methods and Influences*

It is, however, also necessary to consider at least briefly Thomas's mode of theological discourse and influences on his work before turning to an account of his ethics. Although his discussion of ethics is situated in and dependent for meaning on his theology, he does not simply use scripture or the Fathers as proof texts, but argues carefully, subjecting any material he uses to the scrutiny of reason.[91] This is equally true in his use of Aristotle and other philosophers, though unlike with scripture, he is at times at odds with Aristotle.[92] His format and mode of argument, in the *Summa Theologiae* is dialectical rather than arguing a thesis. In his treatment he takes opposing views with great seriousness and courtesy, sometimes altering his own stated position in some way so as to include those elements that he finds correct. As Josef Pieper puts it, this dialectical method is indicative of the conviction that arriving at truth requires

---

87. See e.g. Boyle, "Setting—Revisited," 8–9.
88. See Porter, *Moral Action*, 107.
89. Pieper, *Introduction*, 30–31; Kerr, *After Aquinas*, 12.
90. Kerr, *After Aquinas*, 5.
91. Ibid., 8. See also Pinckaers, "Sources of the Ethics," 19–20.
92. Pieper, *Introduction*, 50–53. For an example of difference with Aristotle, see *ST* I-II.61.5 ad 1, referring to exemplars of virtue and whether virtues may be found in God).

more power than an individual possesses, and that it necessitates working together with others.[93]

It may be that this dialectic method itself was a product of philosophical influence on Thomas. Of the classical philosophers, Aristotle was certainly a major influence on Thomas's work, though perhaps not as great as has often been assumed. Such influences are wide ranging, including not only, as one would expect of a theologian, the Scriptures and the Fathers, but also a Muslim philosopher (Ibn Sina), Plato and others.[94] He was involved in the debates of his day, as is seen in his *Disputations*, but also in the ecumenical dialogue (the Council of Lyons) of East and West.[95]

With this historical and theological setting in mind, I turn now to a brief account of his virtue ethics in the *Summa Theologiae*.

3.2.3: Thomas Aquinas's Virtue Ethics

3.2.3.A: Framework

Following on from his discussion of the nature of God in the *Prima Pars*, the *Prima Secundae* begins to consider questions related to ethics. The link between these sections for Thomas is integral: because a human is made in God's image, her end is also in God, she has real freedom to act, as well as responsibility and control.[96] Throughout his discussion of ethics, these are his basic assumptions about humanity. The human telos, the end, or purpose, is of vital importance in his ethics. Time and again in later questions he bases his answer on the relationship of the question at hand to the human's proper end of receiving the face-to-face vision of God. This is the ultimate end (I–II.3.8); there can be many other ends motivating human behavior, though secondary goods in some sense anticipate the consummate perfection (I–II.1.6). True happiness does not exist in riches, honors, fame and glory, power, health, pleasures, or indeed in any created good (I–II.2), but in union with God (I–II.3.8). All human beings desire this

---

93. Pieper, *Introduction*, 82.

94. Kerr, *After Aquinas*, 7 n. 13.

95. If he was seeking in his own work to bring many different strands of thinking together, the interpretations of his work have been at least as wide-ranging, and often conflicting, as Kerr shows in *After Aquinas*.

96. Forward to *Prima Secundae*, vol 16. In this section all references in brackets in the main text refer to *ST*. See Boyle, "Setting—Revisited," 10–11, for his discussion of how the various sections of the *Summa Theologiae* were disseminated separately even during Thomas's lifetime.

happiness, but not everyone knows where to seek it (I–II.5.8). Yet importantly, a person is not capable through her own resources of attaining this end, but she is created with the capacity to receive this beatitude. Nonetheless, she is required to do something herself, namely to show the motion of activity towards happiness. Thus the framework is in place for considering ethics: the purpose is not salvation by works (humans are only created with the [passive] capacity to receive salvation/beatitude), but to move through actions towards this beatitude. Thus Thomas's work includes a eudaemonist and teleological framework that incorporates philosophical concerns and Christian revelation.

3.2.3.B: VOLITION

It is Thomas's contention that some acts open the way to happiness (though without being able to attain it), while others block the way.[97] For acts to be fully human they must be voluntary (I–II.6.1). Duress renders an act involuntary (I–II.6.5), though emotions and passions such as fear and lust do not (I–II.6.6–7). Ignorance is a special case because it renders an act involuntary (because to be fully human, an act must be based on knowledge and reason), but does not necessarily remove culpability; for there are things that a person is capable of knowing and has a responsibility to know (I–II.6.8). Furthermore, to assess any act it is necessary to consider the circumstances, those things that border on an act without being a necessary part of the act itself (I–II.7.1–2). Such things include the answers to the interrogatives who, what, where, by what aids, why and when, but the most important circumstance that must be considered is the "why" of motive (I–II.7.3–4). In this consideration of voluntariness, it is plain that Thomas has in mind the complex nature of the circumstances of human life and activity.[98] Here he is drawing on reason more than revelation, but not at the expense of revealed truth.

Since volition is required for an act to be *human*, he further elucidates his premise that every act is for an end (I–II.8). He then considers whether the will is set in motion by mind, emotions, heavenly bodies (which he rejects in article 5, whilst accepting the others) and God (I–II.9), and the mode of volition (I–II.10). Aquinas also gives place to the role of

---

97. Forward to question 6, *ST* Vol 17.

98. Though discussion of motive now requires a more careful account of the possibility of self-deception, and ulterior motives, such that neither the agent herself nor an observer may be sure of analysing motives correctly.

enjoyment, not only of our ultimate end (which we can enjoy even now in anticipation) but also of other, earthly ends and goods (I–II.11). He then turns to the intricate process he sees at work in coming to action: the will formulating an intention, making a choice of what to do now, consenting to the means chosen for reaching an end, applying the means, and commanding the action (I–II.12–17). In all this discussion, Aquinas's view of the human person is both complex, recognizing a whole host of forces at work within her (and even God working on her), and highly nuanced, fully aware that although he sometimes treats the will or reason, for instance, as if they were subjects in their own right, that they are nonetheless actually properties of the person.

3.2.3.c: Good and Evil Acts

From the aspects of volition in human acts, Thomas turns to the consideration of moral good and evil in human acts. First he sets out that some acts are good and others evil, but the evaluation is complex, taking into account the objective, the circumstances and the end intended (I–II.18.1–6). Furthermore, it is possible for acts to be neutral, or for acts that generally speaking are neutral, to be made good or bad by the circumstances, etc. (I–II.18.8–10). In addition there is the potential for good and evil in the will's inner activity, not just in the external act, depending again on the objective, the circumstances, the mode of reasoning and on its relation to the eternal law (divine reason) (I–II.19.1–4; 7–10). Thomas considers that even when the conscience is mistaken, its dictates are binding on the person (I–II.19.5), though, analogous to what was said of ignorance, whether the act based on the mistaken conscience is culpable or not will depend on whether the ignorance in question was of something that could and should have been known by the person (I–II.19.6). The good or evil of an outward act depends to a large degree on the aspects of the will discussed in question 19, but the reasoning by which the will is set in motion must also be considered (I–II.20.1–2). Because the same outward act can be good or bad depending on the individual case, aspects of the act itself need to be addressed also—such as the consequences, if they were foreseen or foreseeable—as well as the internal aspects, such as intention (I–II.20.5–6). From here Thomas moves to the category of "sinful," stating that an act will be good or bad dependent on whether or not it is sinful (I–II.21.1), and from that questions of praise-worthiness or blame-worthiness, merit or demerit are decided (I–II.21.2–4). Again, it is noteworthy that he begins with more philosophical terminology (good/bad) and moves towards integration with religious language (sin), which he then gives prime importance.

3.2.3.D: HABITUS

Only when he has laid such foundations does Aquinas come to speak more specifically of the virtues, first in a general discussion of "dispositions" or "habits" (*habitus*), those qualities that are good or bad for the possessor according to how they enable action (in accordance with reason, and therefore with the final end, or not), and which are a necessary part of how humans move from potentiality, which may be expressed in a wide variety of ways, to actuality (I–II.49).[99] A human has various dispositions (and even disposition-like states of the body) of the faculties of the soul, of the senses (insofar as these are controlled by reason), of the intellect, and of the will—in short, there are dispositions that enable her through rational means to move from potentiality to actuality in any sphere of action (I–II.50.1–5). Certain of these dispositions may be to some limited degree innate, but generally speaking they are acquired through repeated actions, or may be infused by God (I–II.51.1–4; I–II.63.1–3). They may grow in strength by being possessed more perfectly, or they may decay or even be destroyed by being possessed less perfectly. Such growth or decay is caused again by action, and whether actions are according to the disposition or not (I–II.52–53). Moreover it is possible to distinguish between good and bad dispositions, depending on whether they are in accordance with human nature or not (I–II.54.3). These he considers more fully as virtues (and vices).

3.2.3.E: VIRTUES

If Thomas's general discussion of dispositions owes much to Aristotle, his closer look at the virtues draws more heavily on the scriptures and the teachings of the Fathers. As W. D. Hughes puts it, "The influence of Aristotle is evident, indeed so apparent in the framework that its importance can be over-estimated."[100] Thomas begins by noting that human virtue

---

99. This is the section to which Kenny referred. Unsurprisingly, Aquinas uses Aristotle's definition for "disposition" here (*Metaphysics* 1022b10–12) and also his notion of qualities (*Categories* 8, 8b26–10a27). See Kent, "Habits and Vices," 116–19, for an account of the meaning of *habitus* in Aquinas.

100. Introduction to *ST* vol. 23, xxi.

is a good disposition that relates to acts (I–II.55.1–3). Here he draws his definition for virtue from a compilation of Augustine's writings: "Virtue is a good quality of mind by which one lives righteously, of which no one can make bad use, which God works in us without us."[101] As ever, Thomas does not use the Augustinian definition as a proof-text, but defends it on the basis of logic: formal, material, final and efficient causes (I–II.55.4). He then considers the "seat" of virtues as being in the "power of the soul," such as the intellect or even such natural aspects as the "appetitive part," which pertains to resistance of obstacles and seeking good and avoiding harm, but most especially in the will (I–II.56).

The intellectual virtues he considers to be both speculative (the ability to seek the truth through wisdom, science and understanding) and practical in the form of prudence, which includes taking good counsel, judging well according to general laws, and judging well in exceptional cases (I–II.57).[102] The difference between these intellectual virtues and the moral virtues is in the powers that they perfect: the intellectual virtues perfect an agent's capacity to seek the truth and judge well and wisely; the moral virtues perfect her ability to act well with regard to her appetitive powers, such as seeking good and avoiding harm, overcoming obstacles, etc. (I–II.58.2). However, prudence provides a special case, being both an intellectual and a moral virtue since it both perfects a person's intellect regarding right judgment and helps her to act (I–II.58.3). The moral virtues and prudence operate interdependently, meaning that they must all be present for any to be fully possessed (and therefore to exist fully as virtues in a person), though the other intellectual virtues need not be present, or can be present independently of the moral virtues (I–II.59.4–5).

The relationship between the moral virtues and emotions is complex. While moral virtue is not itself a passion, it occurs together with passions, and can be seen as a mean between two passions.[103] Human beings by

---

101. He believed this definition to come from Augustine, but Hughes relates in a footnote it is thought to have been garnered from Augustine by the French scholastic theologian and student of Peter Lombard, Peter of Portiers. See however Kent, "Habits and Virtues," who attributes the compilation to Peter of Lombard (119). Thomas notes that this definition is correct for infused virtues, but if one leaves out the phrase "which God works in us without us" it fully pertains to acquired virtues, *ST* I–II.55.4.

102. In article 3 he defends an Aristotelian notion that art is an intellectual virtue, a disposition which gives the ability to act well in the domain of one's art. This he contrasts with other virtues: to act against the "rules" of art knowingly is better than unknowingly; whereas with other virtues it is less blame-worthy to act against "rules" out of ignorance.

103. He discusses virtue as a mean more fully in I–II.64.

nature have emotions, therefore perfect virtue does not consist in any notion of rising above emotions, even sorrow: despite Thomas's dependence on philosophy, his understanding of emotion is both Christian and plausible according to the insights of psychology. Because the moral virtues perfect the appetitive aspect they often have to do with the emotions, though justice relates to the will, not the passions (I–II.59). After some further discussion of the relationship between the moral virtues, acts and emotions (question 60), Thomas turns his attention to the cardinal virtues.

Aquinas defends the position held by prudence, fortitude, temperance and justice in philosophical ethics, even against the notion that the theological virtues should be given a higher place, on the grounds that faith, hope and charity are superhuman, whereas the cardinal virtues (at least as acquired) are human. Among the cardinal virtues, prudence is principal because of its central position as both an intellectual and a moral virtue.[104] The four virtues are to be distinguished because of their different objects, but nonetheless there is an overflow—perfect courage must also be temperate, etc. (I–II.61). This overflow can also be called the reciprocity of the virtues, and means that a person may differ in the strength of her natural inclinations towards different virtues, but cannot actually possess the virtues properly in differing degrees (I–II.66.2).

The theological virtues of faith, hope and charity are needed, says Thomas, because a human's final end is ultimately beyond human reach. Only God can give these virtues such that a person may receive the face-to-face vision of God and partake of God's divine nature. Thus Thomas's virtue ethics is not, as stated before, "salvation by works." The theological virtues are to be distinguished from the other virtues because their object is God himself, while the other virtues have objects comprehensible to reason. The principal of the theological virtues is charity because through it faith and hope also come alive, and because of its central place in God's nature.[105] Furthermore, God can also infuse other virtues (I–II.63.3). Following on from his assertion of the reciprocity of the virtues, Thomas states that acquired human virtues can exist without charity, but for our acts to be directed towards our "supernatural" last end, charity is required, and can only be received from God. Yet charity does not exist without the moral virtues, at least in their infused state if not as acquired; however, it is more difficult for the infused moral virtues to lead to virtuous acts than for the acquired virtues, because the opposing dispositions (vices) may

---

104. See also I–II.66.1.
105. See also I–II.66.6.

remain, whereas the acquisition of virtues necessarily means the decay of their opposing vices.[106] Likewise, he says, faith and hope may exist in some incomplete state without charity, but charity does not exist without faith and hope (I–II. 65).[107]

Since Aquinas discusses the virtues in relation to how a person might attain her final end, it is not surprising that he is also interested in whether these virtues also remain eternally. The moral and intellectual virtues remain as regards human reason, though without the potential for vice. Faith and hope he sees as imperfect and will no longer be required when face to face with God, though certain desires may remain, such as for the salvation of a wayfarer. Charity, however, remains, and will then be possessed perfectly (I–II.67).

3.2.4: What Kind of Theology?

In looking at Augustine it was necessary to ask what kind of ethics he was writing; that question does not arise in relationship to Thomas, rather what kind of theology. There can be no doubt of the philosophical framework behind Aquinas's work, the rigorous attention to reason in setting out the order of his questions, the use of Aristotle's categories and frame of reference. What is disputed is whether this is pagan philosophy (which St Paul might warn against, as perhaps taking us captive—Col 2:8) that has only been superficially touched up, or whether this is Christian theology of a philosophically rigorous nature. One point that should carry some weight in this discussion is what Fergus Kerr refers to as "the anguish of philosophy," namely that Thomas imagined the state of natural philosophers to be one of anguish, because apart from revelation the most cogent natural reason could not allow them to reach their true fulfillment of beatitude.[108] Moreover Kerr claims that for Thomas it would have been impossible to imagine philosophy or natural reasoning apart from theology because

---

106. This is a helpful observation, and explains the possibility of salvation for the person who trusts in God (and so has infused virtues), but whose life disappointingly lacks the cardinal virtues and the acts they enable.

107. In I–II.65.5 ad 3 Thomas falls into what I consider to be faulty Christology, suggesting that Jesus didn't have faith or hope because these have inherent imperfections, whereas he possessed the face-to-face vision which they anticipate. To my mind this does not do justice to Jesus as fully human, as well as fully God.

108. Kerr, *After Aquinas*, 65–66, citing *Contra Gentiles* 3.48. This is close to Augustine's reference to the pagan's virtue as being only splendid vice without love for God, cited in Meilaender, *Theory and Practice*, 30.

they investigate only those things that God has created and using only those means that God has given.[109] Evidence that Kerr is correct may be found, for instance, in the fact that Thomas is careful to distinguish those (earthly) goods which a person may attain by her own effort and through her natural resources from the final good (the face-to-face vision of God), which she may only receive through grace (I–II.65.2). Furthermore, behind anything that might be called "natural" Thomas always means (and often makes explicit) "God-given." For these reasons, I believe that he did not expound a heathenish philosophy with a thin veneer of theology, but an intellectually rigorous and robustly Christian theology. Moreover, it is a theology that is suffused with luminous glimpses of the bliss to come in seeing God face to face.

More important, however, for this study is to ask how Thomas's virtue ethics is to be described theologically. There is a clear eudaemonist, teleological framework, similar to Augustine's. Yet unlike the patristic bishop, Thomas is content to appropriate the cardinal virtues as defined in classical philosophy, though adding both the notion of these virtues being infused by God in the believer as well as the theological virtues, which must be infused. While accepting the possibility of acquiring virtues through practice and human effort may be seen to presuppose that postlapsarian human nature still has a high degree of integrity (the potential to recognize earthly good, to will it and to do it through human strength), the addition of theological virtues and discussion of infused virtues nonetheless shows reliance on grace for anything that could be termed salvific.

3.3: Alasdair MacIntyre

Having looked at virtue ethics through the lens of one of the most influential theologians of the patristic era, and of the middle ages, I turn now to look at a more contemporary treatment. Following the Reformation, virtue ethics was largely the domain of Roman Catholic ethicists, and often was neglected even there.[110] In the twentieth century proponents from the Catholic tradition such as Pieper and Peter Geach advocated Thomist ethics.[111] Only since the publication of Alasdair MacIntyre's *After Virtue*

---

109. Kerr, *After Aquinas*, 65–66. See also Pieper, *Introduction*, ch. 12. For more provocative current interpretations of Thomas, see Stout and MacSwain, eds., *Grammar and Grace*.

110. Cessario, *Moral Vision*, 3.

111. Pieper, *Cardinal Virtues;* Geach, *Virtues*.

has it gained a central place in the wider debates both in philosophical ethics and in Protestant theological ethics.[112] The sheer volume of writing on virtue ethics seen in the last twenty-five years would have been unimaginable before this watershed. Thus it is right to look more carefully at MacIntyre's work, even if he did not set out to expound virtue ethics in a Christian theological context.[113]

3.3.1: *His Analysis*

In *After Virtue*, MacIntyre offered the following analysis. Contemporary moral philosophy consisted of remnants of earlier systems. These remnants had lost their meaning because the frameworks of which they were once a part were no longer understood or commonly assumed. He then tried to show from a philosophical and historical perspective indebted to Hegel and Collingwood how this state of affairs came into being.[114] His analysis was not in itself new, for Elizabeth Anscombe had sketched out such a proposition in 1958.[115] Yet MacIntyre pursued this at a time in which the ground had been somewhat prepared for him—not least by Anscombe, Iris Murdoch, Stanley Hauerwas and Philippa Foot, among others—and in such a way that his analysis seemed to be forceful and cogent, and to demand consideration and response.[116] He began by presenting an evocative parable, which he used to introduce the notion that through historical events the language of morality was in a "state of grave disorder" that could not be apprehended through analytical philosophy (which is descriptive of what is) or other academic disciplines, since they had been affected by the same historical events that caused the disorder, and since their "value-neutral" stance did not allow them to see decline and fall or disorder as such.[117] Moreover, MacIntyre admitted that he saw "no large remedies" for the disorder (2-5).

---

112. MacIntyre, *After Virtue*. This point is made by Hauerwas, *Character*, xv. See also Meilaender, *Theory and Practice*, ix, 2–3; Kotva, *Christian Case*, 1; and Yearley, "Recent Work."

113. Though he later advocated a form of Thomism. See *Rival Versions*. I will return to this later.

114. MacIntyre, *After Virtue*, 3. Further references to this work in this section will be in brackets in the main text.

115. Anscombe, "Practical Inference," 26.

116. See e.g., Anscombe, "Practical Inference"; Murdoch, "On 'God' and 'Good'"; Hauerwas, *Character*; and Foot, *Virtues and Vices*.

117. Though see Stout's questioning of just how great the disorder is and whether

Virtue Ethics in the Christian Tradition

To illustrate the difficulties in using the language of morality, he presented examples of debates in which the arguments were conceptually incommensurable—each argument was coherent in its own terms, and no rational means existed for proving one argument right and the others wrong, thus causing the debates to disintegrate into assertion and counter-assertion (6–7). He characterized these debates as incommensurable, but also as inconsistent, in that they were nonetheless carried out with a claim of "impersonal rational arguments" (7–10).[118] Where once these various arguments were at home in contexts of "larger totalities of theory and practice" (the traditions now facing epistemological crisis), these contexts are now largely lost, and the words used in current debates have changed meaning over the years (10–11).[119]

A significant part of his thesis concerned what MacIntyre described as the Enlightenment's project of providing ethics with an "independent rational justification" divorced from any discussion of theology, law or aesthetics.[120] He traced this project back in time through the work of Søren Kierkegaard, Immanuel Kant, Denis Diderot, and David Hume (chapter 4)—considering the work of great thinkers whom one could not suppose to have failed because they were not equal to the task. Nonetheless, fail they did, according to MacIntyre, and moreover, he claimed they had to fail. The reason for this had to do with the nature of the framework these thinkers had inherited, a teleological framework that was based on a) some notion of what a human actually is, contrasted with b) an understanding of what she could be if she realized her potential, and c) ethics supplying the function of helping her to move from a) to b). In this conception there was a rational coherence in that any duty was shown to be part of her true end (and consonant or coterminous with divine law) (52–53). However, in the Enlightenment there were two independent concepts: one of what humanity as it happens to be is, and one of ethics. Without the teleological concept of what a person should become (with the help

---

the disagreements among ethicists are so great as to preclude discourse, *Ethics after Babel*.

118. MacIntyre later discussed these divergent forms of moral discourse as relying on differing notions of rationality, and resulting in differing accounts of justice, in *Justice? Rationality?*

119. Although the history of these changes is clearly important in MacIntyre's thesis, this is not germane to my study.

120. Though see Schneewind's rejection of the idea of such an "Enlightenment project," given that many of the moral philosophers in question were not atheists but anticlericalists, *Invention of Autonomy*, 8.

of ethics), these two concepts were now free-floating (54–55). The newly enshrined principle that one cannot derive an "ought" from an "is" makes sense only when the subject of the factual statement is not seen to be of a functional nature (such as clock or farmer), which gives awareness of what it is for (its *telos*) and the possibility of evaluation. MacIntyre insisted that within the teleological framework of the earlier virtue ethics there was an understanding of function or purpose of humanity such that ethics in that context was indeed a fully rational enterprise. From a Christian perspective there may be unease regarding his notion of teleology: so construed, ethics appears to be works salvation, since a human's proper end is loving God and enjoying God for ever. Yet if ethics is seen to be not the means to that end, but as constitutive of that end, his criticisms of non-teleological ethics are still valid.

Crucially, MacIntyre's analysis of the situation of moral philosophy (and theological ethics) was both vivid and representative enough of debates to be compelling, even if many have differed sharply on a variety of points and offered robust criticism.[121] However, his analysis of the state of moral philosophy is of lesser interest to this study than his positive suggestions for reinvigorating or reformulating virtue ethics.

3.3.2: *His Proposals*

While MacIntyre saw the results of the failure of the Enlightenment project not merely in ethical discourse, but in the very fabric of Western society,[122] it is sufficient to note that he considered one major result to be the "Weberian" character of society in terms of its irreducible plurality (109).[123] The only alternatives he saw to this were a form of Aristotelian ethics, such as had preceded modernity, and the reaction against the Enlightenment typified by Nietzsche (111).

In *After Virtue* MacIntyre's positive proposals for resolution of the difficulties of incommensurable debates focused on a form of Aristotelian virtue ethics in which "practices" would play a central role. A "practice" he defined as a "coherent and complex form of socially established

---

121. See e.g., Horton and Mendus, eds., *After MacIntyre* for a variety of critiques and MacIntyre's response to them.

122. I shall not discuss here his depiction of the typical "characters" in Western society in ch. 7-8. See 2.4.1.a, p. 35–37.

123. MacIntyre characterized this plurality in terms of "liberalism" in *Justice? Rationality?* In this book he considered at some length the connection between systems of moral thought and the societies which produce them, and which they in turn affect.

Virtue Ethics in the Christian Tradition

cooperative human activity through which goals internal to the form of activity are realized in the course of trying to achieve those standards of excellence which are appropriate to, and partially definitive of, that form of activity, with the result that human powers to achieve excellence, and human conceptions of the ends and goods involved, are systematically extended" (187). Among the examples of "practices," he cites chess, farming, music, football, and enquiries such as physics and chemistry (187).[124] When writing *After Virtue*, he was content with a notion of individual virtues as separate from one another, and of "practices" that themselves may be neutral (or even morally wrong) in their content, but which have internal goods that may only be enjoyed through developing moral and intellectual virtues.[125] Naturally, there are problems inherent in this account. Cricket as a practice may indeed teach many virtues (including justice) to the extent that the game became synonymous with fairness, but would a person learn justice adequately if cricket is the only mode in which she learns it?[126]

Moreover, he proposed that a narrative construal of human life is necessary to his proposal, with its sense of life in its unity, with its structure that includes a beginning and an end, and with its capacity to make sense of the variety of roles a person inhabits (in family, profession, people, nation, etc.).[127] Not surprisingly, there are those who reject the form of virtue ethics that he proposes, and see hubris in his attempt to formulate a scheme of virtues "more compelling than the rival versions he has discussed," which include Homeric, Aristotelian and medieval schemes.[128]

MacIntyre later came to revise this appropriation of Aristotelianism, embracing instead a form of Thomism that meant accepting the notion of the unity of the virtues.[129] Yet MacIntyre proposes that what is needful is not the details of Aquinas's thought, but the "overall specific mode of enquiry," namely a dialectical approach.[130] The happiness at stake in this eudaemonism is dependent on the very nature of human beings. There is interrelationship between rules and virtues such that rules can only be

---

124. MacIntyre points out that virtues are also exercised in contexts other than the "practices."

125. MacIntyre, *After Virtue*, ch. 14.

126. See Miller, "Virtues, Practices and Justice." See also Taylor, "Justice After Virtue."

127. MacIntyre, *After Virtue*, ch. 15.

128. Coleman, "MacIntyre and Aquinas," 81.

129. MacIntyre, *Rival Versions*, chapter 3; Kerr, *After Aquinas*.

130. MacIntyre, *Rival Versions*, 77.

formulated (not as abstract or categorical commands) in terms of a *telos* that can be articulated and understood: negative rules set boundaries in which the good can be found.[131] Furthermore, progress in moral enquiry must go in tandem with progress in moral life—one cannot adequately learn about virtues without acquiring them. Integral to his vision of moral enquiry is the integration of theological, political and philosophical dimensions of thought. "The virtues which conjointly inform the actions of an integrated self are also the virtues of a well-integrated political community."[132]

3.3.3: Some Implications

Whether or not MacIntyre's account does justice to the Thomist tradition he seeks to inhabit in *Three Rival Versions of Moral Enquiry* is somewhat peripheral to the question I seek to address.[133] Yet an important part of his trilogy is the awareness that Thomist virtue ethics is not a monolithic, self-enclosed system, but has had a variety of formulations at various times and in various places. Indeed, given Thomas's dialectical approach, perhaps it is not unreasonable to claim that Thomist virtue ethics must always be in the process of being formulated and in the process of being changed. If so, to engage in Thomist ethics demands a dynamic approach that may commit the researcher to fewer certainties of outcome than many might desire.

However that may be, the difficulty raised by John Haldane as to how one should respond to MacIntyre, given that his stance has changed quite considerably in the course of the three books discussed here is one that needs to be addressed.[134] Yet for three reasons I think it is appropriate to engage with MacIntyre's early proposal to define virtues in relationship to "practices." First, one could hardly engage in debate at all if such emerging and provisional positions cannot be assumed to be fixed enough to merit discussion. Secondly, and therefore, it cannot be unreasonable to interact with ideas MacIntyre put forward, as ideas in their own right and not

131. This has resonance with Bonhoeffer's notion of ethical boundaries, see *DBW* 6:368–71.

132. MacIntyre, *Rival Versions*, 138–43, quote, 143.

133. I shall also ignore the questions of whether his assessment of the state of moral debate is accurate, and how debates which currently seem to be at an irresolvable impasse might be taken forward towards resolution. These are important considerations, but require a different study than I am undertaking here.

134. Haldane, "Thomist Revival," 91–92. See also Miller, "Virtues, Practices and Justice," 246–47.

Virtue Ethics in the Christian Tradition

utterly discredited by the fact that he himself has since focused on other matters. Thirdly, I consider it at least possible, if not likely, that MacIntyre's later emphasis on Aquinas's dialectical approach, rather than the content of Thomist virtue ethics, reflects MacIntyre's overarching concern to seek ways of bringing what he sees as an impasse to resolution, more than any move away from virtue ethics. If I am right in this assumption, it would lend increased support for considering more carefully his own form of virtue ethics put forward in *After Virtue*. This I propose to do, not least because, if I read him rightly, his stance by the time of writing *Three Rival Versions of Moral Enquiry* had moved close enough to a Thomist position that discussing it here would add but little to what has been said in relation to Aquinas himself.[135]

It is MacIntyre's suggestion that a certain core within the variety of conceptions of virtue ethics (from Homer and Aristotle, to Benjamin Franklin and Jane Austen) is discernible. He assumes that in all of the construals he discusses there must be a prior acceptance of some account of social and moral life, of a narrative conception of life, and of an account of what constitutes "practices" that train a person in virtues (186–87). In this account of virtue ethics, it would seem that such "practices" come to the fore, with an emphasis on the social nature that they presuppose. For whether practices are forms of the arts, sciences, games or politics, these "practices" and the virtues they instill can only be learnt within a social construct and tradition. He claims moreover that these "practices" not only have benefits for the individual but for the whole community and how persons relate to one another within the community (188–92). MacIntyre's emphasis is much more on the practical question of how a person develops virtues, rather than the theoretical issue of defining individual virtues and considering their relationship to one another. Problems arise, however, in his account pertaining to the question of the relationship of the virtues one to another precisely because at the time of writing *After Virtue* he rejected the notion of the unity of the virtues. Thus he refers to Peter Geach's example of a "courageous" Nazi and his insistence that "either it was not courage that he possessed or that in that kind of case courage is not a virtue," and states that it is indeed courage and a virtue, which might be the point of moral contact that would enable the process of moral re-education to begin (179–80).[136] Many would agree with MacIntyre that

---

135. Though MacIntyre's interpretation of Aquinas has been called into question. See, e.g., Coleman, "MacIntyre and Aquinas."

136. MacIntyre does not give a reference, but see Geach, *Virtues*, 160–61, and MacIntyre, *After Virtue*, 274.

any notion of the "unity of the virtues" seems unempirical, and no doubt all could cite along with him instances of "vicious violinists and mean-spirited chess players"—people who seemingly possess both strong virtues associated with their "practices" and strong vices (178–79, 193).[137] Yet the question remains, is the "courage" of someone so patently vicious a virtue, as MacIntyre here claims, or does it only have the semblance of courage, is it a counterfeit, a simulacrum, as Thomas Aquinas would have it? The question was not merely abstract for Bonhoeffer, who, as we have seen (2.3.1), wrote, "The most shining virtues of the apostate are night-black compared to the darkest weakness of the faithful."[138] Surely, the "courage" of the Nazi would be included here. It is a pity that in writing *After Virtue* MacIntyre did not apply to this question the criterion of teleology, which he otherwise so often invoked; had he asked towards what this "courage" tended, it might have prompted a different stance regarding the relationship of the virtues. MacIntyre's account of the virtues in relationship to the practices fails to convince particularly when placed in the context of Nazi Germany. The love of music and art, of sciences, a highly developed sense of aesthetics, as well as industry, discipline and other positive traits are almost legendary among many of the leading Nazis who were involved in or responsible for a whole host of atrocities. Yet history does not suggest that they learned from the "practices" of music and the arts, etc. what might be called "moral virtues," or that the "practices" were points of moral contact that enabled re-education. Thus, at least in this respect, MacIntyre's account seems to be inadequate, even if the "practices" can offer training in virtue(s).

Beyond MacIntyre's notion of defining virtues in relationship to practices, his statement that a society is dependent on prior acceptance of some account of social and moral life is worth consideration. At the present time, with questions regarding corporate identity in the setting of a pluralist society, it seems improbable that widespread agreement on

---

137. The issue of how the virtues are related (unity, reciprocity, interconnection, etc.) is widely debated. Porter, for instance, calls herself committed to a "connection" of the virtues as a "program for all those who want to grow in personal goodness," *Moral Action*, 65. Geach seems ambivalent, *The Virtues*, 160-68. Meilaender considers the unity of the virtues an end result, but not necessarily found in the stages along the way, *Theory and Practice*, 61. Foot holds that a virtue used to an evil end is not in that person or case a virtue, *Virtues and Vices*, 17. And Hursthouse considers it possible that a situation may force a virtuous person to do something unjust, but that a virtuous person would not act unjustly, to wit, as an unjust person would, "Applying Virtue Ethics," 65.

138. *DBW* 6:63.

Virtue Ethics in the Christian Tradition

any such account might be achieved. Yet precisely because these are real challenges today, it would seem that there is an increasing awareness of the problems attending the lack of a shared account of what it means to be human, let alone how to depict society, or how to understand the moral life. In this setting, MacIntyre's words may seem almost a utopian dream, but they may yet provide an attractive, even evocative, and visionary statement of hope.[139]

Another major strand of MacIntyre's account is the presupposition of a narrative construal of human life. This resonates widely in our culture, not least in theology with renewed interest both in how God's people are formed by the telling and retelling of God's story, as well as in how narrative passages in the Bible may be used appropriately to develop theology, and indeed in narrative forms of preaching and teaching. Whether such interest has come precisely in reaction to (or against) the increasing fragmentation of contemporary life, or from postmodern discontent with didactic and atomistic modes, the awareness is acute that a person is formed by the stories she has been told and tells about God, herself and the world. In the context of a number of current ethical discussions, gaining a sense of how the beginning and end of human life belong to the middle may be something that is best seen and articulated with the help of a sense of narrative unity. These issues are tangential to this study, although interesting, since Bonhoeffer concerned himself with such issues as abortion and euthanasia as they arose in the Nazi context in his discussion of the natural life. Thus even if it seems necessary to set to one side MacIntyre's proposal in *After Virtue* of defining the virtues in relationship to "practices," his emphases on the need for a shared account of the social and moral life and on the importance of a narrative construal on human life bear further consideration, in comparison and contrast with the accounts of Augustine and Thomas Aquinas.

3.4: Three Rival Versions of Virtue Ethics?

The accounts of virtue ethics found in Augustine, Thomas Aquinas and MacIntyre differ not only in their specifics, but in some of their major assumptions. Augustine's redefinition of the cardinal virtues as forms (order) of love is distinct from Thomas's adoption of the classical conception with the addition of infused (and) theological virtues. MacIntyre's account

---

139. The work of Hauerwas has been influential in this area. See especially his *Community of Character*.

is different again, even if both he and Aquinas are indebted to Aristotle. Are these then, borrowing from MacIntyre, three rival versions of virtue ethics, or are there commonalities that make them compatible or even complementary rather than rival versions?

While all three have as their framework some form of teleological eudaemonism, with emphasis on the nature of human flourishing and how it is achieved, there are differences in their notions of the human good. MacIntyre's account is, at heart, communal; he is concerned with society as a whole, and traditions and cultures. At the time of writing *After Virtue*, his teleology seemed focused on this life, and his discussion of the good for humans was, like Aristotle's, rooted in what a person can become here and now. This is very different from Augustine and Thomas, with their insistence that God is the supreme good that is only fully realized in the eschaton when a believer receives the face-to-face (or beatific) vision of God.

Similarly, how human beings may attain the supreme good is different in the three accounts. For Augustine, a person is utterly dependent on grace to be able to will or do such good as she knows. She is to exercise virtues, but she is dependent on grace to be able to do so, and they must to some degree be infused by God. For Thomas the theological virtues must be infused, and a person cannot attain the supreme good without them, but she is capable to a large degree of acquiring the cardinal virtues. This is an issue that carries little weight in MacIntyre. He is concerned in *After Virtue* with how a society promotes, values, teaches, and learns virtues, and seems to assume that there is no difficulty doing so. By the time he has adopted a Thomist view, he emphasizes the potential of a dialectical approach to overcome differences in ethical theory and does not deal directly with these issues in virtue theory.

The differences and similarities in these accounts are of particular interest in the context of this study, since some basic definition is required before it is possible to explore how Bonhoeffer's *Ethics* may be related to virtue ethics. What, then, can one say is necessary for a construal of ethics to be rightly classed as virtue ethics in the Christian tradition? No doubt certain issues that pertain to the person are essential: character, character formation, what it means to be human, and what the (supreme) human good is.[140] This perspective will include development, which necessitates a view over time, so a narrative account may be useful, even if it is not

---

140. I think eudemonism in this form is necessary, though it need not be the organizing principle or the starting point, as in "What is a happy life?"

Virtue Ethics in the Christian Tradition

strictly necessary. An approach that sees life in its entirety may also be helpful, though like Thomas one must accept that only God truly has that view. Teleology is also an integral part, both in the sense of looking towards what/who a person is becoming, and in the sense of recognizing that a human's goal is one that can only be fully attained/granted beyond this life, being formed in the likeness of Christ.[141]

An important consideration is whether it is necessary for virtue ethics to have aretaic notions, good or excellent traits, at its heart. This may be generally assumed, yet Hauerwas's distinction between virtue (or character) and virtues (character traits) and his proposal to base ethics on the former rather than the latter makes it possible to speak of "virtue ethics" without sustained focus on particular virtues.

Furthermore, there is the question of the purpose of an ethic. If a theory is to help analyze behavior, the discussion of issues internal to the agent, such as motives, is important.[142] Yet according to Aristotle and Aquinas, the point of moral enquiry is living rather than merely understanding the moral life; thus progress in enquiry is dependent on growth in virtue. In this case attention should be paid to how such growth occurs and may be fostered.

As well as having different starting points in philosophy (Augustine with Neo-Platonism, Aquinas with Averroist/Aristotelian philosophy and MacIntyre with awareness of all of those as well as numerous others), there is a complex relationship between their starting points in Christian doctrine. Thus Thomas built on what he knew of Augustine, and MacIntyre, latterly, has adopted a Thomist tradition. All of this makes for complex relationships between them, as well as wide areas of overlap in thought.

Another important area to consider is how to define the complex relationship between law and virtue, and there are real differences between these thinkers. In Augustine the two greatest commandments have such a central place that he is often seen as a kind of deontologist. Thomas treats law as it relates to the eternal law, with which human laws may or may not be in accordance, and whether or not they are binding will depend on this relationship. One often speaks of "natural law" in Thomas, but, as mentioned before, "nature" is that which is God-given and is never seen separately from God or "supernature." Meanwhile, MacIntyre does not

---

141. Meilaender also stresses the importance of teleology, *Theory and Practice*, 6–7. See also Hauerwas, *Character*, xxx; and Kotva, *Christian Case*, 23.

142. See, e.g., Slote, *Morality to Virtue*, 89, and Hauerwas, *Character*, 89–106.

speak at length about the role of law in his own proposals.¹⁴³ This may be due to his more prominent concerns about learning virtues (*After Virtue*), rationality (*Whose Justice?*) and overcoming incommensurability (*Three Rival Versions*), but the interplay between law and virtue is discussed only generally in terms of MacIntyre's approval of Aristotle's notion that communities require both lists of virtues and laws prohibiting certain actions (because virtues alone do not ensure a well-ordered society) (151–52, 200). There seems little doubt that some account is necessary, yet proposals vary widely, not just among the three thinkers I've treated in some detail, but among others as well.¹⁴⁴

3.5: Questions from Bonhoeffer

Having considered virtue ethics in three distinct construals, it is now necessary to see if the questions raised in the last chapter when looking at Bonhoeffer's *Ethics* can be addressed.

3.5.1: Is a virtue-based ethic necessarily a private one? Is it necessarily legalistic? How is it related to the hypocrisy Bonhoeffer calls "Phariseeism"?

To answer whether virtue ethics is necessarily private, some brief observations about what Bonhoeffer meant by "private" must suffice. Bonhoeffer's concern is that a "virtuous" person would seek to do good according to her ability and opportunity, and avoid doing anything evil; yet in the context of Nazi Germany he sees such a person as turning a blind eye and a deaf ear to the injustices perpetrated all around.¹⁴⁵ So I take it that the "private" virtue here would exclude anything involving the public arena, political action or speech, or involvement in others' affairs. Insofar such a distinction between "private" and "public" would seem to be not wholly unrelated to the kind of two-sphere thinking common in Lutheranism at that time,

---

143. Though he does speak of the relation of law and virtue in stoicism, *After Virtue*, 168–70.

144. On the issue of how rules relate to virtue ethics, see Hauerwas, *Character*, 3; 208–10, where he places command "in a larger framework of moral experience." See also Slote, *Morality to Virtue*, 10, 160–63, and ch. 10; and Hursthouse, "Normative Virtue Ethics," esp. 27; and Porter, *Moral Action*, 126, 130–38, Hursthouse, "Applying Virtue Ethics," 67–70. All emphasize the importance of some integration of the two.

145. DBW 6:66.

which separated the church and from the world, and which Bonhoeffer utterly rejected.[146] If this is right, perhaps Bonhoeffer's comments about private virtuosity are aimed as much against the "private" aspect as the "virtuosity." Surely any such discrepancy or dualism between one area of life and another would receive similar treatment from Bonhoeffer. Yet, even if this surmise is correct, is virtue ethics necessarily private?

From what we have seen regarding the centrality of the dual commandments to love God and neighbor in Augustine's understanding of ethics, it seems clear that such virtue ethics could not be accused of supporting the kind of virtuosity that could happily ignore others' distress. The love of neighbor that God commands is defined by Augustine as both doing no malice (which might be true of Bonhoeffer's privately virtuous person) and as neglecting no good, which is far removed from stopping one's ears and closing one's eyes to horrors all around.

Similarly, in Thomas's careful treatment of act, it is clear that the omission of a good action is not simply a "neutral" act, but would require the full range of considerations regarding the objective, the circumstances, the motives, and so on, before one could speak of it as good, neutral or evil. Doubtless, ignoring the needs of others out of a desire to keep out of trouble with the authorities, which is at least one reading of the motives of Bonhoeffer's privately virtuous person, would not be classed as good or neutral by Thomas any more than it was by Bonhoeffer.[147]

The account offered in *After Virtue* is quite nuanced in this regard, for he is aware of the possibility of "virtues" being employed to evil ends.[148] It is partially with this in mind that he speaks of the need for the virtues to be related to some conception of moral law, though of course there is no law to forbid the omission of help.[149] More tellingly, he insists that it is the *whole* of a person's life that must be considered.[150] With this holistic view, it would be difficult to speak of "virtue" if the whole of the person's life is marked by inaction in the face of injustice, or if that inaction could rightly be described as collusion with injustice.

Thus Christian virtue ethics is certainly not necessarily private, and it may even be that the opposite could be claimed: ethics conceived in terms

---

146. See, e.g., *DBW* 6:41–52.

147. See *ST* II–II.57.1, where he discusses justice in terms of the agent's relations to others.

148. See especially *After Virtue*, 274–75, where MacIntyre clarifies his position.

149. *After Virtue*, 200.

150. Ibid., 200–201.

of virtue addresses omissions as much as commissions, the whole of a person, and the totality of life are involved such that divisions of "private" and "public" cannot be allowed to stand.[151]

Moving to the second question, to ask whether virtue ethics is legalistic involves some irony, given that the recent resurgence of virtue ethics has been fuelled in part by a desire to overcome certain forms of legalism.[152] However, Bonhoeffer's critique of Roman Catholic moral theology as being "almost unbearably legalistic" is in reference to that church's teachings regarding the issues he was addressing in his section on marriage, including sterilization and contraception.[153] Clearly he regarded the positions endorsed by Roman Catholic teaching not only as legalistic but also casuistic, but the question here is whether virtue ethics necessarily ends in legalism and/or casuistry.[154] Certainly, although Augustine worked with a form of virtue ethics, he at no point seems to work casuistically, let alone legalistically. Similarly, many more contemporary virtue ethicists would even say that different virtuous persons might (for reasons of varying personal constitution or circumstance etc.) choose different courses of action in similar situations, a notion that surely rejects any possibility of legalism. (Of course such a position could lead to casuistry if one then tried to elucidate the features of the various agents or circumstances that would require a virtuous person to act one way or the other, but such an attempt need not be made at all.)

Yet to answer this question satisfactorily it is necessary to ask further how virtue ethics is related to rules more generally, and here MacIntyre's comments may be helpful: rules should be formulated in terms of the *telos* for human beings rather than as abstract or categorical commands; and negative rules provide boundaries in which the good can be found.[155] As already mentioned, this is not wholly unlike Bonhoeffer's insistence that ethical decisions are boundary issues that must not be allowed to swamp all of life, and that God's command (permission to live as humans) is for the entirety of human life, not just those parts that are seen as morally

---

151. MacIntyre shows in his work deep interest in public affairs, as well as being a proponent of virtue-based ethics. See especially part 3 of his *Ethics and Politics*.

152. See e.g., Meilaender, *Theory and Practice*, 4–5. See also Pieper, *Cardinal Virtues*, xii.

153. DBW 16:138–39.

154. See Pieper, *Cardinal Virtues*, 31, and Cessario, *Moral Virtues*, 3, 13–14. For a more positive assessment of casuistry, however, see Biggar, "Case for Casuistry;" and Jonsen and Toulmin, *Abuse of Casuistry*.

155. *After Virtue*, 151–52, 200.

good or bad. From this it is possible to say not only that virtue ethics is not necessarily legalistic, but that in some formulations there may be affinities with Bonhoeffer's own notion of how ethics for the whole of life is related to rules.

Thus, virtue ethics should not be considered private or legalistic. Yet can it defend itself against the charge of hypocrisy? In "The Love of God and the Decay of the World" when Bonhoeffer speaks of Pharisees, it is to say that they recognize only their virtues and vices, not the infinitely more important fact that they have fallen away from God.[156] So the question must be asked whether a virtue-based ethic so focuses the agent on her development of virtues (or ridding herself of vices) that what is essential in terms of her relationship to God might be lost from view. It is important to distinguish between the form of ethical thinking (virtue ethics) and the focus and motivation of the agent (which need not be the acquisition of virtues).[157] Just as Burnaby noted that loving because it is commanded is not actually love, it is certainly the case that the motive for action in a truly virtuous person cannot simply be the desire to be virtuous. According to Augustine, the only virtuous motive is the desire (the weight or pull of love) to love God and neighbor. Thus it is possible, and in relation to Bonhoeffer it is important, in Christian ethics to say that the agent's focus is not primarily on acquiring virtues or eradicating vices, but on God in Christ and the love for God and neighbor that follows.

3.5.2: Is virtue ethics necessarily an example of humans trying to reach God?

In the previous chapter (2.3.1) it became apparent that there is a potential problem regarding whether virtue ethics should be seen as a form of "religion" in the sense of the Barthian critique of human attempts at approaching God (instead of relying on God's gracious self-revelation and coming to humanity). If the starting point of virtue ethics is necessarily the question of how a person can be/become good (and thereby please God, or merit her salvation), then this critique may well apply. Again, O'Donovan's comments are apposite: the quest for human happiness may not be the starting point most appropriate to Christian ethics, and

---

156. DBW 6:318.

157. Meilaender's distinguishes between first (e.g., generosity) and second order (e.g., desire to be generous) of motivation, *Theory and Practice*, 14-15, 77-78. Cunningham makes little mention of such distinction, *End of the Law*, ch. 1 and 2.

humans cannot discover "the whole of our Christian duty by consulting our self-interest, even though the whole of our Christian duty does serve our self-interest."[158] In looking at Augustine, Thomas and MacIntyre it was apparent that each of these writers did accept this legacy of classical philosophy, yet it is important to note that not every conception of Christian virtue ethics has this starting point. Moreover, even if virtue ethics is situated within a eudemonistic conceptual framework, this does not necessarily result in the expectation of reaching God through human effort. This being so, virtue ethics is not necessarily a form of "religion" in Barth's sense.

3.5.3: *Is virtue ethics necessarily based on natural law?*

The question regarding natural law is more vexed: for Bonhoeffer, natural law seems to have been opposed to revelation in a way that many would now find questionable.[159] Furthermore he seems to have assumed that Thomas based his ethics on (this negative understanding of) natural law, an assumption that is problematic.[160] For Thomas natural reasoning or natural law would be incomprehensible apart from theology, since human reasoning is at all events a gift of God and since he employed it in attempt to understand things of God's creation.

In the case of Augustine's teaching, we have seen that at the time of writing *De moribus ecclesiae* his thought was often led by the concerns of philosophy or natural reasoning, and in places Christian teaching and biblical emphases were even distorted. However, his later works become increasingly dependent on biblical teaching and revelation, while still holding to the foundations of virtue ethics. Thus from the later Augustine it is possible to state that virtue ethics is not necessarily based on natural law. Likewise, Hauerwas's conception of an ethic of character is not grounded in natural law. Thus, whether or not Bonhoeffer's assumptions

---

158. O'Donovan, *Self-Love*, 141, 157.

159. See, e.g., Grabill, *Rediscovering the Natural Law*; and Biggar and Black, eds., *Revival of Natural Law*. Cf Hauerwas's treatment of natural law and natural theology in *With the Grain of the Universe*. However, see also Black's proposal for integrating Hauerwas's concerns with those of the Finnis/Grisez school, *Christian Moral Realism*.

160. See e.g., Pope's "Natural Law and Christian Ethics": Aquinas considered that revealed divine law is required for a person to know what leads to her true end, the beatific vision; the natural law he believed was sufficient only for her to know her earthly good, 80–81. See also Grabill, *Rediscovering the Natural Law*.

about natural law should be seen to be correct, his objection to it need not be a stumbling block for seeing his ethics as related to virtue ethics.

3.5.4: How might virtue ethics relate to the question of how Christ takes form among us here and today? Is virtue ethics necessarily abstract, or a form of system, or based on an abstract catalogues of virtues?

If one of Bonhoeffer's central emphases, concretion, is articulated in the question of how Christ takes form among us here and today, it is worth considering how virtue ethics might address this. It may be possible to construct theories involving the virtues being acquired through the training of habits or being infused by God, thus leading to a virtuous character that might be shown to be in some way in likeness to Christ. Such a formulation might be possible drawing on Augustine's early writing, seeing Christ as virtue, wisdom and truth. However, I imagine Bonhoeffer would utterly reject such a proposal as being abstract: it is not immediately clear how such virtues relate to the person of Jesus Christ, incarnate, crucified and resurrected, nor how virtue ethics so formulated relates to Christ's winning form in the believer.

Yet it might be possible, still drawing on Augustine, for a virtue-based ethic to speak convincingly of how Christ wins form among us: that through closeness to God, God's own holiness, truth and love may so pervade the believer's character that she becomes more and more Christ-like. Glossing this further, suggesting that it is precisely Jesus Christ (not abstract notions of God, such as holiness and truth, but the historical person Bonhoeffer refers to as incarnate, crucified and risen) whom she follows and who transforms her, it is possible to claim that virtue ethics might say more than most models of ethical thinking about how Christ wins form among us. Indeed the tradition has long been concerned with how a person is trained in the virtues, the kinds of influences and commitments required for her to gain the virtues. For such an account to relate well to Bonhoeffer's ethics, a fuller account would be needed regarding the relationship of justification and sanctification in virtue ethics, an area that will be addressed in the next chapter.

Concerning abstract ethics, the forms of virtue ethics expounded both by Augustine and Thomas would seem to be characterized often by abstractions, with Augustine referring to Christ as virtue and wisdom, for instance, and Thomas using Aristotelian categories. Nonetheless, it is also possible to suggest that even in their accounts the seeds are present that could grow into a less abstract form. I have already suggested that Augustine's notions of conformation to the good could be made less abstract by concentration on the person of Jesus Christ rather than abstract notions such as wisdom and virtue. In Thomas Aquinas's account, one could emphasize his awareness of the plethora of circumstances that border any ethical act: who the agent is and who any other people are who might be affected by an act is important in his understanding, as are other questions of place, means of acting, timing, and so on. Such construals would not be open to the charge of being abstracted from Christ or real life.[161]

Yet it may be of greater help to draw on the Hellenistic notion of philosophy as a way of life, not an abstract mode of thought. This could apply at least as well to a follower of Christ using virtue ethics: she cannot learn more about the virtues without acquiring them, and she cannot learn more about how Christ wins form among us without focusing on him. Thus I believe it is possible both to formulate virtue ethics in ways that are not abstract, and to live in such a way that moral enquiry is not in any way abstracted from Christ or everyday life.

The question regarding systems overlaps in some ways with the previous question, given that certain forms of system are clearly abstract. We have, however, already seen that Augustine does not expound any system, and that Thomas's "system" is not closed, self-referential, or constructed to deduce answers from first principles. Thus it seems right to say that if this is to be called a "system," it not of the kind Bonhoeffer found objectionable. Likewise, MacIntyre's attempt at formulating virtue ethics in a fresh way, while it is wide-ranging, is not systematic, and in the later parts of his trilogy he was quite as forthright in his rejection of such systems as Bonhoeffer. Thus this question also can confidently be answered, no.

The question regarding an abstract catalogue of virtues could be answered positively if Thomas Aquinas's treatment of virtue ethics were seen to be normative. There is no doubt that he has a "catalogue," the four cardinal virtues and the three theological virtues; and there is little doubt that each of these could be seen as abstract concepts.[162] Other accounts, however, are less open to this criticism. Augustine's redefinition of the cardinal virtues as forms of love would make it difficult to speak of a "catalogue" at all, and MacIntyre's emphasis on how we might learn virtues

---

161. See also Hursthouse, "Applying Virtue Ethics," and Cottingham, "Partiality and the Virtues."

162. That such virtues need not be abstracted either from Jesus Christ or from daily life could also be argued.

Virtue Ethics in the Christian Tradition

means that he undermines any perceived importance of such a catalogue. Furthermore, Hauerwas's emphasis on *virtue* (or character) rather than *the virtues* offers an account that avoids any catalogue of virtues.[163] Thus virtue ethics need not be based on an abstract catalogue of virtues.

In view of all these things, virtue ethics need not be abstract, or based on a system, or involve an abstract catalogue of virtues. Importantly, virtue ethics may be well able to articulate how Christ takes form among us here and today. Thus although some care may be needed in how virtue ethics is articulated, it need not be antithetical to Bonhoeffer's insistence on concrete ethics.

3.5.5: Does virtue ethics demand a view of human nature in general and human reason in particular that Bonhoeffer would perceive to give too little account of the Fall? Is virtue ethics opposed in some way to grace that one must categorize Bonhoeffer's thought as not one but the other?

It may be that Bonhoeffer's criticisms of Thomas's theology did not fully do justice to Aquinas's understanding of human nature as fallen and in need of grace to receive the beatific vision. Yet this observation cannot be the only answer to the first question, since there are too few references in Bonhoeffer's *Ethics* to Thomas to be sure just what Bonhoeffer believed about his theology. Yet whether or not Bonhoeffer's estimation of Thomas's anthropology is right or not, virtue ethics does not necessarily demand Thomas's position. Augustine's emphasis on the Fall and its effects in his later works makes it impossible to claim that his view of human nature (and reason) would be seen by Bonhoeffer as giving too little attention to human nature as fallen. Thus if I am right in suggesting that Augustine is best seen as advocating a form of virtue ethics, the answer to this question is a firm "no."

In a related matter, the question of grace, though it comes last in my list from the previous chapter, is by no means the least important, given that the Reformation assertion of *sola gratia* is of central importance to Bonhoeffer's theology as a whole. If it could be demonstrated that virtue ethics were in some fashion opposed to grace there could be no possibility of seeing his ethics as related to virtue ethics.[164] Certainly in Hellenistic

---

163. Hauerwas, *Character*, 15–16, ch. 3.
164. See Geach, *Virtues*, 46, for one example of virtue ethics that has an almost

forms there is no sense that humans are not utterly capable in their own strength of acquiring all such virtues as might be seen as needful for living a happy, flourishing life. Yet despite the young Augustine's use of this framework, even at the early stage when he was writing *De moribus ecclesiae* he underscored the need for grace to live virtuously.[165] In his later writings he emphasized this more, to the point of seeing both love and indeed all virtues as forms of grace, while still maintaining the basic outlines of his earlier virtue ethics.

Similarly, we have seen that Thomas Aquinas stated repeatedly that the most needful virtues can only be infused, not acquired through human effort, and even those which can be acquired through practice may also be infused. Thus both of the Christian writers, despite their dependence on various forms of Greek philosophy, are well aware of human dependence on God's grace at least for receiving the beatific vision, and perhaps for any development of virtues.

3.6: Conclusion

Having followed up, in the light of these three major treatments of virtue ethics, the questions that arose out of an exploration of how Bonhoeffer treated important themes in this tradition, it is possible to say that there is nothing that would preclude the possibility of seeing Bonhoeffer's *Ethics* as being in some way related to virtue ethics. However, for that to be possible it will be necessary to discuss the relation of virtue ethics to sanctification, and examine how Bonhoeffer sees the relationship between justification and sanctification, which will be the first task of the next chapter. There I shall also explore the ways in which his ethics shows affinities with virtue ethics, and the specific themes that seem most closely related.

Pelagian feel. See also Hauerwas, *Character*, xxxi, where he felt the need to defend himself against criticisms that he had too little emphasis on grace. Cf. Meilaender, *Theory and Practice*, 19, 122.

165. See e.g., *De moribus ecclesiae*, 13.22–23, and 30.64.

4

Bonhoeffer's *Ethics* as Virtue Ethical

4.1: Introduction

THUS FAR WE HAVE SEEN IN CHAPTER TWO THAT IN BONHOEFFER'S *ETHICS* the notion of "virtue" is often used negatively or ambiguously (2.3.1). Yet Bonhoeffer's use of the term "virtue," his references to the Thomist tradition, and his allusions to classical philosophy and myths are all so nuanced that it would be incautious to assume therefore that Bonhoeffer necessarily rejected virtue ethics as it might be conceived now (2.3.1–3). However, such evidence internal to his *Ethics* is also not sufficient to speak unequivocally about the possibility of the presence of some correlation.

Furthermore, we have seen that other commentators have been diverse in their assessment of Bonhoeffer's mode of conceiving of ethics (2.4). Nonetheless, those who take seriously the themes both of ethics as formation and ethics as command seem most faithful to Bonhoeffer's thought. Thus on the basis of the analyses of other commentators no case could be made for Bonhoeffer's *Ethics* to be seen as related to virtue ethics, but neither could such a case be conclusively refuted.

Perhaps more importantly, we have seen in chapter three that issues raised in chapter two regarding the nature of virtue ethics which might have precluded any correlation between that and Bonhoeffer's *Ethics* were found not to be problematic: virtue ethics is not necessarily private, legalistic or "Pharisee-like"; it is not an example of Barthian "religion"; nor need it be based on natural law; it is not necessarily abstract; nor does it require a view of human nature which Bonhoeffer might think takes too little account of the Fall, but can emphasize the role of grace (3.5).

The conclusion of these findings has been that, while no correlation has yet been shown, various possible objections to seeing Bonhoeffer's *Ethics* in relation to virtue ethics have not been substantiated.

In this chapter I shall first of all attend to the question which has already been raised as theologically necessary for virtue ethics in a Christian context, namely, how Bonhoeffer saw the relationship between justification and sanctification (4.2). Since virtue ethics is focused on the agent, and developing those qualities that enable right and good living, there is an obvious relationship theologically speaking to the question of sanctification. For if it is the case that a Christian is primarily enabled to act well in an atomistic way (being given grace to withstand this particular temptation, say), then virtue ethics cannot be the most natural form in which to think about how she lives well. However, if it is the case that God desires to make her holy (or, at least holier) in this life, to sanctify her, then this involves making her the kind of person who is able to act well, even in the face of this or that particular temptation. Such a theological stance would make virtue ethics a likely form for considering how Christians are to live.

Following from the question of how Bonhoeffer sees the relation of justification and sanctification, I shall explore the concerns that seem to underlie the ethics manuscripts taken as a whole (4.3). The reason for doing this is that if there is any meaningful correlation between Bonhoeffer's *Ethics* and virtue ethics, this should be discernable in relationship to the concerns that seem to motivate his writing.

I shall also ask if there are general aspects of his treatment of ethics that show possible relation to virtue ethics (4.4). Yet because not only general concerns are important to this study, I shall finally look to see if there are specific themes in Bonhoeffer's *Ethics* that have a virtue-ethical flavor that might give real evidence for the existence of a correspondence between the two (4.5).

4.2: Justification and Sanctification

In the previous chapter, I deferred further exploration of how virtue ethics relates to the question of how Christ takes form among us here and today until the nature of justification and sanctification in Bonhoeffer's thought has been explored. The reason for this is simply that virtue ethics in a Christian context must relate to sanctification, in that both presuppose the ongoing change and formation of the agent's actual character.[1] Thus how

---

1. Though see Stanley Hauerwas's comments that in 1985 he was "no longer convinced that justification and sanctification are the best means to spell out the

Bonhoeffer's Ethics *as Virtue Ethical*

Bonhoeffer viewed sanctification is of no small moment for this study. A claim made by David Fergusson holds good particularly if Bonhoeffer's *Ethics* is to be seen as related in some way to virtue ethics: "Attempts to articulate a contemporary doctrine of sanctification must surmount at least three obstacles," which he names as charges of individualism, Pelagianism, and detachment from the concerns of the world.[2] This, he claims, is because traditional accounts of growth in holiness have often seemed to emphasize an individual's private spiritual experience rather than the role of the community, have suffered from Reformation polemics which often placed sanctification in tension with justification, and have seemed to imply some rescue from a world presumed to be doomed.[3] In this chapter Bonhoeffer's rejection of individualism (4.4.1) and his affirmation of humanity's utter dependence on grace (4.3.1) will both be demonstrated. His attention to the concerns of the world is addressed more obliquely in the following section (4.2.1).[4] It will be seen then, that if Bonhoeffer does articulate a doctrine of sanctification, it will be one that avoids the obstacles named by Fergusson.

4.2.1: *Sanctification in Earlier Works*

In a sense, it is noteworthy that it is unproblematic to speak of Bonhoeffer's stance not only on justification but also sanctification, because it was not particularly common in his context to address this. Arvid Runestam claimed in 1929, "The concept of discipleship is the stepchild of Lutheran ethics."[5] The word "discipleship" should not be misinterpreted as meaning something essentially different from the concept of sanctification. Both concepts require that the believer's behavior is changed in the light of Christ by the working of the Holy Spirit.

At least one of Bonhoeffer's teachers was also aware of this lack in Lutheran teaching. Adolf von Harnack stated,

---

theological significance of the emphasis on character for the moral life"; he felt what he had said earlier was correct, but that he didn't say enough, *Character*, xxviii–ixxx; and 194–224 for his views in 1975.

2. Fergusson, "Doctrine of Sanctification," 380.

3. Fergusson, "Doctrine of Sanctification," 381, 383, and 384. As Fergusson shows in the article, these are misrepresentations of how the doctrine of sanctification should be understood.

4. See also e.g. *DBW* 8:511, 541–43, and 558.

5. Runestam, "Nachfolge Jesu," 747, quoted by Gremmels, "Rechtfertigung," 87, my translation.

> Luther is not responsible for the comfortable misunderstanding which arose out of that [the doctrine that good works are unnecessary for salvation]; but from the very beginning one has had to lament over moral laxity and a lack of seriousness regarding sanctification in the German Reformation churches. The saying, "If you love me, keep my commandments" receded inappropriately. The Pietist movement was the first to recognize once again its central importance. Until then, in opposition to the Catholic "works righteousness," the pendulum of behavior was swung precariously on the opposite side. Yet religion is not only conviction, but rather conviction and deed, faith which is active in sanctification and love: that is what the Protestant Christians must learn more securely if they are not to be shamed.[6]

Given this insight, one might expect that he would treat sanctification or ethics seriously, yet in the same book, whose title means "the essence of Christianity," there is hardly any reference to ethics at all, let alone sanctification.[7] Yet in his defense one must note that other theologians categorically discounted the possibility of speaking of Christian ethics.[8]

Thus it is indeed noteworthy that it is possible to speak of sanctification within Bonhoeffer's work from very early in his career. In his doctoral dissertation, he holds justification and sanctification together in discussing ecclesiology, not expounding their relationship, but using them to make another point: "Real sanctification is merely a sign of the last things. Here we are still walking in faith in God's gracious judgment on our doing. Here the center is justification, not sanctification (although the former is not real without the beginning of the latter). That is, here we see only our sin and believe in our sanctity."[9] Even at this early stage in his theological development, Bonhoeffer shows an insistence on the intrinsic relationship

---

6. Von Harnack, *Wesen des Christentum*, 180, my translation.

7. He does note that one could present the gospel as an ethical message "without devaluing it," and he defends the righteousness of the Pharisees, 45, and criticizes medieval Catholicism as teaching that true discipleship was only possible for monks, with only a second-class form possible for those in everyday life, 51 and xi, and he recognizes some form of self-denial is required to flee from or destroy mammon, worry and selfishness, 53–54. As regards Bonhoeffer's respect for Harnack, see Eberhard Bethge, *Biography*, e.g., 43, and 66–67; *DBW* 8:179, 246 (note 13), 304, 415 (note 4), 509 (note 10), 559 (note 21). Cf also *DBW* 8:531 (note 21).

8. For instance Albrecht Ritschl and Paul Tillich: see Trillhaas, "Albrecht Ritschl"; and Ratschow, "Paul Tillich."

9. *DBW* 1:275 n. 253. In the final form of his dissertation, he cut the latter part of this quote, which improved the flow of his argument. Given his further use of justification and sanctification, it is unlikely that he changed his mind; see *DBW* 1:75, 100, 103, 143, 196. See also John Godsey, *Theology*, 42, paraphrasing *DBW* 1:108–9.

between justification and sanctification, whilst holding open the eschatological dimension of the completion of sanctification.

In his early insistence on the necessary relationship between justification and sanctification, he may well have been influenced by Karl Holl's interpretation of Luther. As Andreas Pangritz sates, "Not least foundational for Bonhoeffer's own understanding of Luther was probably Holl's interpretation of justification as truly being made righteous, as found in his book on Luther: 'The goal which God pursues in justification is only then reached when he has made the person truly righteous. Justification and being made righteous belong intrinsically together.'"[10] Whatever the source for Bonhoeffer's thinking, what is important is that he did hold the two together in his early writing.

However, it is in *Discipleship* that he makes the unity of justification and sanctification most explicit. In Eberhard Bethge's estimation, *Discipleship*, written during Bonhoeffer's time as head of a seminary of the Confessing Church, was intended to address the question of justification and sanctification, and to recover Luther's teaching of *sola fide, sola gratia*.[11] Bonhoeffer wrote to Barth while he was working on the book, saying that he had been having a dialogue in his own mind with the older scholar about the nature of justification and sanctification in Pauline theology and in the interpretation of the Sermon on the Mount.[12] Barth's reply was to say that he "never could, nor wished to, deny" the doctrine of sanctification, but that he nevertheless had concerns about the concrete treatment, specifically that it might suggest its "realization in some sphere that is humanity's own."[13] In other words, Barth was concerned that an articulation of the doctrine of sanctification might place an emphasis on human activity rather than divine. In Godsey's view, *Discipleship* "represented Bonhoeffer's above-mentioned silent controversy with Barth over the question

---

10. Pangritz, *Barth in der Theologie Bonhoeffers*, 28, citing Holl, *Luther*, 123, my translation. On Holl's influence on Bonhoeffer, see Bethge, *Biography*, 46. On Holl's interpretation of Luther's understanding of justification and sanctification, see Berkhouwer, *Faith and Justification*, 15, and Althaus, *Theology*, 236–37 and 241–43. On Bonhoeffer's critical reception of Holl, see Pangritz, *Barth in der Theologie Bonhoeffers*, 28; DBW 10:357–78; and DBW 11:184–85. See also DBW 10:422 for another early example of his holding justification and sanctification together.

11. "Challenge of Dietrich Bonhoeffer's Life," 55.

12. DBW 14:235–36.

13. DBW 14:250–51. However, see his positive assessment of the book, CD IV/2, 533. In the following section Barth uses *Discipleship* as a foundation for his own discussion.

of the relationship between justification and sanctification."[14] There can be little doubt that Bethge and Godsey are right about Bonhoeffer's intention in *Discipleship* to discuss justification and sanctification.[15] Here he argues with forceful words against any notion of justification that does not include sanctification: "We have gathered like ravens around the carcass of cheap grace; from it we received the poison that killed the discipleship of Jesus among us."[16]

Indeed, Bonhoeffer's focus in *Discipleship* is on the necessity of recognizing the costliness of grace, not presuming upon a cheap grace that demands nothing of the believer. Christian Gremmels sees Bonhoeffer as following Luther's own theology in this, which he summarizes as: "Because we have received unmeritedly our justification from God, therefore we can, as a result of this, do what is righteous among people."[17] Gremmels notes that Bonhoeffer recognized in the years of the church struggle that Lutheranism had lost its heart, the connection of justification and doing what is righteous. "Out of the Because-Therefore came an If-Why: If I have already been declared righteous anyway, why should I still have to do anything?"[18] This, of course, is simply another way of stating the problem of cheap grace.

Although *Discipleship* is one of Bonhoeffer's best-loved works and has become a modern classic of spirituality, there is often a discernible discomfort among scholars with regard to this book. One reason, apart from scorn for the popular, could well be his seemingly direct and non-academic style of writing with little mention of his "dialogue partners."

Another possible reason for the general lack of scholarly interest in *Discipleship*, however, may relate to his comments in prison: in a letter to Bethge of July 21, 1944, he wrote of his earlier desire to learn to have faith by trying to live something like a holy life. "I probably wrote *Discipleship* as the end of that path. Today I see clearly the dangers of this book, though I stand now as then by what I wrote."[19] As Ann Nickson said, many

---

14. Godsey, "Barth and Bonhoeffer," 23.

15. See e.g., the final two sections, "The Saints" and "The Image of Christ," *DBW* 4:269–304.

16. *DBW* 4:52. See the whole passage, 52–56 and 43.

17. "Rechtfertigung," 89, all citations my translation. For an example of Bonhoeffer's comments on Luther, see e.g., *DBW* 4:36. For Luther on sanctification, see Mokrosch, "Gewissensverständnis," 88–89; Althaus, *Theology*, 234, 236, 245–46, 257, 273, 355; and Ebeling, *Word and Faith*, 64, 77–78; cf 62–64.

18. "Rechtfertigung," 94.

19. *DBW* 8:542.

commentators overemphasize the dangers without giving due attention to the fact that he still stood by what he had written.[20] They seem to suggest that, in his new understanding, this had been an attempt to escape from the world and live a holy life in quasi-monastic seclusion. Yet given that Bonhoeffer still stood by what he wrote, the comment surely must not be read as a retraction, even if he would from his perspective in prison have wanted to add some caveat. Certainly, part of the change in Bonhoeffer's thought relates to living fully in the world, because after the above quote he continues, "Later I experienced, and I am still experiencing right up to this very hour, that it is only in the full this-worldliness of living that one learns to believe."[21] Yet, I am not convinced that a changed perspective regarding living fully in the world is truly the thrust of his comments and partial revision. He goes on to say,

> When one has fully given up on making something of oneself, whether it be a saint, or a repentant sinner, or a churchman (a so-called priestly figure!), a righteous or an unrighteous person, a sick or a healthy person—and this is what I call this-worldliness, namely living in the fullness of tasks, questions, successes and failures, experiences and perplexities—then one completely throws oneself into the arms of God, then one no longer takes seriously one's own sufferings but the sufferings of God in the world, then one watches with Christ in Gethsemane, and I think, that is faith, that is *metanoia*; and so one becomes a human being, a Christian (cf. Jer. 45!). How could one become incautious in success, or crazed through failure, when one shares in this life in God's sufferings?[22]

Bonhoeffer refers in this letter to his study in America and conversations with Jean Lasserre at that time, his development and work during his training of seminarians, and his further experience in the time of his involvement with the conspiracy and finally his imprisonment. His increasing sense of the Christian life as being "this-worldly" is important here, referring to it as not "the shallow and banal this-worldliness of the enlightened, the busy, the comfortable, or the lascivious, but the profound this-worldliness, which is full of discipline and the constant awareness of death and resurrection."[23] Yet this does not tell the whole story of what

---

20. Nickson, *Freedom*, 97. See Green, *Sociality*, 178–79, for one example of such interpretation.
21. *DBW* 8:542.
22. *DBW* 8:542.
23. *DBW* 8:541.

Bonhoeffer probably meant with regard to "dangers" of this book. For the conversation with Lasserre to which he refers is about what they wanted to do with their lives. The French pastor wanted to become a saint; Bonhoeffer wanted to learn to believe, and later thought he might do so by living a holy life. I think the greatest danger he saw in prison was that of trying to make something (no matter what) of oneself.[24]

How, then, does this understanding of the "dangers" of *Discipleship* affect how one should view his account of justification and sanctification in that work? The answer to this question is dependent on how sanctification itself is understood. For if sanctification is seen in terms of the believer having to try to become something it is clear that Bonhoeffer had distanced himself from that by the time he was in prison.[25] However, another text from prison, "Thoughts for Baptism" would suggest that he had not changed his mind on sanctification. He wrote there, "our being Christian will consist now in two things: in praying and in doing what is righteous before people."[26] Therefore, it is important to look at how he treats justification and sanctification in the *Ethics*, to see if the views he expressed there would also seem to fall under his concern about making something of oneself.

4.2.2: *Sanctification in the* Ethics

4.2.2.A: "Christ, Reality and the Good"

In the first manuscript, "Christ, Reality and the Good," Bonhoeffer undermines in important ways all ethical systems, especially those dependent on a dualistic conception of reality. He states, "In the place which in all other ethics is characterized by the opposition of 'ought' and 'is,' of 'idea' and 'realization,' of 'motive' and 'deed,' in Christian ethics stands the relationship between reality and becoming real, of past and present, of history and event (faith), or to utter instead of terms capable of many

---

24. This would accord with what Bonhoeffer's twin sister, Leibholz-Bonhoeffer has written about views in the family, *Portrait of a Family*, 53. See also Ford's claim that this is not a denial of selfhood: "It simply is freed from concern or anxiety about any formation or transformation of self apart from what happens in the course of worship and responsible living in the world (or 'prayer and righteousness')" (*Self*, 260–61).

25. See for instance Webster, *Word and Church*, 95, who appears to construe sanctification in terms of "self-conscious self-cultivation"!

26. *DBW* 8:435. See also *DBW* 8:178, 226, 356, 415, 433, and 549 for further examples of themes from *Discipleship* still current in his prison writings.

Bonhoeffer's Ethics *as Virtue Ethical*

interpretations the clear name of the matter itself: of Jesus Christ and the Holy Spirit" (34).[27] Inherent in this claim is not only the rejection of dualisms found in secular ethics, but also any dualism between justification (as the work of Jesus Christ, completed in history, reality) and sanctification (as the work of the Holy Spirit, ongoing in believers in the present, still becoming real).[28]

Later in this manuscript, as he argues against the then current notion of "two kingdoms" (which involved a stark division between what was secular, in which the church could have no say, and what was sacred, which was largely seen to be private life and about which the church was allowed to speak) Bonhoeffer is happy to speak directly of sanctification. In this context he states that the first concern of all Christians must not be simply to "live a pious life" but to be "witnesses of Jesus Christ to the world. The Holy Spirit equips those, to whom he gives himself. That such a witness to the world can only happen in the right way, if it comes from a sanctified life in the church of God, is a self-evident precondition" (50). Such a usage of the word "sanctified" should, of course, not be overburdened by great claims that this passage is really about sanctification. Clearly it is not, except in terms of how sanctification relates to his main concern here of the church's need, because of who it is, to be reaching out to the world, for there to be visible, holy deeds that point to Jesus Christ.[29] This brief reference to a sanctified life indicates *in nuce* important emphases for Bonhoeffer: sanctification is the work of the Holy Spirit, and takes place within the context of the Christian community.

4.2.2.b: "Ethics as Formation"

The manuscript and theme of "Ethics as Formation" is the one some have already suggested might be seen to be related to virtue ethics.[30] One might therefore expect to find more sustained passages relating to sanctification.

---

27. All page numbers in brackets in the main text refer to *DBW* 6.

28. It is interesting that Jones, among others, finds Bonhoeffer lacking "an adequate pneumatology" for how we discern God's will, living in the penultimate and pointing to the ultimate, "Cost of Forgiveness," 164–66. It would seem from the above passage at least that Bonhoeffer took seriously the role of the Holy Spirit in enabling right living.

29. It would also be interesting to follow up how in Bonhoeffer's thought sanctification is related to ecclesiology, another strand of continuity in his writing from the time of his doctorate. See also conformation as occurring in the church, *DBW* 6:84–85.

30. See e.g. Sagovsky, "Bonhoeffer, Responsibility and Justice."

In this manuscript Bonhoeffer memorably depicts a variety of ethical types, only to show how each of them fails and must fail in the exceptional circumstances of Nazi Germany. Instead of trusting to reason, fanaticism, conscience, private virtuosity, or even acting in one's own freedom, all of which he likens to rusty weapons, Bonhoeffer points to the shining ones of simplicity and cleverness, drawing on Matthew 10:16 (64–70). After giving a Christological preface, he begins to unfold his theme of ethics as formation, or more precisely, as being conformed to Christ or as Christ winning form in the believer. "The form of Jesus Christ wins form in the person. The person does not win his own independent form, but what gives him form and sustains him in the new form is always only the form of Jesus Christ himself. It is therefore not some aping imitation, nor a repetition of his form, but his own form that wins form in the person" (83).

This manuscript and its theme are important in looking at sanctification in the *Ethics*, despite the fact that there is no overt discussion of the topic. Nonetheless, it is clear that Bonhoeffer expects that the believer will be in some way truly and visibly changed through being conformed to the person of Jesus Christ, and this is surely another way of speaking of being sanctified.[31] Moreover, in such a formulation of sanctification there can be no suggestion that the person is trying to make something of herself.

4.2.2.c: "Ultimate and Penultimate Things"

Yet if "Ethics as Formation" is an implicit account of sanctification, the theme of the ultimate and the penultimate is the context in which Bonhoeffer is explicit about justification and sanctification. Sadly, the relationship between his notion of the ultimate and the penultimate and the doctrine of justification and sanctification has not been apparent to all of Bonhoeffer's interpreters, but the following should make this correlation clear.[32] He defines the ultimate (final both temporally and qualitatively) as the justification of the sinner by grace (137–40). The penultimate is potentially all of earthly life, which cannot lead to the ultimate but can either prepare for it or can place hindrances in the path of Christ's coming

---

31. See also *DBW* 6:125, 129–32.

32. See e.g., Burtness, *Shaping the Future*, 72–73, where he sees the ultimate and penultimate as ethical structures, later relating the penultimate to evangelism and social gospel, 76; and Dumas, *Theologian of Reality*, 158–59.

to justify sinners (141–42).³³ There are two categories he considers under the penultimate, being human and being good (151).³⁴

Penultimate things are discussed for the sake of the ultimate, and another way of speaking about this pair is *Vorbereitung und Einzug*: preparation and entry, words he thought of using for the title of his book at one stage (153 n. 55), which are borrowed from ecclesial Advent language and from Isaiah. Christ prepares his own way and his coming cannot be forced or prevented by human activity, but "we can oppose his coming in mercy" or we can prepare the way (154). Thus he advocates whatever supports humanity and goodness as being part of preparing the way for Christ's coming. "Only the coming of the Lord will bring the fulfillment of being human and being good" (157).

Although Bonhoeffer begins by defining the ultimate as justification, he does not work through in detail how his account of ultimate and penultimate relates to justification and sanctification. The ultimate as justification is quite clear: it is God's final word, qualitatively different from all that might precede it (140). The temporal finality is important because it counters any tendency towards a "cheap grace" (141): since justification is only ever the *final* word, there is no possibility of reasoning, "since I am saved, therefore it doesn't matter what I do."³⁵ The qualitative finality is equally important because it demands that there is no continuity between the penultimate and justification, that nothing a person does can force (or indeed hinder) the coming of Christ. This is grace, and it is a sovereign act of God. Thus in one succinct definition Bonhoeffer safeguards justification by faith, rejecting any notion of works righteousness.

This he does, however, without ceding any ground regarding the necessity of a sanctified life:

> Christ comes indeed, and creates his own way, whether the person is ready for it or not. No one can prevent his coming, but we can oppose his coming in grace. There are conditions of the heart and life and the world which particularly hinder the reception of grace, that is which make it infinitely more difficult to be able to believe. We say, "make difficult, hinder," but not "make

---

33. There are similarities in this to Thomas's views. See 3.2.3.b, p. 73.

34. See *DBW* 6:151 n. 52 regarding his earlier intention of speaking also of "being evil." Being evil would not fit his definition of the penultimate as being open to the coming of Christ in mercy. Equally, Bonhoeffer may have understood evil as an absence, rather than a reality in itself. This would accord better with his rejection of dualism.

35. See Gremmels, "Rechtfertigung," 94.

> impossible," and we also know indeed that even the straight way, the removal of hindrances cannot force grace.... But all of this does not release us from preparing the way for the coming of grace, from removing all that hinders or makes it more difficult to come to faith. (154)

And in the next paragraph he continues:

> Yet all this does not exclude the task of preparation. It is rather a task of immeasurable responsibility for all who know of the coming of Jesus Christ. The hungry need bread, the homeless shelter, those denied their rights justice, the lonely companionship, those lacking discipline order, the slave freedom. It would be blasphemy against God and neighbor to leave the hungry starving because precisely the one in greatest need is closest to God. For the sake of the love of Christ, which belongs to the hungry as well as to me, we break bread with them, share shelter. When the hungry do not come to faith, the guilt falls on those who denied them bread. To get bread for the hungry is preparation for the coming of grace.
>
> It is something penultimate that is happening here. Giving the hungry bread does not mean proclaiming the grace of God and righteousness, and having received bread does not mean standing in faith. But for the one who does it for the sake of the ultimate, this penultimate stands in relationship to the ultimate. (155)

What I hope is clear from these passages is the utter seriousness with which Bonhoeffer upholds the doctrine of justification by grace, by faith, and not by works, as well as the uncompromising insistence on works of righteousness, exemplified by feeding the hungry, tending to those in poverty, giving shelter to the homeless, and so on, precisely because of belief in justification, "for the sake of the ultimate." He does not use the word "sanctification" in this context, but his reference is still in terms of "being human" and "being good," and both are to be defined in Christ. Moreover, it is not the outcome for the neighbor thus served, but the motivation of the Christian ("the one who does it for the sake of the ultimate") that allows Bonhoeffer to speak of acts as having penultimate character. From this it should be clear that the notion of preparing the way is closely related, if not identical, to sanctification. It is possible therefore to see that Bonhoeffer did not change his position expounded in *Discipleship* regarding justification and sanctification, but nor did he speak of the latter in the terms that he rejected in prison, namely an attempt to make something of oneself. Furthermore, the theme of the ultimate and penultimate is one that Bonhoeffer referred to in later manuscripts as well so that it must be accorded a fairly central place in his overall thought in the *Ethics*.[36]

4.2.2.D: "The Natural Life"

It is not far-fetched to claim that the manuscript "The Natural Life" is a prolonged elaboration on the two things Bonhoeffer considered to be penultimate: being human and being good. As such it may be read as an exposition of what kind of life may be seen to be open to the coming of Christ in grace (natural, rather than what is unnatural, i.e. closed to Christ's coming, 165). Intriguingly, it is precisely in this manuscript that Bonhoeffer is able to do what he considers to be so important: to be concrete in addressing the burning issues of his time and place, such as euthanasia and forced sterilization. Although Bonhoeffer does not speak directly of justification and sanctification, he continues to use the closely related one of the penultimate, being open to the coming of Christ.

4.2.2.E: "History and the Good"

This manuscript contains in both of its versions some of the central ideas of Bonhoeffer's *Ethics*, including his insistence on a concrete ethic based on love, responsibility and grace. Again, although he does not specifically speak of justification and sanctification, he holds the two together without compromise. The Christian acts responsibly in freedom, not trusting in any principles for the justification of her actions, but relying on grace (220). Yet the grace required for justification does not in any way obviate the need to act in a way that indicates sanctification. Everyone lives in relationships that give her responsibility for such action, which is choosing to do God's will (287–88).

4.2.2.F: "The Love of God and the Decay of the World"

In this manuscript, written in late 1942 and clearly under the influence of having read Barth's *Church Dogmatics* II/2, Bonhoeffer's central concern is that Christian ethics can only be about doing the will of God. Human knowledge of good and evil, he claims in an argument very close to his earlier work *Creation and Fall*, is a product of the Fall (301–2). God-given

---

36. See e.g., *DBW* 6:350, and 369.

simplicity (*Einfalt*) as seen in Jesus creates unity with God, the possibility of a right understanding of things and "direct action," a concern of his addressed in *Act and Being* (315–22).[37] Again it is clear that Bonhoeffer is upholding the doctrine of justification by grace with the need for the believer to act in accordance with God's will. His terminology is not that of justification and sanctification, but in this manuscript also, Bonhoeffer holds the two together theologically.

From this short look at how Bonhoeffer handles the issues of justification and sanctification and related concepts in the *Ethics*, it is clear that he at all times upholds the doctrine of justification by grace, and is careful to treat ethics not as works righteousness, but also as related to grace: Christ wins form in the Christian, the command of God frees her for simplicity of action in accordance with God's will. This is how "Christ wins form among us here and today." It is clear, even if he hardly uses that word, that Bonhoeffer expects the believer to be sanctified as much in his writing of the *Ethics* as he explicitly did in *Discipleship*. Moreover, if he was concerned about some element of "making something of oneself" in *Discipleship*, there is no hint of that in the way he treats sanctification in the *Ethics*. From all of which it is possible to say not only that Bonhoeffer's notion of sanctification meets all of Fergusson's criteria, but also that his theological stance offers a framework in which it is possible for virtue ethics to be present.

I now turn to a consideration of how some of Bonhoeffer's overarching concerns expressed in the *Ethics* manuscripts relate to virtue ethics. This is to ensure that, if some relationship to virtue ethics is to be established, it can be shown to relate to the broader outlines of his thought and not just to isolated themes.

4.3: Overall Concerns of *Ethics*

In my reading of these manuscripts, I have tried to identify issues that seem to motivate Bonhoeffer's work, and it is his underlying aims rather than specific themes that I address in this section. The concerns that seem to drive much of his work include: the need to develop Christian theological foundations for ethics (4.3.1), especially its relation to grace (4.3.1.a), to Christ (4.3.1.b), and to the Fall (4.3.1.c); the need for a concrete ethic for his own time and place (4.3.2); the need to articulate the historical

---

37. See e.g., *DBW* 2:23, 48, 126, and 158–59. See also *DBW* 6:384, and 404, where Bonhoeffer returns to these themes.

setting for his ethics (4.3.3); the need to explore the relation of the church and the world and how that affects ethical discourse (4.3.4); and the structures of ethical life (4.3.5). The questions regarding each of these concerns are how well they accord with virtue ethics, and how well working in a virtue-ethical mode would enable these concerns to be met.

4.3.1: *Christian Foundation for Ethics*

One of the overarching themes in Bonhoeffer's *Ethics* is elucidating a foundation for Christian ethics. Several of the manuscripts, both in earlier and later periods of writing, are devoted to developing a fully Christian foundation for ethics. "Christ, Reality and the Good," "Ethics as Formation," "Ultimate and Penultimate Things," "The Love of God and the Decay of the World," and "The 'Ethical' and the 'Christian' as a Theme" all attempt to make clear how ethics can be conceived within Christian doctrine. Thus systematic questions pertaining to the role of grace, the Fall, and (not unrelatedly) justification and sanctification, all focused on the person of Jesus Christ, are central to the conception of ethics Bonhoeffer was attempting to articulate. Thus it is also crucial in this current study to show that seeing his ethics as related to virtue ethics would do no injustice to his theological concerns.

4.3.1.A: GRACE

One of the foundational issues that was deeply important to Bonhoeffer and which recurs throughout the manuscripts is that of justification by faith and the need to establish ethics in such a way as not to undermine this central doctrine. Thus he emphasizes throughout the manuscripts human reliance on grace. In the first manuscript, "Christ, Reality and the Good," he underscores the centrality of grace in his conception of ethics by his use of the unusual word, *teilbekommen*, to receive a share, to participate by gift (38). We have already seen his insistence in "Ethics as Formation" that it is Christ who wins form in the believer (4.2.2.b), as well as his safeguarding of the role of grace in his discussion of the penultimate (4.2.2.c). Unsurprisingly, throughout the manuscripts there is a clear emphasis on ensuring that ethics does not become a human work apart from grace.

We have seen in the previous chapter that virtue ethics can be articulated in ways that uphold this doctrine (3.5.4). This can be done in two ways. The first is to highlight infused virtues rather than acquired virtues.[38] This path would underscore the believer's dependence on God's gracious action and not allow for any whiff of works righteousness. Yet it could be open to just the abuses that Bonhoeffer sought to address in *Discipleship* and which still concerned him in writing the *Ethics*, namely cheap grace.

The second, however, is to follow Bonhoeffer in his treatment of penultimate and ultimate in saying that the behaviors that one might call "virtuous" or see as a sign of sanctification in the agent's life do not *lead* to justification. His discussion of the relation of the penultimate and the ultimate may be a genuine contribution Bonhoeffer has to make to Christian virtue ethics by showing how sanctification (the practice of true virtue) is part and parcel of salvation.

4.3.1.B: CHRISTOLOGY

Equally unsurprising is the fact that Christology is a central part of Bonhoeffer's foundation.[39] Thus one of the two central strands of his ethics, ethics as formation, is focused on Christ. Bonhoeffer does not particularly hold before the reader a portrait of Christ as the gospels portray the actions and teachings of Jesus, but a dogmatic formulation: incarnate, crucified, and risen (70-83). Within this framework, Bonhoeffer is able to present a theology of incarnation and the acceptability before God of what is human and what belongs to human earthly life (which of course links closely with his treatment of the natural life), while at the same time showing that what is sinful comes under the judgment of God and that Christ was crucified to reconcile sinners to God, and to bring not only new life but new creation. This is the basic Christological emphasis that informs Bonhoeffer's concept of ethics as formation. "Being conformed to the incarnate One means being a real human being. . . . Being conformed to the crucified One means being a person judged by God. . . . Being conformed to the risen One means being a new person before God" (81-82).[40]

---

38. See 3.2.3.e, p. 77-78 regarding Thomas's treatment of virtues and his notion that the theological virtues must be given (infused) by God, while the cardinal virtues may be acquired either by practice (through human effort) or infused by God.

39. See e.g., Torrance, *God and Rationality*, 78; Feil, *Theology*, 84-89; Godsey, *Theology*, 171-72, 205; and Nickson, *Freedom*, 145.

40. See also *DBW* 6:33 regarding the source of ethics as "the reality of God in his revelation in Jesus Christ," and *DBW* 6:34-35 and 40-41, where Bonhoeffer defines the good in terms of participating in the reality of God in Christ, and thereby encountering equally the reality of God and the world in Christ. See also his definition of the penultimate as everything which is open to the coming of Christ in mercy, *DBW* 6:151-52.

Bonhoeffer's Ethics as Virtue Ethical

Again, this theological foundation for ethics is one that is compatible with virtue ethics, as was seen in the previous chapter (3.5.3). Christological concerns can be included in virtue ethics by focusing on Christ himself as the example of what human virtuous living means. Thus one might not only ask the question "what would Jesus do?" but also "how would Jesus do this?" and "for what reasons would Jesus do this?" and so on. A myriad of accounts from the gospels may inform such thinking, but Bonhoeffer's (Barthian) dogmatic approach of thinking in terms of Incarnation, Crucifixion and Resurrection may also be seen as a kind of shorthand way of holding various aspects in balance.

4.3.1.C: THE FALL

Another doctrine that has a foundational role is the Fall and its consequences for all of human life. It forms a central motif for the manuscript "The Love of God and the Decay of the World."[41] One of the most intriguing ways in which Bonhoeffer uses the concept of the Fall is in averring that Christian ethics must not have as its goal the knowledge of good and evil, which according to Genesis 3 only became available to humanity at the cost of separation from God.[42] Thus Christian ethics must bring the foundation of all other kinds of ethics into question and critical scrutiny (301–2).[43]

This is another theological emphasis that virtue ethics, as we have already seen (3.5.4), can honor. Analogous to the traditional viewpoint that virtue ethics (philosophy) is a way of life, virtue as perhaps conceived by Bonhoeffer is shown and shaped by Christ (who wins form in the believer). Thus what is sought is not in the first instance "knowledge," but Christ himself. A more Thomistic conception might highlight the role of infused prudence in giving the believer right perception and thus an awareness of ethics not based on the fallen knowledge of good and evil.

From all this it is possible to say that virtue ethics need not be a hindrance in the articulation of these foundational theological concerns. Both regarding grace and the effects of the Fall, it seems that Bonhoeffer potentially has real strengths to offer a Christian account of virtue ethics.

---

41. See *DBW* 6:301, note 1 regarding the possibility that this manuscript was written with the intention of making it a preface or the first chapter.
42. In this he follows closely his argument in *DBW* 3:84, 114.
43. See also *DBW* 6:277.

In the case of Christology, however, it may be that virtue ethics has particular strengths that would support Bonhoeffer's emphases.

4.3.2: Concrete Ethics

We have seen that one of Bonhoeffer's concerns in the *Ethics*, to provide a Christian theological foundation for ethics, could be supported within a virtue-ethical framework. Another issue that appears throughout the manuscripts is his insistence that ethics must be specific to his time and place, not abstract.[44] In chapter 2 (2.3.4.a) I offered a summary of the variety of ways and places in which Bonhoeffer insisted on the need for ethics to be concrete,[45] and in the previous chapter (3.5.3) we saw there is no doubt that virtue ethics need not be abstract. Indeed, its attention to the particularities of the agent may make virtue ethics more capable of meeting Bonhoeffer's concerns for concrete ethics than many other modes.

4.3.3: History

Another of Bonhoeffer's concerns is directly related to his insistence that ethics must be related to his own time and place: history. Indeed, one might claim that it would be ludicrous to insist on the necessity of addressing one's own context if one were not attentive both to the current situation and to the history that led to it. Hence Bonhoeffer attempts to address questions of history in at least three of his manuscripts, "Inheritance and Decay," "Guilt, Justification, Renewal," and "History and the Good."[46] It seems to me that his historical analysis is not always persuasive,[47] however

---

44. See e.g., *DBW* 6:32, 39, 85–86, 87, 235, 246, and 263. Regarding the particularities of each agent's family, friends, profession, etc., see *DBW* 6:256–60. Regarding concrete ethics and the authorization to speak ethically, see *DBW* 6:373 and 354–64.

45. There is an oddity about abstract ethics which has received little attention: Bonhoeffer frequently insists on its necessity, but most of the material in the manuscripts is not concrete. His early philosophical interest and this fact lead me to suspect that, although he saw the dangers of abstract ethics and desired to write specifically and concretely, this did not come naturally to him. See 32 n. 37. Regarding Bonhoeffer and philosophy, see 32 n. 36.

46. That he shows himself to be influenced by Hegel in this area is also true, but not pertinent to this discussion. See Wayne Floyd, "Encounter with an Other."

47. For instance, his claim that one can only speak of "historical inheritance" in the Christian West is one I would not make, *DBW* 6:94. Also, his insistence on the unity of the West is correct in some important ways, but also obscures significant differences of peoples, languages and cultures, *DBW* 6:100–101.

Bonhoeffer's Ethics *as Virtue Ethical*

for this study the correctness of his notions is not as important as the question of what he was trying to achieve. In the manuscript "Inheritance and Decay," for example, it is more obvious what his goal is (namely, countering Nazi ideology) than that his historical claims are sound. In disputing pre-Christian, mythological foundations for Germany (93–94; 98–100), and in arguing for the unity of Europe precisely through Christianity (99–101), Bonhoeffer is arguing against prevailing Nazi claims for a Germanic master race, drawing on Norse gods and legends.[48] The key to his thought in this manuscript is his statement, "With the loss of its unity that was created through the form of Jesus Christ, the West stands before nothingness" (118). This notion he fleshes out: "Faced with the abyss of nothingness, the question of an historical heritage (whose reception means both processing in the present and passing on to the future) dies out. There is no future and no past. There is only the present moment, snatched from nothingness, and the desire to seize the next moment" (119). Again, whether Bonhoeffer is correct in the etiology or not, he is certainly describing the reality of life first in the Weimar Republic but also in the Nazi era, with the sense of loss of ties to Germany's imperial past and, because of the drastic economic situation, the loss of ready assumptions about the future.[49]

The least that must be said of Bonhoeffer's interest in history in his *Ethics*, is that it is integral to his notion of concrete ethics,[50] as well as his understanding of the ethical agent, which, as has already been noted, affirms the contingent realities of particular relationships, ties, and setting. Thus an interpretation that seeks to do justice to his concerns must take this emphasis on history seriously. This seems something virtue ethics (at least as expounded by MacIntyre and Hauerwas) does quite easily, both through its focus on the agent (including all her particularities of interrelations and circumstances) and the assumption that virtues are developed

---

48. See *DBW* 6:94 n. 5.

49. See *DBW* 6:124 regarding the partnership of the church with others in Nazi Germany. See also "Guilt, Justification, Renewal" as a reading of Germany's recent history and Bonhoeffer's hope for the future. If Bonhoeffer was not wholly convincing in his perception of history in "Inheritance and Decay," the acuteness of his depiction of the guilt of the church in Nazi Germany is startling. If there is any question of how clearly he saw his own context (and therefore how well equipped he was to do what he set out to do in writing an ethics for his time and place), that should be fully answered by his awareness of the then current situation. See also "History and the Good," which may have been intended to replace "Inheritance and Decay" (*DBW* 6:245 n. 1). If so, this would have been an improvement in that he avoided the less persuasive historical analyses and created a tighter composition.

50. See especially *DBW* 6:245–46.

over time and practiced in concrete historical settings. Furthermore, taking seriously Bonhoeffer's notions of European history, it can be said that virtue ethics belongs firmly in the history and culture he envisaged. Finally, as MacIntyre demonstrated in *After Virtue*, the notion of virtue ethics has been variously defined and fleshed out in different cultures and times; thus it is clear that virtue ethics can be appropriated for other historical settings in ways that Bonhoeffer would deem necessary for being concrete and for a specific time and place.

4.3.4: *Relation of the Church and the World*

Another general concern that Bonhoeffer addresses at various points in his manuscripts is the conceptual question of the relation of the church and the world, a concern that had different relevance in his context than it might have in ours. This is both because of Lutheran theology and polity of "two kingdoms," which posited that the church had no remit to address questions of state or politics, and, relatedly, because of what was actually happening in Germany and the difficulties the churches were experiencing in trying to address the evils inherent in National Socialist policies. This, like so many other issues already discussed, has foundational character, in that Bonhoeffer first had to make a case for why the Church (and he as a theologian) should even be discussing certain questions in Christian ethics.

One manuscript that treats this theme overtly is "Church and World," in which Bonhoeffer explores his experience that those in Nazi Germany who valued the goods of high humanism sought the proximity of the church. In doing so, he develops the notion that all these goods (reason, law, education, humaneness, freedom, tolerance, etc.) actually derive from Christ, and in seeking protection through the church, these people were actually seeking Christ himself, if only unwittingly (347–48).[51] Thus, the relation he sees between the church and the world is not necessarily one that would be affirmed outside the church.

---

51. This is closely related to his theme of unconscious Christianity; see *DBW* 8:545, 547, and 582. See also his question of how the church can encourage "good" people to turn to Christ, *DBW* 6:350–51; and *DBW* 8:407–8, and 455. See also "On the possibility of a word of the church to the world," though it was probably not written for his book, (*DBW* 6:354 n. 1). Also his rejection of such church/world duality is of importance. See "Christ, Reality and the Good," especially *DBW* 6:42–43.

Bonhoeffer's Ethics *as Virtue Ethical*

Furthermore, it is instructive to look at the confession of the guilt of the church in "Guilt, Justification, Renewal," as it were, as a worked example of the relationship of the church and the world.

> With this confession the whole guilt of the world falls on the church, on Christians, and, in that it is not denied here but confessed the possibility of forgiveness is opened up. For the moralist it is completely incomprehensible that the essentially guilty person is not sought here, that the righteous atonement as punishment for the evil ones and as reward for the good ones is not demanded . . . but rather people are here who take upon themselves all, truly all, guilt, not in some heroic decision of sacrifice but simply overwhelmed by their most personal guilt against Christ, and who can no longer think in this moment about retributive justice against those principally guilty, but only about the forgiveness of their own great guilt. (127)

The confession of guilt that follows is deeply insightful and moving as it addresses the passive complicity of the church in the atrocities of the Nazi regime through not raising its voice against the oppression, hatred, murder of innumerable innocents, "the weakest and most vulnerable brothers of Jesus Christ" (130). Such a confession is only possible if one presupposes the relation of the church and world advocated by Bonhoeffer, which does not neatly delineate between the sacred and the secular and which not only allows but demands that the church have a voice in all areas of life.

Much more could be said,[52] but for this study it is enough to note that the theme of the relation of the church to the world is an important issue, and to ask how virtue ethics can address it. This could be done perhaps by focusing on the agent, who cannot be divided into sacred and secular compartments, thus emphasizing a holistic conception of life as Bonhoeffer himself does. Also, a Christian account of human flourishing (defining, as Bonhoeffer does, the good in Christ) may enable the relation of the church and the world to be appropriately articulated, since the well-being of the whole world is not independent from the church.

4.3.5: *Structures for Ethical Life*

The final general concern that occurs repeatedly in Bonhoeffer's *Ethics* is the notion of "structures" for ethical life. Although I think André Dumas

---

52. It is worthy of some reflection that Bonhoeffer does not offer a political theology, but rather a theology which demands the integration of all spheres of life.

is mistaken in seeing "*Gestalt*" in terms of structure, there are other quite central themes that clearly are about structure: the responsible life, and mandates.[53] In the subsection of the second version of the manuscript "History and the Good," headed "The Structure of the Responsible Life," Bonhoeffer considers the dual ties both to God and neighbor as structuring factors: the person is responsible before God (must answer, respond to God), and through her relations with others she is called to act on their behalf, which introduces his significant theme of representation, *Stellvertretung* (256).[54] Such "structures" are determining boundaries that affect action, whether she is aware of them or not. These structures are God-given, as are the contingent parameters of context and the responsibility of others that limit a person's responsibility (267–69).

The second "structure" that appears in Bonhoeffer's ethics is the notion of mandates. It is not unrelated to responsibility, in that Bonhoeffer discusses them also in a further new subheading of the second version of "History and the Good," "The place of responsibility" (297-98). This is not a full discussion of the mandates, but throughout this section it is clear that Bonhoeffer considers each area of life that he calls a divine mandate to be a sphere in which God calls a person to account regarding acting with responsibility for others (291–93).[55]

The fact that he used the concept in early and later manuscripts and in prison seems more important to me than the issue of the changes in his

---

53. That, as Dumas claims, "form" is problematic because of possible confusion with Aristotelian concerns of form and content would seem to be unfounded in the actual context of what Bonhoeffer writes, *Theologian of Reality*, 219 n. 7. Clearly the translation of words from German to English, from German to French and then again to English is fraught with perils for the interpreter. In some cases it certainly could be that "*Gestalt*" (or the related verb "*gestalten*") could be translated either as "form" or "structure," and these two English words may in some cases be synonyms. Nevertheless, Bonhoeffer's use of "*Gestalt*" often refers to persons or characters from fiction and should be translated with words which have such possible connotations. See also Plant, "Uses of the Bible," 96, where he argues that "*Gestalt*" should not be translated: "At the very least it is a tragic obfuscation of the richness of the term 'Gestalt' to translate it in every instance with the English word 'form.'" There are advantages and disadvantages to both options, though I believe "form" is as rich (and mostly in quite parallel ways) as "*Gestalt*." My suspicion is that for native speakers of English the richness of "form" may not be apparent, simply because it is taken for granted.

54. Regarding the translation of *Stellvertretung*, see my "'Felicity to the Original Text?'" 351.

55. See also *DBW* 6:54–59, where he speaks of the mandates in relation to concretion, scripture, and the unity of the person who lives simultaneously under these mandates.

thinking concerning their content, most famously the change regarding work/culture and marriage/family (cf 54, 383 and 392).[56]

Both in his discussion of the structures of responsible living and the mandates Bonhoeffer attempts to give his ethics a structure that is demonstrably biblical and which cannot take on an independence that becomes dangerous, as had the notion of "orders of creation" that had been used by others.[57] Furthermore it seems important that Bonhoeffer was using these categories to show that all of life is the arena where the person is held to account for acting responsibly on behalf of others and according to God's will, and in this sense his broadening of categories is instructive. The concept of mandates thus does double duty, fighting both faulty theology and the malaise in Nazi Germany that allowed average people (who probably wanted to be good and do what is right) to imagine that the evils around them were not their responsibility, even if through their work, say, they participated in them.[58]

The relationship of virtue ethics to responsibility is not as straightforward as it may seem.[59] It is inaccurate to speak of responsibility as a virtue, even if one may describe acting responsibly as virtuous. This is, first of all, because of Bonhoeffer's emphasis on the fact that everyone is responsible before God (called to respond) for all her actions: seeing responsibility as a virtue is a different conception. Secondly, his vision is of a person *de facto* being in positions of responsibility, rather than speak-

56. See von Bismark and Kabitz, eds, *Love Letters*, 161 for an example of his continued use of the concept in prison. See also *DBW* 8:290–92.

57. It can of course be debated how dangerous his own category of "authority" as one of the divine mandates might be. His continuing insistence on the necessity of having an "*oben*" (above) and an "*unten*" (below) in society may appropriately be interpreted as coming from his own bourgeois background. Yet it is at least possible that he was making a comment about the nature of human societies as they *de facto* are, and ruling out the possibility of an ideal of some egalitarian utopia. See *DBW* 7:32, 112, and 181; and *DBW* 8:23, 39, and 75. On the dangers of independent structures, see Scholder, *Vorgeschichte*, ch. 3. See also Biggar's comments, *Hastening*, 53–54; the editors' comments *DBW* 6:421; and Barth, "Nein!"

58. Brock's claim that the mandates are best understood in relationship to ideas found in Psalm 119 (seeing Torah as a dynamic way of life) is not accurate for Bonhoeffer's own conception, but it may make this theme more accessible for people today, Brian Brock, "Bonhoeffer and the Bible," 11.

59. Lehmkühler's claim that the concept of responsibility is grounded in ethics as formation will not quite do: the reason he gives (that Bonhoeffer had written the formation manuscript first and must therefore have been presupposing it in writing about responsibility) does not necessarily hold because of the fragmentary nature of the manuscripts and the possibility that he may still have revised or even cut the manuscripts we have. See Karsten Lehmkühler, "Einwohnung."

ing of responsibility as something that she must exercise as she might, for instance, patience or courage. Thus I believe that responsibility must be seen as a structure of life that impinges on action. Notably, responsibility as Bonhoeffer discusses it is about interrelatedness: humans are not independent beings but creatures dependent on and answerable to God, and are connected in myriad ways to others. Although many accounts of virtue ethics may not deal directly with these issues, they are to some degree implicit in any Christian account. Certainly the focus of virtue ethics on the person entails that the variety of relationships and their demands on the agent are taken seriously. It is hard to imagine, for instance, that a mother be considered a virtuous person if she neglected or abused her children, even if she were, say, a good parliamentarian. Nonetheless, an interpretation of Bonhoeffer's *Ethics* related to virtue ethics needs to spell out what otherwise might only be implicit: the fact of human interrelatedness has implications for what is necessary for a person to be virtuous.

How virtue ethics relates to the mandates is perhaps simpler to consider, as the mandates seem to have the twin concerns of safeguarding against the dangers of creation orders and ensuring that all of life is understood to be the arena for ethical action. The problematic issues related to creation orders often stemmed from the sense that these areas of life were in some way autonomous and had their own rules and codes (*Eigengesetzlichkeit*) that even theologians did not dare critique. Such division of spheres of life does not belong within virtue ethics, though it may well recognize that some variance in what is virtuous may relate to context and suitability. The second issue of perceiving all of life as needing right behavior and action is implicitly a part of virtue ethics, since it is necessarily concerned with the whole person at all times and contexts. Thus although the structures that Bonhoeffer outlines in his *Ethics* are not necessarily replicated in virtue ethics, I believe his concerns are actually well met, especially if the theological underpinnings include the understanding that the person is, in all her doings and being, responsible before God.[60]

In summary then, the most basic concerns within Bonhoeffer's *Ethics* are easily addressed within virtue ethics. If such is the case, it will be important to see if there are particular facets of his ethics that relate well to virtue ethics, so I turn now to examine that.

---

60. I am not persuaded that current formulations of virtue ethics would necessarily benefit from adopting Bonhoeffer's notion of the mandates, but being explicit about the ways in which human interrelatedness confers responsibility for others and may demand representational action could be helpful.

4.4: Specific Aspects Related to Virtue Ethics

The aspects of Bonhoeffer's thought that seem to relate well to virtue ethics include his anthropology, which, as has just been seen, is foundational for his concepts of responsibility and representation (4.4.1), and somewhat relatedly, his holistic conception of human life (4.4.2).

4.4.1: Bonhoeffer's Anthropology

One feature of Bonhoeffer's *Ethics* that I believe relates better to virtue ethics than any other mode of ethical thought is his basic understanding of humanity.[61] As Clifford Green has amply demonstrated, Bonhoeffer always sees persons in their connectedness with family, friends, church community (if Christians), and wider society (as shown here also in terms of nation, culture, and history).[62] One issue within this broader category that seems particularly interesting is his notion expressed in the second version of "History and the Good" of responsibility: "I stand *simultaneously* for Christ before people, and for people before Christ. My responsibility, which I take on in the hearing of people for Christ, comes simultaneously with my responsibility for people in the hearing of Christ. The responsibility *for* Christ before people is the responsibility for people before Christ and only within that the responsibility for myself before God and people. Called to account before people and God, I can only give an account of myself [*mich verantworten*] through the testimony of Jesus Christ, who stepped in for God before people and before God for people" (255, his emphases). It is only possible, I would suggest, for a person to answer for others before Christ if she somehow belongs to them and they to her. Likewise, the possibility of answering for Christ before others depends on her being in Christ, belonging to him. In both cases it is clear that what is at stake is the very identity of the person, both in Christ and in relationship with others.

Moreover, this is not a single instance on which I draw but the conception of human life that underlies all of the *Ethics*. The concept of representation (*Stellvertretung*) makes this explicit again, where Bonhoeffer reiterates his claim that the isolated individual as ethical agent is a fiction (257). It is fully harmonious with his assumption of human interrelatedness

---

61. Though there are convergences here with relational ethics in that both presuppose a relational ontology.

62. Green, *Sociality*.

that Bonhoeffer considers that the responsibility of one person is limited by the responsibility of others, which prevents representational action from becoming the imposition of one's own will (268). Building on such assumptions of interrelation, Bonhoeffer's conception of the church in "The Concrete Command and the Divine Mandates" sees the church as a corporate person who can act representationally, and which has relationships to the other areas of human life considered as "mandates" (147–48). While any mode of ethical discourse may be presented in conjunction with a presupposition of the communal nature of human life, it seems to me that only virtue ethics and relational ethics necessarily focus on the person of the agent, and take seriously interrelationships and particular bonds that they denote and create.[63]

A second aspect of Bonhoeffer's conception of humanity that relates well to virtue ethics is a narrative sense of life.[64] As Stephen Plant puts it, "'Ethics as Formation' predates what theologians have learned to speak of as 'narrative theology,' but his *Ethics* at this point is strikingly suggestive of the insight of narrative theologians that human life is story-formed."[65] Even if, as Plant says, Bonhoeffer's work predates current notions of narrative theology, it seems especially in "Ethics as Formation" that he sees the person as being formed by the story (even perhaps as thumb-nail sketch: incarnation, crucifixion, resurrection/ascension) of Jesus. He even seems to be working with other stories and narratives as he goes, such as Shakespearian characters and Don Quixote (62, 35). Also in one of the latest of the manuscripts to be written, "The 'Ethical' and the 'Christian' as a Theme," he speaks of the "flow of life from conception to the grave" (388), again suggestive of a narrative sense of life, or at least of a holistic view of human life as it occurs over time. This appears also in this manuscript as Bonhoeffer considers the importance of maturity (not personal maturity as a character trait, but the maturity he seems to assume goes hand in hand with positions of authority, 373–74, 377–78), as well as the necessity of ongoing and developing relationships between the one who speaks of ethics and those who are addressed (377–78). Although he does not explicitly speak of a narrative quality of life (and as Plant notes, it would be anachronistic to expect him to), he clearly presupposes something like this. As said of Bonhoeffer's sociality, it would be possible for various modes of

63. See e.g., Hauerwas, *Community*; MacIntyre *After Virtue*, ch. 15; and Blum, "Community and Virtue."

64. This is, of course, not part of the classical tradition but through the work of MacIntyre, Hauerwas and others it has gained a place in current virtue ethics.

65. Plant, *Bonhoeffer*, 120. See also Plant, "Uses of the Bible," 81, 89–94.

ethical thought to include the presupposition that human life and relationships grow and develop over time. However, this is an assumption that is often integral to virtue ethics and would be more difficult to incorporate in any version of ethics that views single acts atomistically.

4.4.2: Holistic Conception of Human Life

In the above discussion there has already been a hint of Bonhoeffer's holistic conception of human life, at least as it develops over time. More specifically it is important to see that underlying Bonhoeffer's understanding of ethics is the claim that all of life is to be lived according to God's will, a subject that he addresses not as "ethics" (which he sees as concerning issues at the boundaries of life) but variously as "the natural life" or as "command." In earlier and later manuscripts the concern remains constant, though the vocabulary changes, namely to consider how the totality of human existence is lived before God, not in continual contortions of scruples or dilemmas, but in God-given freedom. This is given expression first in the manuscript "Ultimate and Penultimate Things," where the penultimate is first described quite generally as all of earthly life (141–42), but later more specifically only insofar as the earthly life is open to the coming of Christ in grace to justify sinners, or "being human and being good" (151). He advocates whatever supports humanity and goodness as being part of preparing the way for Christ's coming. The challenge to most forms of ethics is to have a broad enough understanding both of the human person and life to accommodate such perspectives. Virtue ethics can do this more easily than most forms simply because its focal point is the whole of the person as developed in the course of a life-time, and there is no distinction between some aspect of life (a point of decision, a particular act) as ethical and some other aspect that is not.

Another early manuscript, "The Natural Life," is in a manner of speaking a worked example of his attempt to address the whole of life in his ethics. His vision stretches from the most basic right to physical life (179–91) to issues such as bodily pleasures (180–82) and intellectual enjoyment (216–17), from reproduction and embryonic life (199–212) to euthanasia (184–91) and suicide (192–99). So from the womb to death, and from the most basic necessities to life to leisure and pleasure, all of life is included in his ethical thought. In this connection what is of greatest interest is his treatment of broader areas of life not always considered as "ethical" such as the section he began on the natural rights of intellectual life, where his intended starting point was to deal with issues of judgment, action and enjoyment (216). From notes he had written in preparation, it would seem that his conception of judgment included "processing reality for one's own perceiving."[66] Regarding "enjoyment" there are subheadings in the manuscript: "playing, enjoying oneself." It is of some interest here that the editors of the critical edition suggest Bonhoeffer may have been influenced by his reading of Pieper's *Temperance* as regards enjoyment. His copy is marked with brackets and an exclamation mark in the margin where Pieper states, "That sensual enjoyment is not excluded from the realm of the morally good by Christian teaching about life does not need to be specially explained."[67] Furthermore, this interest in enjoyment carries over into his prison letters where he writes, "Who can for instance in our times still light-heartedly care for music or friendship, play and be joyful? Certainly not the 'ethical' person, but only the Christian. Precisely because friendship belongs in the realm of this freedom ('of the Christian person') it must trustfully defend itself against all the raised eyebrows of 'ethical' existence—certainly without the claim of the necessity of a divine commandment but with the claim of the *necessity* of *freedom!*"[68] In this context Bonhoeffer speaks also of the "latitude of freedom" (*Spielraum der Freiheit*), which again is an aspect of Bonhoeffer's moral and theological vision.[69] Bonhoeffer sees real theological significance in such things as art, education and friendship, and furthermore his theological reflections here are utterly connected to his ethical thinking in general and to the themes in his *Ethics*. So although he uses the language of the "ethical" in quite a narrow way (as he had already done in the manuscript "The 'Ethical' and the 'Christian' as a Theme"), his moral theology has a wide compass indeed.

For this reason I think Jean Bethke Elshtain is not right in saying, "Human life, Bonhoeffer insisted, was pathologically overburdened by the ethical."[70] She quotes at some length from the "The 'Ethical' and the 'Christian' as a Theme" where Bonhoeffer cites Ecclesiastes 3 that there

---

66. *DBW* 6:216 n. 148, referring to Ethics Notes 49 and 51. His preparatory notes indicate that he saw "character" as important here. It is a pity for this study that he did not complete this section.

67. *DBW* 6:216 n. 149. See p. 24, n. 18.

68. *DBW* 8:291–92, his emphases, with playful reference to Luther's treatise "*Von der Freiheit eines Christenmenschen.*" For other examples of this holistic view of human life in his prison writings, see *DBW* 8:511, 455, and 501.

69. *DBW* 8:291.

70. Bethke Elshtain, "Freedom and Responsibility," 279.

is a time for all things, eating, drinking, sleeping, as well as consciously deciding and acting, working and resting, etc. (367). Indeed, at first glance much of this manuscript may seem to negate the claims I have been making about Bonhoeffer treating the whole of human life in his *Ethics*, for he states here that the ethical must be at the borders of life, not normally of import but only in exceptional cases. The middle of life is natural, everyday life, protected at the borders by the Ten Commandments (367–69). And yet the fact that he chooses to speak of this natural everyday life in his *Ethics* (and also in the later letter already quoted) underscores that his moral vision includes this "middle" as well as the boundaries. Later in this manuscript he becomes more specific: God's command gives a person permission to live as a human in freedom, enabling her to move, act and decide, giving her peace, trust, equanimity and joy (385–86). What is at stake is not that Bonhoeffer wants to suggest that certain areas be excluded from ethical thought or to claim that life is "pathologically overburdened by the ethical," but to allow that some parts of life are not under specific divine mandate (commandment requiring obedience). Indeed, whatever terminology he uses (the natural, command, creaturely existence, living as humans before God, the latitude of freedom) the totality of human existence is within his moral compass. If anything, his treatment of command at the centre of life allowing persons to live fully human lives before God strengthens similar concerns already addressed in the language of the "natural" or the "penultimate."

In these manuscripts and other writings it should be clear that Bonhoeffer conceived of all of human life as belonging within the realm of moral, theological reflection.[71] As said of other areas that accord well with virtue ethics, it is again the case that his concern for the totality of life may be brought into many conceptions of ethics. Yet again here it seems to me to relate naturally to virtue ethics in that the focus on the agent does not allow the possibility of considering only certain times or aspects of life to have ethical importance. Every part of life is lived by the agent and must be seen to be ethically relevant.

However, it is now necessary to ask if there are aspects of Bonhoeffer's moral thought that seem in some sense to be related to virtue ethics more specifically than those considered already.

---

71. See also e.g. *DBW* 3:75–87.

4.5: Virtue Ethical Themes in Bonhoeffer

The most obvious theme to be treated here is, naturally, that of conformation (4.5.1). However, I shall also address those aspects that Bonhoeffer treats in virtue-like ways (4.5.2), notably simplicity and cleverness (4.5.2.a), and prudence as it is implied in the notion of responsibility (4.5.2.b). Finally, I shall also discuss virtue-ethical concerns Bonhoeffer addressed in other contexts (4.5.3).

4.5.1: *Conformation*

The most fundamental theme in Bonhoeffer's *Ethics* that seems to be somewhat like virtue ethics is, of course, "Ethics as Formation." Although I would reject an attempt to link Bonhoeffer's *Ethics* to virtue ethics based on this theme in isolation from the whole of his ethical thought, it must be conceded that this theme offers a strong starting point. As Nicholas Sagovsky stated,

> Bonhoeffer discusses not only the theological ground for such action (focusing very much on Christology) but also such action as the outcome of the process of formation (Gestaltung). Bonhoeffer talks more in terms of character (cf Hauerwas) but his thought could be linked with the "virtue" ethics of MacIntyre and others at this point. "Responsible action" does not come out of nowhere. It comes from being "conformed to the image of Christ" through membership of the Church, reading of the Scriptures, meditation and committed action. It comes through the formation of a Christian "conscience" (a knowledge and awareness of both God and reality). It is this which Bonhoeffer was seeking to teach and develop at Finkenwalde.[72]

There are issues one could critique here, including whether it is appropriate to take the Finkenwalde books as fleshing out what Bonhoeffer meant in the *Ethics* by formation. Certainly the concept of the "Church," and the practices of reading and meditating on scripture and committed action remained central in his own thought and life. The language of "conscience" or "image of Christ" is much more problematic, since neither represents his categories. Of conscience he writes in "Ethics as Formation" that it has not enabled people to act well: "The innumerable honorable and tempting disguises and masks in which evil approaches him [sc. the

---

72. Sagovsky, " Responsibility and Justice," point 11.

person of conscience] make his conscience fearful and insecure until he is finally satisfied by having a soothed conscience rather than a good conscience, thus until he deceives his own conscience so as not to despair; for the man whose only security is his conscience is never capable of grasping that a bad conscience is more healing and stronger than a cheated conscience" (65).[73] What makes using the notion of "conscience" more problematic, however, is his extended treatment of it in the manuscript section "The Structure of the Responsible Life." Here he sees the conscience as a result of the Fall, because of which humans lost their creaturely unity with God and thereafter seek unity in themselves. As such it is directed not towards union with God in Christ but towards self-justification (276-78). Even when a person is in Christ and her conscience is freed by him, her conscience remains in its essence a call to unity with herself rather than God and may hinder her from taking on guilt when responsible action may demand it (281-82).[74] Thus it is probably not helpful to speak of the formation Bonhoeffer intended in terms of the "formation of a Christian 'conscience,'" notwithstanding Sagovsky's scare quotes. This is not improved by Sagovsky's parenthetic gloss on "conscience" as "a knowledge and awareness of both God and reality" since Bonhoeffer's claim is that humans know both God and reality only in Christ, and in Christ the reality of God and the world are not to be separated (34-35, 39-41).

Sagovsky's language of "image" of Christ is also problematic, though perhaps not to the same degree. Bonhoeffer consistently speaks of the "form" (*Gestalt*) of Christ, which need not necessarily differ greatly from what might be meant by "image" of Christ.[75] Yet to speak of the "image" (which would most naturally be *Bild*, also in biblical usage) of Christ may seem to import certain devotional practices and a spiritual heritage that Bonhoeffer was consciously avoiding. In one section he had struck out of "Ethics as Formation" he says, "Recognize in him [sc. Christ] God, who takes care of humanity. Every individual and the whole of humanity should recognize in him, themselves, their own nature, their own image" (70, note 25).[76] In a later passage in the same manuscript his use of "*Bild*"

---

73. See also *DBW* 6:89.

74. See also *DBW* 6:308-9 for another example of this usage, this time in relation to shame. Cf more positive instances, *DBW* 6:144 and 293, and a neutral one, 206-7. See also *DBW* 6:278-79, where he counters the Nazi slogan "Adolf Hitler is my conscience" with "Jesus Christ has become my conscience."

75. I am indebted to Dr. Sibylle Rolf for her comment that Bonhoeffer's use of "form" follows Luther's usage.

76. See also *DBW* 6:83, where he speaks about humans recognizing their own image in Christ.

is once again linked not to the image of Christ but humanly constructed image of humanity (74). I think it unlikely that it is a mere coincidence that precisely in the manuscript on formation Bonhoeffer avoids any use of "image" in relation to Christ.[77] He explicitly rejects the language of the "imitation" of Christ, which is often related in thought to the "image": conformation to Christ "does not happen through striving 'to become like Jesus,' as we are accustomed to expressing it, but rather through the form of Jesus Christ impressing itself so strongly on us that our form is stamped with its own [form]" (81). The editors rightly point out that here Bonhoeffer is expressly distancing himself from the notion of *imitatio Christi*.[78] However, it does seem to me a mere detail whether one uses the language of "image" or "form," so long as one keeps in mind Bonhoeffer's reservations regarding this part of the traditional usage of "image."

Even though these aspects of Sagovsky's claim are carelessly worded, it seems to me that the basic claim stands: the notion of formation is more closely related to character and virtue ethics than any other mode of ethical thought. The most obvious reason for making this claim is quite simply that the manuscript "Ethics as Formation" (and the others that specifically draw on it) has as its central concern the agent and the development of her character. In one of his typically stark formulations, Bonhoeffer says,

> Being evil is worse than an evil deed deed. Indeed, it is worse when a liar tells the truth than when a lover of truth tells a lie, worse when a misanthrope practices philanthropy than when someone who loves people is once overwhelmed by hatred. A lie is better than the truth told by a liar, hatred is better than an act of brotherly love by a misanthrope. Thus one sin is not the same as another. They have different weight. . . . Falling away is infinitely worse than falling. The most shining virtues of the one who has fallen away are black as night compared to the darkest weakness of the faithful. (62–63)[79]

---

77. See also *DBW* 6:302 and 319 for language of "image of God" (*Bild Gottes*), which is ambivalent in tone, and 288 for creation in the "image of God" (*Ebenbildlichkeit*).

78. See *DBW* 6:81 n. 65, and see also Lehmkühler, "Einwohnung," 326. Cf Rasmussen, "Ethik des Kreuzes," 147, 150. See also Frick, "Imitatio Christi," though he does not refer specifically to the *Ethics*.

79. See Tödt's comments on this passage, "Paradoxical Obedience," 11. See also Puera's "Christ as Favor," where he discusses Luther's notion of *conformatio Christi*, and the assumption that the believer is transformed through continuous change into the form of Christ, 60–63.

Bonhoeffer's Ethics *as Virtue Ethical*

In this passage Bonhoeffer is clearly marking the overall character of the agent as being of much greater importance than single acts, even if character might be said to be developed over time through many acts such that the two can hardly be separated.

If virtue ethics and formation both have as their central concerns the person, it is also the case that the examples given are necessarily persons. Thus one might ask what a virtuous person would do in this or that situation, or how a virtuous person would perform this or that act. For Bonhoeffer the exemplar can only be Jesus Christ: "Since however there is only one place where God and the world's reality are reconciled with one another, in which God and human have become one, therefore and only therefore is it possible to hold God and the world at the same moment in view. This place does not lie beyond reality in the realm of ideas; rather it lies in the centre of history as a divine wonder; it lies in Jesus Christ, the world reconciler" (68). Here follows an extended passage with "*ecce homo*" (behold the human) as its leitmotif. Being conformed to Christ incarnate means permission to be truly human; being conformed to Christ crucified means being mortal, being subject to sin, suffering and death; being conformed to the risen Christ means carrying the hidden glory of Christ within us, perceiving the shimmer of that which is coming, willingly carrying the cross with the indwelling Holy Spirit (80–82). Thus while one can say that just as virtue ethics has the "virtuous person" as its example, Bonhoeffer's formation has Christ, not in the form of narratives from the gospels but in creedal formulae.

It would be, however, too simplistic to distinguish sharply between the two, and such a distinction may say more about one's own formation than Bonhoeffer's intentions. There can be little doubt that the central focus of Christology for Bonhoeffer is *who Christ is* rather than what a person believes about Christ.[80] Similarly, in speaking of biblical meditation, Bonhoeffer emphasizes the encounter there with the living God, rather than the gleaning of information about God.[81] Thus, Bonhoeffer's dogmatic categories should be seen as a shorthand that calls the person of Jesus Christ to mind, whether in vivid scenes from the gospels or moments of personal encounter. An imagination formed by such meditation will see the sights of the stable and smell the odors of the animals when thinking of Christ incarnate. To speak of the crucifixion is to see the blood dripping from the crown of thorns and hear the jeers and taunts of the crowds. To

---

80. Pangritz, "Who is Jesus Christ," 137.
81. *DBW* 5:70–71.

contemplate the resurrection is to smell the fish Jesus is cooking on the beach and to see Thomas in his need to touch the very wounds before he would believe. These and many other parts of the gospel narratives need to be embedded in these Christological categories. Christ as Bonhoeffer depicts him is the figure of the church's creeds, but known to his followers fleshed out in the myriad stories from all four gospels as well as the Acts of the Apostles.

Unsurprisingly, the author of *Sanctorum Communio* also shows the place of conformation being the church (84–85). Finally Bonhoeffer focuses on how formation enables ethics to be concrete: Christ is always the same, but in transforming real people there is always an element of particularity (85–87).

> The question, how Christ wins form among us today and here, respectively how we are conformed to his form, includes however further difficult questions: what does it mean "among us," "today," "here"? If it is impossible to determine what is good for all times or places, so the question is raised for which times and places an answer to our question can even be given. . . . It concerns at first quite generally the times and places that have to do with us, in which we have experience, which for us are realities. It concerns the times and places that direct concrete questions to us, which give us tasks and place responsibility on us. Thus "among us," "today" and "here" concern the area of our decisions and encounters. (87–88)

Thus we have crystallized in this one manuscript many of the concerns already identified as central to Bonhoeffer's thought: a concrete ethic focusing on Christ and based on grace. It is most clearly an ethic that looks foremost to the agent being formed by Christ himself and in his likeness.

The question then arises whether this virtue-ethical facet is more like Hauerwas's ethic of *virtue* (character) or *virtues*. It is therefore necessary to ask if there are aspects of Bonhoeffer's ethics that function like virtues.

4.5.2: *Virtues*

Given that Bonhoeffer does not have extended treatments of any of the classical or theological virtues, to answer the question whether his ethics has any notions of "virtues" one must look at other themes he addresses. Here I shall address two, simplicity and cleverness (4.5.2.a), and prudence as it is implied in the concept of responsibility (4.5.2.b).

4.5.2.A: SIMPLICITY AND CLEVERNESS

The first characteristics that might be seen to be something like "virtues" in Bonhoeffer's thought are simplicity and cleverness. Though he notes the failure of an ethic that focuses on virtue (as he does with other forms, including those based on rationality, conscience, duty, and even one's own freedom, 64–66), he begins to flesh out what it means to be formed by Christ, basing his discussion on Matt 10:16 where Jesus tells his disciples to be innocent as doves and wise as serpents (67–68). Bonhoeffer's words are *"einfältig"* and *"klug,"* which mean "simple" and "clever," and the aspect of singleness inherent in *"einfältig"* is important.[82] The simple person

> belongs only to God and God's will. Because the simple person does not look in two different directions at God and the world, he is capable of seeing the reality of the world freely and without prejudice. Thus simplicity becomes wisdom. Clever is the person who sees reality as it is, who sees the ground [*Grund*, perhaps "reason"] of things. Clever is therefore only the one who sees reality in God. Recognition of reality is not the same as knowledge of external processes, but rather the perception of the essence of things. Not the best-informed is the cleverest. Precisely he is in danger of missing the essential because of the manifold. On the other hand, often the knowledge of an apparently lesser detail facilitates looking in the depths of things. Thus the wise person will seek to gain the best possible knowledge of processes without however becoming dependent on it. Recognizing the characteristic in the factual is cleverness. . . . The liberated view of God and reality as it has existence only in God unites simplicity and cleverness. There is no proper simplicity without cleverness and no cleverness without simplicity. (67–68)[83]

I quote this at length partly to show the importance of singleness that is built into Bonhoeffer's conception of simplicity. It is worth noting that "the manifold" (*das Vielerlei*) threatens to obscure the essential, just as the

---

82. See *DBW* 4:204, where Bonhoeffer treats this biblical text, and moves from the use of "innocent" (*ohne Falsch*, from the Luther Bible) to "simple" (*einfältig*). Although *"klug"* can mean wise or prudent (as a closer parallel to typical English translations of the biblical passage), usually it means "clever," "shrewd," or even "cunning." Given its relation to "serpent," the most natural understanding would be one of these latter words, though in *Discipleship* Bonhoeffer is careful to distinguish between "worldly cunning" and "spiritual wisdom." I have chosen to translate using "clever" as being the most neutral or ambiguous, to allow both understandings to be heard.

83. See also *DBW* 6:155, where Bonhoeffer glosses simplicity as "devotion of the heart to Jesus Christ."

simple/clever person is not distracted by trying to look simultaneously in different directions, both at God and the world.

Several other things, perhaps minor (in themselves) are worth noting. First, as seen in the long quote above, at the end simplicity and cleverness form a unity that is articulated in much the same way Thomas explains the unity of the virtues—although seemingly they are separate and might occur in isolation from one another, they are only truly themselves and only operate fully when they are found together. So it would seem also with simplicity and cleverness: they are dependent on each other and bound up together.

Secondly, they are given by God (again emphasizing grace) much as Thomas speaks of virtues as being infused: it is being in Christ that frees the Christian to have such simplicity and cleverness. When simplicity reappears in the later section "The Structure of the Responsible Life," Bonhoeffer states, "Alone proceeding from him [Jesus Christ] there is human action that is not ground down by conflicts of principle but rather comes from the completed reconciliation of the world with God, an acting that does what is according with reality in soberness and simplicity, an acting in representational responsibility" (266).

Thirdly, returning to Bonhoeffer's focus on the person of Jesus Christ, simplicity is defined in Christ—Matt 10:16 is interpreted "as every one of his words: only by himself" (68).[84] In one of his last manuscripts, "The Love of God and the Decay of the World," Bonhoeffer writes,

> The freedom of Jesus is not the arbitrary choice of one of innumerable possibilities, rather it consists precisely in the complete simplicity of his acting, [a simplicity] for which there are never several possibilities, conflicts, alternatives, rather always only One. This One Jesus calls the will of God. He calls it his food that he does this will.[85] This will of God is his life. He does not live and act from the knowledge of good and evil, but from the will of God. There is only *one* will of God. In it the Source is regained, in it freedom and simplicity of all doing is founded. (315, his capitalizations and emphasis)

Fourthly, just as Thomas's virtues are seen as enabling right action, simplicity is seen as liberating and allowing new, godly life. "In no way, however, is the new unity with the will of God, the simplicity of doing repealed or even just disturbed. . . . Submission to the will of God only

---

84. See also *DBW* 6:404.
85. John 4:34.

happens in doing. In doing the will of God, the person renounces his own rights, his own justification; in doing he abandons himself humbly to the merciful Judge" (329).[86] These last two quotes have also opened up the relationship in Bonhoeffer's thought between simplicity and doing the will of God, which will be explored in greater detail in chapter 6. What I hope is apparent here is the important point that simplicity (like the virtues in a Thomist construal) is not something to be considered primarily as a possession but to be valued as it enables right action, doing the will of God in Bonhoeffer's terms.

Fifthly, it seems to me that in some senses simplicity operates like prudence in Aquinas. As prudence enables the virtuous person to see a situation aright (recognizing what are the salient features, how it is even to be described) as well as knowing what is the right action to take, so simplicity enables her to "see the ground [*Grund*, foundation or reason] of things" (67), to perceive beyond the "manifold" what is "essential" (68). It is precisely this simplicity that Bonhoeffer claims allows her to see God and the world at one and the same time in Christ, which is, of course, one of his central Christological points in the *Ethics*. Moreover, when Bonhoeffer returns to simplicity in the later manuscript "The Love of God and the Decay of the World" he brings, as was shown above, this concept into relationship with another of his great themes in the *Ethics*, command and the will of God. In this context the prudence-like character of simplicity comes again to the fore. "The impression that the simple [*einfältig*] recognition of the will of God must take the form of intuition, the elimination of all consideration, the naïve grasping of the first thought or feeling that presses [on us], thus that psychological misunderstanding of the simplicity of the new life that has dawned in Jesus, receives here a radical correction" (323). In the following passage he begins to elucidate what things might be part of the "consideration" that is part of simplicity that allows the Christian to recognize the will of God: heart, mind, observation, experience all have a part to play, all of which will need to have been transformed and conformed to the form of Christ (324).[87] All of this is

86. See also *DBW* 6:321–23 and 326–27 for more on simplicity and the will of God. See e.g. Meilaender on virtue and the importance of perception, and the need of virtue to perceive reality aright, *Theory and Practice*, 17, 25; and Hauerwas, *Vision and Virtue*.

87. See also *DBW* 6:326: "Mind, perception and attentive awareness of what is given step into lively action" in the testing in simplicity of the will of God. "Past experience will speak in confirmation or in warning." Even possibilities and consequences will be considered. "The whole apparatus of human powers will be put in motion where the concern is to test what God's will is."

bound up, furthermore, with living and growing in love, which also means in the reconciliation and unity with God and people (325), and is possible in the knowledge of "being protected, sustained and directed by the will of God" (326). "Therefore, it is neither a petulant nor a despairing but rather a humble and trusting testing, a testing in freedom for the word of God, which is always new in the simplicity of the always only one word of God" (326). Yet it also includes self-examination in awareness of the danger of self-deception (326-28). Bonhoeffer's perception (perhaps paradoxically) of the complexity of what is involved in the simplicity that can recognize God's will for her action is not unlike Thomas's description of the many things that go into the operation of prudence, the many things that may influence how a situation and right action are rightly to be perceived.

Finally, however, there are elements of simplicity that are not like prudence. At the outset Bonhoeffer speaks in terms of singleness or even purity of heart. Also, the simple person "has God," and therefore she "depends on God's commands, judgment and mercy, which proceed afresh daily." She belongs solely to God and God's will (67). This is probably best described as a picture of the Christian disciple. Yet I think it does not stretch the point to observe the link between discipleship and sanctification, and again between sanctification and virtue. The simple person is a follower of Christ, being sanctified (made virtuous, conformed to Christ). As such, simplicity may best be seen not merely as a prudent-like virtue, but as Bonhoeffer's concept of Christian virtue, which is cast in terms redolent of divine command ethics.

Thus in five ways it seems to me that simplicity and cleverness operate something like virtues in Bonhoeffer's thought: there is the unity of these two concepts, as well as the insistence of God-givenness. They are to be understood primarily with reference to Jesus himself (with a virtue ethic-like focus on his person). They enable right action. More specifically, simplicity seems to function somewhat like prudence, which itself seems telling, given that it is prudence that is seen to hold all the virtues together in Thomist thought. However, in important ways simplicity seems to be a way of speaking of discipleship, sanctification, or virtue itself.

4.5.2.B: Prudence in Responsibility

I have already suggested that responsibility as such is not properly aretaic in Bonhoeffer's thought; it is a given aspect of human existence based on humanity's communal nature. What is interesting about responsibility

Bonhoeffer's Ethics *as Virtue Ethical*

in relationship to possible "virtues" is how it relates (like simplicity) to something very like prudence. In the manuscript "History and the Good" he claims that the responsible person must act in freedom, without cover from any people or principles, taking responsibility for the consequences, not applying any principle, but seeking "to grasp and to do what is necessary, 'commanded' in the given situation" (260). She must observe, consider, evaluate, decide, and even consider what the likely consequences of her acts will be, and to test her own motives, her heart (267). Thus although responsibility itself does not seem to be a "virtue" in Bonhoeffer's conception of ethics, the discernment of what responsible action must be taken involves the whole person in ways that (as with simplicity and cleverness) resemble prudence in Thomist ethics.[88]

4.5.3: *Virtue-ethical Concerns in Other Contexts*

Given, as many have argued, the high degree of continuity in Bonhoeffer's thought, it is important to see if there are signs of virtues or virtue-ethical thinking in his other writings.[89] One of the earliest examples of which I am aware comes from *Sanctorum Communio*, where Bonhoeffer's notion of sin is not based on individual acts but on being, namely "being in Adam."[90] In this it is not so much "sins" that he discusses as "sinfulness," the image of God destroyed, no longer being human as intended by God. Although this is at some remove from virtue ethics as such, again the emphasis on the person and avoidance of an atomistic view of individual acts accords well with the emphases of virtue ethics.

Finally, there is at least a hint of virtue-ethical concerns in the outline for a book Bonhoeffer prepared in prison.[91] As well as continuing to ask the question who Jesus Christ is for us (really) today, or maybe as a part of that, in his outline for a short book he hoped to write, the second part was to treat the question of what Christian faith essentially is. In this connection he intended to write about the encounter with Jesus Christ, and

---

88. Wannenwetsch's "Responsible Living" is good on responsibility in Bonhoeffer and popular abuses and misconceptions of this theme.

89. On continuity in Bonhoeffer's thought, see ch. 2, note 3.

90. *DBW* 1:71, his note 1. See also *DBW* 2:69, 99, and 135–48. See also Plant, *Bonhoeffer*, 74.

91. It is worth noting that, as in the *Ethics*, in Bonhoeffer's prison writings, the use of the word "virtue" (*Tugend*) is not usually positive. See in his novel a description of an "old maid who goes through the world using her virtuosity and excellence as an accusation against all others," *DBW* 7:142.

the "experience that there is here a reversal of everything of human existence in that Jesus is only 'there for others.' The 'being-there-for-others' of Jesus is the transcendental experience! From the freedom from his self, from the 'being-there-for-others' even to death springs the omnipotence, omniscience and omnipresence. Faith is the participation in this being of Jesus."[92] Here we see again the pre-eminence accorded Christ's being (existence for others), and the emphasis on the being of the believer and church (as participating in the being of Christ). This has obvious resonance with *Act and Being* where the discussion centers on being in Christ (rather than being in Adam), but it also shows a fundamental focus on the person (whether Christ or the believer).[93]

What I hope this section has shown is that there are profound affinities between Bonhoeffer's *Ethics* and virtue ethics, particularly as found in the theme of ethics as formation. Moreover, there are a variety of ways in which the notions of simplicity and cleverness have an aretaic function in his thought. Given that these are the only "virtues" that Bonhoeffer names, and that he seems most concerned with those aspects that seem similar to prudence, it may be right to agree with Sagovsky and see an ethic of character rather than an ethic of virtues.[94] Beyond this, I have tried to show some continuity in the basic contours of the virtue ethical concern of focusing on the person and being of Christ and the agent.

4.6: Conclusions

What we have seen in this chapter is, first, that Bonhoeffer's theology has a strong place for the doctrine of sanctification, especially in *Discipleship*, which is a sustained treatment of justification and sanctification, issuing its stern warning against the cheap grace that does not recognize the necessity of being sanctified. Moreover, it is clear that Bonhoeffer did not revise his views as he was writing the *Ethics* manuscripts. Here he continued to work with the theme from *Discipleship* of conformation to Christ, or sanctification, as a work of Christ himself in the believer. However, he also developed what was to become an important theme, namely referring to justification and sanctification in terms of the ultimate and the

---

92. DBW 8:558–60.

93. See also Plant, *Bonhoeffer*, 95, "In Christology, reflection upon the person of Christ always precedes reflection upon what he does, since our understanding of Christ's person makes every difference to our understanding of his works."

94. Sagovsky, "Responsibility and Justice," point 11.

penultimate, a theme that appears in manuscripts written in the early and late periods of writing. Furthermore, Bonhoeffer continued in prison to refer to things in terms of the ultimate and penultimate, which suggests that he did not in any way revise his thinking either in terms of the importance of a right understanding of the relationship of justification and sanctification, nor in terms of how best to express this. This emphasis on sanctification is important in considering how Bonhoeffer's *Ethics* is related to virtue ethics, because in a Christian context virtue ethics can be expressed theologically in terms of the growth in holiness or Christ-likeness that is sanctification.

Secondly, we have seen that the overall concerns expressed in the *Ethics* are, at the very least, not inimical to virtue ethics, and in many cases seem to accord particularly well. The Christian foundations he is attempting to lay, with his emphasis on the Fall, grace, and Christology are all appropriate in Christian virtue ethics. His repeated insistence on the need for concrete ethics may sit no better or worse with virtue ethics than any other type; certainly there are construals of virtue ethics that are quite abstract. Yet, with its inherent focus on the agent and the specifics surrounding the act in question, there is already an element of particularity to virtue ethics. This makes it easy, I think, for virtue ethics to take his concern seriously, and perhaps a formulation of virtue ethics which does so would be the stronger for it. Similarly, Bonhoeffer's interest in the historical placement of his concrete ethics sits easily with virtue ethics, at least for a twenty-first century reader familiar with more recent formulations of virtue ethics that take seriously both the historical setting, and the narrative quality of human life. In the case of Bonhoeffer's treatment of the relation of the church and the world, with his stark refusal to countenance any dualism, it seems to me that virtue ethics, again, accords particularly well. Since it is concerned with the whole of life, rather than specific decisions or discrete acts treated in an atomistic way, there is less scope for compartmentalizing or for dualistic thinking. Finally, Bonhoeffer's interest in structures for ethical life, including his treatment of responsibility and his development of the notion of divine mandates, is not necessarily mirrored within most accounts of virtue ethics. However, the interrelatedness of persons that underlies his treatment of responsibility is an understanding that fits well with virtue ethics, and the clear insistence that every part of life requires right action (virtuous living) is quite clearly related to virtue ethics' concern with living well.

The Virtue of Bonhoeffer's Ethics

Thirdly, I have identified two aspects of Bonhoeffer's *Ethics* that seem to be related to virtue ethics. One is his understanding of human nature, which sees humans as communal beings, and sees life as ongoing and developing, rather than assuming people to be isolated or existing without past or anticipated future. Another is his holistic conception of human life: his moral scope is for the entirety of life, including everyday life. While these things are not "ethical" as such, they are foundational for the kind of ethics one can then formulate, and it seems to me that Bonhoeffer's anthropology and his treatment of the whole of life accord better with virtue ethics than with other approaches to ethical thought.

Finally, there are themes within the *Ethics* that may be seen as virtue ethical. Most notable is the theme of "conformation" or "ethics as formation" with the focus on the agent being formed by Christ into his likeness. This has little affinity with acquiring virtues, but much with God's infusing virtues in the believer. Moreover, there are certain aspects that seem almost to function as virtues in Bonhoeffer's thought, namely simplicity and cleverness, and something Bonhoeffer often does not name but which looks very like prudence, enabling the right perception of what is required. Additionally, there are elements of virtue-ethical thinking that can be found in a number of his other works.

However, lest this discussion remain solely analytical or theoretical, it is important to ask how Bonhoeffer in fact does argue when he becomes more concrete in his ethical discourse. I turn my attention to that now.

5

Mode of Ethical Discourse

In the previous chapter we found that Bonhoeffer's theology assumes the interconnection of justification and sanctification in such a way as to make a link between his ethics and virtue ethics not implausible. We have seen also that his overall concerns in his *Ethics* are in no way inimical to virtue ethics. We have also seen two ways in which his underlying assumptions regarding human nature make a link with virtue ethics seem natural. Finally, we saw that the theme of conformation has strong virtue-ethical resonances, and that there are even motifs which can be seen as aretaic. Therefore it is now appropriate to ask whether, when Bonhoeffer addresses concrete issues, he argues in a virtue-ethical fashion.

An examination of Bonhoeffer's way of arguing when he addresses specific issues may uncover a variety of things. For if his mode of discourse does not show any resemblance to what one might expect of virtue-ethical thought, it could be indicative either that my analyses thus far have not been correct, or that Bonhoeffer himself is inconsistent. Either possibility would, of course, present important difficulties for the remainder of this study. However, if his way of handling discussion is consonant with a virtue-ethical approach, this would add further confirmation to what has been shown hitherto.

Therefore, I will look in some detail at that portion of the *Ethics* where he treats concrete issues. First I shall attend to the setting for this, the manuscript "The Natural" (5.1.1). Then I shall examine his prime category of discussion, "*Suum cuique*" (5.1.2). With this groundwork laid, I shall look at what Bonhoeffer considers to be the most fundamental right, that to bodily life (5.1.3). This is the overall setting in which his further discussions take place, and I shall examine two topics, one of which is representative of how he generally argues, and the other the one real exception (5.1.4–5). From what is seen in these examples, it should be possible to assess how Bonhoeffer makes his arguments regarding concrete issues (5.1.6).

Because of the possibility that Bonhoeffer's way of handling specific questions may be thought to have changed during his imprisonment, I shall then look at an example from this later period (5.2).

5.1: Ethics

In turning now to an analysis of his mode of argument, it is necessary to be clear about the various ways I shall categorize his methods. My most basic categories are to distinguish between what is essentially a theological argument from what is not. Theological modes of argument may depend on belief in God or specific beliefs about God (in this case, most frequently that God is Creator), or they may depend explicitly upon belief that the Bible is authoritative, indeed revealed by God. These distinctions within Bonhoeffer's theological arguments are simple enough to see and acknowledge. What is more difficult is the question of how to describe his modes of argument that are not overtly theological. I have chosen to refer to them as "philosophical," though using this term quite loosely, for I do not mean to suggest that he might be seen to be following any particular school of thought in such instances, nor that his arguments could necessarily be seen as appropriate in a philosophical work. What I mean is that they are based on observations, or reasoning, or the analysis of a situation and language usage, and thus are open to dialogue and discourse without particular belief in God or the authority of scripture. There may be many kinds of value judgments that one could make on the appropriateness, persuasiveness, or usefulness of the various modes of argument, which I will not discuss here. Instead, what I hope to highlight is simply how he handles the issues he discusses.

Also it is important to outline the kinds of argument that may be indicative of differing modes of ethical thought. While Roger Crisp notes that a "pure virtue ethics . . . will suggest that the only reasons we ever have for acting or living in any way are grounded in the virtues,"[1] I will not claim that this is the case for Bonhoeffer. Rather the mode of arguing that seems related to virtue ethics will focus on the agent, and her motives. By contrast, I would take a deontological mode of debate to focus on particular laws, rules or commandments; while a utilitarian style would centre on

---

1. Crisp, "Modern Moral Philosophy," 7.

outcomes; and a situationist one would focus on the circumstances and features of the case in question.

5.1.1: "The Natural": The Setting for Concrete Issues

The only extended discussion of concrete ethics in these manuscripts appears in "The Natural." Before looking in detail at the way in which Bonhoeffer argues regarding the specific issues he treats in this section, it is important to consider more generally the place and significance of this manuscript in his *Ethics*. Beyond the general importance of any context, it can hardly be without significance that Bonhoeffer only addresses concrete issues in this one manuscript, despite his almost constant refrain regarding the necessity of a concrete ethic, not an abstract one.

First, I have already hinted that there could be possible significance in the fact that Bonhoeffer was working in the Roman Catholic monastery of Ettal when he wrote this manuscript, and the possible influences of his conversations with people there as well as his reading of Pieper and other Catholic theologians (2.3.2).[2] At all events, Bonhoeffer was more open to discovering and learning from the moral theology of his Roman Catholic brethren than most German Protestant theologians of his day would have been,[3] even if he did not accept uncritically all he read and heard, for instance in the case of natural theology (167).[4] Importantly, however, it appears that he found there a rich foundation for making the concrete statements for his time and place that he felt were most needed.

Secondly, in considering the importance of the section on "the natural" as I consider how Bonhoeffer mounts his arguments when he is being concrete, it is vital to recognize that this lies not primarily in its being rather surprising (not least in its apparent Catholic influence) for

---

2. Note the concern some friends had regarding his becoming too Catholic, Fritz Figur (56) and Juluis Rieger (95-96), in *I Knew Dietrich Bonhoeffer*. See also some of Bonhoeffer's comments regarding Catholicism: *DBW* 16:70-72. See also 25.

3. See *DBW* 1:121: "But are we not approaching dangerously the Catholic teaching of thesaurus [treasury of merits], which is in the centre of the whole modern Catholic view of the sanctorum communio? Certainly, we are approaching it totally aware; we want to know, along with Luther, that the good core which threatens to be lost to us will be preserved in Protestant dogmatics."

4. All page numbers in brackets in the main text refer to *DBW* 6. See *DBW* 16:72-73, 114, and 138-39. See also Feil, *Theology*, 145; and Feil, "Zukunft," 164. See also 2.3.2, p. 23-24 regarding Bonhoeffer's understanding of reason.

a Protestant of his generation.[5] More to the point, it is also connected to what was clearly a central theme to him, namely that of the "penultimate":

> We speak of the natural in distinction from the creaturely so as to include the fact of the Fall; we speak of the natural in distinction from the sinful so as to include the creaturely. The natural is that which, after the Fall, is directed towards the coming of Jesus Christ. The unnatural is that which, after the Fall, closes itself against the coming of Jesus Christ. Of course the difference between what is directed towards the coming of Christ and what closes itself against the coming of Christ is a relative one; neither can the natural force the coming of Christ, nor can the unnatural make this coming impossible; in both cases the real coming is an event of grace, and only through the coming of Christ is the natural confirmed in its character as penultimate, and the unnatural definitively exposed in its character as destruction of the penultimate. Thus there remains even before Christ a difference between the natural and the unnatural that cannot be removed without grave harm. (165)

It is, therefore, clear that Bonhoeffer did not write this section in isolation from his thinking in other manuscripts, and since the theme of the penultimate and the ultimate, as we have already seen, appears in later manuscripts as well as earlier ones, this is an important connection.

Finally, in Bonhoeffer's attempt to write an account of Christian ethics that would be for his time and place, it is noteworthy that he addresses one of the theological issues that made right discernment of that context difficult for many Protestants: the dynamic of divine providence and human free will. In the theological climate of Germany in the early twentieth century, many people believed that the success of any undertaking was the proof of its being ordained by God, hence the position (even of some who did not like Nazism) that Hitler's power was part of God's will and must be supported.[6] In this context, then, Bonhoeffer gives a theological framework for saying that temporary success (whereby "temporary" may even extend over the period of a lifetime) does not prove that something is God's will. Yet if something is starkly against God's will, against what is natural, the natural itself will correct it. What is unnatural can only be "organized" and sustained through force or violence, but what is natural

---

5. Feil rightly claims that Bonhoeffer is expounding a "theology of the natural" rather than a "natural theology." See his "Philosophische Theologie" and "Standpunke der Bonhoeffer-Interpretation."

6. See Scholder, *Vorgeschichte*, ch. 5 on "political theology," and ch. 9 on the stance of various theologians.

simply exists through God's creation and will (168-70). "For this reason it can come to a temporary overcoming of the natural through the unnatural. In the long term every organization breaks apart, whereas the natural remains and gets its way through its own power; for life itself is on the side of the natural. Of course there may first be grave shocks and upheavals of external forms of life. But so far as life sustains itself, the natural makes its own way" (170). This, in substance, is not greatly different from his assertions in other places regarding how success and failure are to be seen theologically. What is interesting is the sense that he sees corrective influences within God's created order, even in the world's fallen (natural) state.[7]

These points taken together suggest that the theme of the natural is firmly linked to some of his other central concerns. It may well have been influenced by his conversations and reading in Ettal, especially of Pieper, though this should not be unduly weighted. Additionally, it is not only in the specific issues that he addressed that he tried to make his ethics appropriate for his context: in this passage he is again trying to help people to see that Hitler's success did not mean that what he was doing was God's will. With these things in mind, I turn now to look at his method of arguing.

5.1.2: "Suum cuique": The Basis

"The most general formulation of rights given with the natural states, in the words of Roman justice: *suum cuique*, to each his own. In this sentence is expressed simultaneously the diversity of the natural and the rights that belong to it, as well as the unity of rights protected in the diversity" (174).[8] Of course, this notion of justice has classical links with virtue ethics, yet it is not apparent that such links are more than historical. Other forms of ethical thought, especially deontology, could incorporate this understanding of justice, though *suum cuique* would be in some tension with

---

7. It is interesting to note that Bonhoeffer was misunderstood in speaking about such issues. See Wilhelm Niesel's contribution in *I Knew Dietrich Bonhoeffer*, where he states, "To our utter amazement he made a speech telling us we had to change our attitude towards Hitler; events [in Poland] had proved that God was with him and we had to recognize it," 147. The editors note that Bethge offered a very different construal of the remarks Bonhoeffer made, but do not provide a reference, and I have been unable to locate it. Nonetheless, given what Bonhoeffer wrote in his *Ethics* not long after Hitler's successes in Poland, it is likely that Niesel did not understand what Bonhoeffer was saying.

8. See also *DBW* 6:173, where he speaks of rights and duties in connection with the penultimate. See also Pieper's treatment of rights, *Cardinal Virtues*, 45-52, and 88-89.

utilitarianism, since it does not recognize the importance of the outcomes of actions. Similarly, the notion of what is due to whom is not essentially situationist, but is focused on the person, albeit the one addressed by the agent rather than the agent. On balance, however, this concern with the nature of persons shows some relationship to the concerns of virtue ethics or perhaps relational ethics. Notwithstanding such considerations, it seems likely that Bonhoeffer was drawing on this notion more because it was being used by other Protestant theologians, rather than any influence from the classical period or even from Roman Catholic moral theology.[9]

Whatever the provenance of his use of the notion of *suum cuique* may be, what is interesting for this study is what he does with this concept. First, as we have seen from the opening sentences of this section, quoted above, he sees *suum cuique* as a statement of the rights related to the natural, thus an integral part of the manuscript "The Natural Life." This he also relates to his notion of the ultimate and the penultimate: "Where justice in the given natural is sought, there the will and gift of the Creator is honored, even in the world that lies in rebellion; and it points simultaneously to the fulfillment of all justice when Jesus Christ through the Holy Spirit will give to each his own. Thus the safeguarding of this sentence may in an authentic sense be spoken of as a penultimate that is determined by the ultimate" (176).

In using the concept, Bonhoeffer first counters one of the assumptions at work in Nazism, namely that the collective (the folk, the race, the state) has rights rather than the individual. "Here the individual is only a means to an end in the service of the society. The happiness of the society stands above the natural right of the individual" (176). He goes on to argue against social eudaemonism, the concept that seeks to maximize the happiness of the collective that is at the heart of utilitarianism, even if that might more usually be expressed in terms of the happiness of the greatest number (with the possibility that it is a number of individuals in question, rather than a race, folk, or state being considered). He continues,

> Thereby however, the natural life itself is attacked and with the destruction of the right of the individual, the destruction of all justice whatsoever is begun and thus the path towards chaos is followed. It is therefore no coincidence that the consequence of social eudaemonism time and again has been the destruction also of the rights of the society through tyranny; the right of the

---

9. See *DBW* 6:174, note 36 for examples from his contemporaries, as well as its barbaric abuse by Nazis.

individual is the supporting power of the right of the society, just as conversely the society carries and protects the right of the individual. That there is a natural right of the individual follows from the will of God to create the individual and to give him eternal life (177).[10]

In this passage two things are of note. First, as regards the mode of ethical thought, is Bonhoeffer's rejection of one major strand of ethical thinking, utilitarianism, or consequentialism. This is interesting particularly since, as noted in chapter two, his ethics has been seen as belonging to this strand (2.4.2.d).[11] Secondly, and of greater substance for Bonhoeffer's aims, the discussion of *suum cuique* gives him purchase in arguing against one of the foundational hallmarks of Nazi practice (the emphasis on the folk, race, state, at the expense of the individual and of whole groups of people), allowing him to do what he considers most necessary: namely to write an ethic for his time and place.

Bonhoeffer's treatment, then, of *suum cuique* is interesting both because of his explicit rejection of one of virtue ethics' rival forms of ethical thought, and because of its historical and inherent proximity to virtue ethics, even if forms of deontology could also use the notion. More concretely, it provides a tool for countering one of the most basic tenets of Nazi ideology, namely the primacy of the collective over the individual, as well as the popular ideology based on Nietzsche's notion of the will to power.

5.1.3: "The Right to Bodily Life"[12]

Following what we have seen in "The Natural Life," and continuing to draw on the points made in "*suum cuique*," comes a discussion of the most basic of rights, that of bodily life.[13] The work he does in this section

---

10. Although Bonhoeffer's arguments may not address utilitarianism as it might be expressed in English, the editors see this discussion in dialogue with that tradition, DBW 6:176, note 43. See also his clear rejection of utility as a way of conceiving the good, DBW 6:38, and 254; or as a way of thinking of human life 172, 187-88, and 214.

11. See 42-43. He also rejects a form of voluntarism based on "blind will" and Nietzsche's notion of the will to power, DBW 6:177-78. This is of less interest, since commentators have not proposed seeing Bonhoeffer's ethics as a form of voluntarism. For more regarding Bonhoeffer and Nietzsche, see Köster, "Nietzsche als verborgener Antipode."

12. See 2.3.2, p. 24 on the planned a parallel section called "The natural rights of intellectual life."

13. It is of some interest that his first category is that of "rights" (and he did not write his planned treatment of duties). In Barth's treatment of similar issues he begins

illustrates his method of arguing when he does what he believes is most necessary, namely writing an ethic that is relevant to his own context. For that reason, it is important to consider carefully how he proceeds at this point. Bonhoeffer's first point is: "Bodily life, which we receive without our cooperation, carries within itself the right to its sustenance. This is not a right that we have stolen or attained for ourselves, rather it is in the most direct sense 'born with us,' a received right that exists before our will, that rests in being itself" (179). Thus, his first statement about this most basic of all rights is one that is drawn from what is observable by anyone (to wit, that a person receives her bodily life without any act of her own will or participation). It is an appeal that can be made to anyone, regardless of faith commitment or lack thereof.

Only then does he continue: "Because according to God's will human life on earth only exists as bodily life, the body has the right to preservation for the sake of the whole person" (179). Thus Bonhoeffer's second appeal is one that is based on faith, but of the most generic sort: many forms of theism might be expected to recognize God's will as being involved in the fact that humans exist bodily rather than as non-embodied spirits on earth.

He then continues with arguments that are philosophical, rather than theological: "Because all rights are extinguished with death, the preservation of bodily life is the foundation of all natural rights whatsoever and therefore is endowed with particular importance. The most basic right of the natural life is the protection of the body from intentional harm, violation and killing. That may sound very sober and unheroic. However, the body is not primarily there to be sacrificed, rather to be preserved. That then from other and higher perspectives the right and duty may arise to sacrifice the body has as its prerequisite the original right to the preservation of bodily life" (179).

Finally, Bonhoeffer makes a Christian theological point:

> Bodily life is, as is life generally, simultaneously a means to an end and an end in itself. It is idealistic, but not Christian, to understand the body exclusively as a means to an end. A means is dispensed with as soon as the end is reached. That is in accord with the view of the body as prison of the immortal soul, which abandons the body for ever at death. According to Christian teaching, the body has a higher dignity. The person is a bodily

---

with God's command, first considering the positive element implied in the command not to kill, and then considering the prohibition itself, CD III/4, 324, 397. (In this section I offer some comparisons with Barth's way of handling similar concerns, since Barthian divine command ethics will feature prominently in the next chapter.)

being and remains such in eternity. Bodiliness and being human belong indivisibly together. Thus bodiliness, which is willed by God as the form of existence for humans, has as its due being an end in itself. (179–80)

This passage I take to be representative of Bonhoeffer's ethical reasoning when he addresses concrete issues (as well as having importance in being the groundwork for the rest of his argumentation). Typically he offers a rationale that is not theological, and only turns to theological arguments, often of a fairly basic level, after he has made his point.[14] I shall examine another instance in the following to demonstrate this.

Before that, however, it is worth looking at the content of one of his claims in this section regarding bodily life as an end in itself, namely his treatment of bodily pleasure: "The body as an end in itself is expressed in the bodily pleasures within the natural life. Were the body only a means to an end, then the person would have no right to bodily pleasures. An expedient minimum of bodily enjoyment should then not be exceeded. That would have very significant implications for a Christian appraisal of all problems related to the bodily life: dwelling, nutrition, clothing, leisure, recreation, sexuality. However, if the body is recognized as an end in itself, then there is a right to bodily pleasures without their being subordinated to a higher purpose" (180). The reason this passage is worth considering is the fact that it (and similar passages) give some indication of what kind of ethics could do justice to this way of arguing. Certainly a deontological ethic (including divine command ethics) could choose to safeguard various rights. However, consequentialist theories could hardly express this notion, since they are generally based explicitly on some notion of intended outcome, which Bonhoeffer considers inimical to the essence of pleasure (180). Even if a consequentialist might argue that allowing for bodily pleasures promotes overall health and well-being of the individual, who is then able to contribute more fully to the happiness of the greatest number, this is an argument for bodily pleasures, but not on the grounds of the body being an end in itself. Similarly, situation ethics could argue for the place of bodily pleasures, but not on the same grounds as Bonhoeffer. It must be said that virtue ethics also need not contain such thought, but unlike the others, it can accommodate both the substance of Bonhoeffer's claims, and the grounds for making them. If bodily existence is recognized as being a condition of being human, then there is every reason for virtue

---

14. Cf Barth's treatment, which begins with a stark theological statement of divine command, *CD* III/4, 324.

ethics, at least one that includes eudaemonism, to consider that a virtuous person will live in a way that allows for full bodily flourishing, including such pleasures.

5.1.4: *Typical Example: Arbitrary Killing*

Bonhoeffer's discussion of the right not to be killed arbitrarily offers the first concrete example of his method of arguing.[15] Again, as was the case in his more general comments, and as is typical of his treatment of almost all other issues, his starting point is philosophical rather than theological.[16] "The body is always 'my' body, it can never, even in marriage, belong to another person in the same way as to me. My body is what separates me spatially from other persons and sets me as a person in opposition to other persons. Touching my body is an interference in my personal existence" (182).

In view of all this, the "first right of the natural life consists in the protection of bodily life from arbitrary killing" (183). He then defines what he means by "arbitrary," which he relates to "innocence," the understanding of which is surely not Christian theological ("all have sinned," Rom 5:12) but legal in nature: "However, in this context every life that is not undertaking an attack upon another life and which cannot be arrested for a criminal deed worthy of the death penalty is innocent" (183).[17] He

---

15. The weighting of philosophical and theological arguments is similar in the cases of the choice of marriage partner, (*DBW* 6:199–203), abortion (*DBW* 6:203–4), contraception *DBW* 6:204–9), voluntary and forced sterilization (*DBW* 6:209–12), and "The Freedom of Bodily Life" (*DBW* 6:212–16).

16. It is undeniable that some of the points he makes on a philosophical basis would now be hotly contested, such as the appropriateness of physical punishment (*DBW* 6:182), the consideration of whether children are to be considered as independent beings (*DBW* 6:182–3), an assumption that capital punishment has its place (*DBW* 6:183), to name but three such examples. Again, contrast his mode of arguing with Barth's almost exclusively theological, deontological approach, *CD* III/4, 413–5.

17. It is worth noting that assassinating Hitler could not be classed as "arbitrary killing," since he was endangering others and committing crimes for which there was a death penalty. However, Bonhoeffer did not follow Aquinas regarding tyrannicide. Barth refers to evidence from the diplomat Erich Kordt's *Nicht aus den Akten*, which suggests that Thomas's views on tyrannicide were known to the conspirators, *CD* III/4, 448–49. But note also Barth's comments regarding the conspiracy and whether they were obeying an exceptional command from God: since the conspirators were not prepared to assassinate Hitler in utter disregard for their own lives, either they had no command or if they had a command from God they failed to hear it, 449. See also Tödt, "Paradoxical Obedience," 7, 12.

Mode of Ethical Discourse

discusses exceptions such as the killing of an enemy soldier in war, the killing of a criminal endangering others, and unintentional killing of civilians in warfare, again not on theological grounds, but on philosophical grounds (183–84).

Thus, his argument largely relies on philosophy rather than theology and even using the legal understanding of "innocence," which is at variance with a Christian interpretation. The motivation of the agent, important in virtue ethics, is of central importance in his category of *arbitrary* killing.

5.1.5: Atypical Example—Suicide[18]

The one topic Bonhoeffer treats that does not follow this pattern of arguing from reason with theological considerations offered only in support is suicide. It was less obviously an important issue in the context of Nazi Germany than certain other issues he addressed, such as euthanasia, yet it is clear that for Bonhoeffer, and perhaps for his co-conspirators, it was one of real personal concern. Bonhoeffer himself worried that he might not be able to keep the secrets that could save the lives of his own friends and family under the pressures of interrogation and torture.[19] In the initial consideration of whether and when suicide may be permissible, Bonhoeffer's reasoning is much as before, namely of a philosophical nature.[20] He first notes that it is a specifically *human* possibility, not open to other animals, and not unrelated to the possibility of sacrificing one's life for a higher purpose, and then states that the possibility of taking one's own life is a right that is conditional upon having the freedom to do so, but this represents "an incomparable power, which can easily lead to misuse" (192). The temptation (and possible misuse) he sees as relating to trying to be the master of one's own fate, escaping from failure, loss of honor, loss

---

18. Bonhoeffer uses the word "*Selbstmord*" (murder of self) throughout most of this discussion. It is the most common term used generally, though German has the possibility of distinguishing between murder and killing (*Selbsttötung*), which Bonhoeffer only uses when he wants to make this distinction explicit.

19. See Bethge, *Biography*, 832–33. It is interesting to note that Bethge discusses Bonhoeffer's thinking on suicide only in relation to his own temptations in Tegel, but it would seem that he thought seriously about its possible validity as early as 1940–41, when he was writing this manuscript. See his explicit treatment of such a case, *DBW* 6:197.

20. See Barth's praise of Bonhoeffer's treatment, *CD* III/4, 404–6. Barth's own arguments are theological and biblical, but also pastorally sensitive, and he is also unwilling to condemn suicide outright, 403–5, 410–11.

of a loved-one, etc. (192–93). As he continues to discuss at length why a person may be attracted to the possibility of suicide, it is clear that his arguments are not going to lead to an absolute condemnation. Indeed, at this point one might expect that his overall evaluation might be that suicide is permissible, yet the tone changes radically when he turns to theological considerations (much earlier and with more weight than when treating other issues):

> However, if it is necessary to speak of the reprehensibility of suicide, then this is valid not before the forum of morality or of humans, but alone before the forum of God. The one who commits suicide is guilty, only before God, who is the creator and Lord over his life. Because there is a living God, therefore suicide is reprehensible as the sin of lack of faith. Yet lack of faith is not a moral shortcoming, rather it is capable of motives and deeds both noble and mean. Lack of faith, however, does not reckon in good or in bad things with the living God. That is the sin. The lack of faith is the reason for which the person grasps for his own justification and its last possibility in suicide, because he does not believe in a divine justification. The lack of faith hides from the person in a fatal way the fact that even suicide does not release him from the hand of God, who prepared for him his fate. (194)

Thus Bonhoeffer carries on his argument via the theological conviction that God is the author of life and therefore has the right to determine its end. Contrary to his usual mode of discourse, here it is the theological considerations that are lengthy and clearly determine his overall stance:

> God stands up for the right to life even against the one who has become weary of life. He gives the person the freedom to risk his life for something greater, but he does not want for this freedom to turn against that life. The person should not harm himself, even as certainly as he should bring his life as a sacrifice for others. The person should place his earthly life, even where it becomes agonizing, completely in God's hand, from whom he received it, and should not consider releasing himself from it through his own means. He only falls, indeed even dying, again in God's hand, which in life had become too hard for him. (196)

Also unlike in his other arguments, here Bonhoeffer considers individual cases that might genuinely test his theological treatment. "Because suicide is a deed of loneliness, the final decisive motives almost always remain hidden" (196). Here he makes the distinction between killing oneself or murdering oneself, whereby killing oneself could actually be an act of sacrificing one's own life for others, a deed that Bonhoeffer sees as possibly valid. "Making a ban on suicide [*Selbsttötung*] absolute over against the freedom of sacrificing one's life can hardly be substantiated in the face of such cases. Even the old church fathers considered suicide among Christians to be allowed in certain circumstances, for instance if chastity was threatened by violence, even if Augustine disagreed and made the ban on suicide absolute" (197).[21] Thus he uses particular cases and common sense reasoning and even church history or tradition to place a caveat on the theological stance he has given. As he continues the argument, he uses examples to show that it might be difficult to know in individual cases whether the act should be considered suicide or what he takes to be a "Christian duty" to give to another the last place in a life boat, or to protect a friend from a bullet, even by taking that bullet oneself (198): "One's own decision becomes here the cause of one's own death, even if the difference remains between the direct suicide and the risking of life, in which life is given over to God" (198).

The whole discussion of suicide juxtaposes arguments from reason that would seem often to allow or even honor suicide with arguments from theology that would forbid it, at least generally. This is the only discussion in which Bonhoeffer's position seems to be ambivalent. The discussion is also unique in that his arguments from reason do not support his theological statements, and it is significant that in such circumstances the theological position has the final say. Although this discussion is atypical in these ways, it follows the pattern of emphasizing the motives of the agent, which is important in virtue ethics.

5.1.6: Assessment of Bonhoeffer's Mode of Argument

What, then, should be made of the way Bonhoeffer goes about making his case when he is dealing with issues of real moment for his own time and place? The first thing that is important to address is that his mode of arguing may or may not relate to how his own views have been formed. Thus when I say that he does not argue often from an explicitly theological standpoint this does not mean that his own thinking was not influenced by theological convictions. To the contrary, the fact that his philosophical arguments almost always coincide with a Christian stance may well be an

---

21. See *DBW* 6:197 n. 101 regarding the views held by a number of the church fathers.

indication that, like Milton, Bonhoeffer perhaps is trying to explain the ways of God to man, using arguments that people without Christian commitments might understand and find persuasive. This would be further supported by the fact that in many cases the theological foundations present are quite basic, and not necessarily even Christian: namely drawing on God as creator, a premise that theists of almost any hue would accept. All of this is not to deny that Bonhoeffer's own upbringing in a kind of Christian humanism might not have played a role in how he chose to argue his case, but simply to underscore that it would be too simplistic to assume that his mode of argument must necessarily correspond to how his own positions were formed.

It would be possible to suggest that Bonhoeffer's mode of argument in this section may have been influenced by the fact, as noted above, that he was working in the monastery in Ettal, having conversations with the abbot, using the library, and was working with at least one of Josef Pieper's texts. It is, of course, the normal mode for Roman Catholic moral theology to address not merely Catholics or Christians but all people of good will. In doing so, arguments are typically mounted on philosophical rather than theological grounds.[22] It is impossible to be sure how much influence there might have been, but it seems to me, given how nuanced he is in taking up the theme of the natural but distancing himself in many ways from Roman Catholic positions, that even if there was influence, Bonhoeffer would not have used this mode of argument unless it suited his own purposes. I would also suggest that he would not do so against his own theological convictions. If he is happy to address ethical issues in ways that might be persuasive to non-Christians, it would at least accord with his notion that everything good is to be claimed and won for Christ (350–51).

Hence, it is important to ask what his purposes and who his intended readers might have been, for it is possible that his choice of mode of discourse might have related to the form of argument he thought might be most persuasive. The internal evidence in the manuscripts otherwise would suggest that Bonhoeffer was writing a work of theological ethics. Yet it would seem that when he attends to specific issues of great moment in Nazi Germany he is not writing with academic theologians, or even necessarily Christians, in mind. Of course this is one of the many areas in which the fact that these manuscripts are unfinished fragments makes it

---

22. However, see Bonhoeffer's later insistence that the Protestant churches cannot speak to the world "on the basis of some perceptions based on reason or natural law, temporarily ignoring the gospel," *DBW* 6:359.

necessary to speak only tentatively and provisionally, and in such a fashion it is at least possible to construe his intended work not only as a concrete ethic for his time and place, but as an ethic that may speak to a broad readership (since at that time there would have been a relatively small number of people who were not theists of some sort).

The relationship between his own philosophical and theological thinking is most severely tested by the issue of suicide, which is the one place where Bonhoeffer's theological stance is not in agreement with the arguments he puts forward from reason, as he claims that suicide can only be condemnable before God but not before the forum of morality or human judgment (194). Thus in this one case only, Bonhoeffer does not make a philosophical case for why his theological stance is right. Indeed, to use his own words written about Barth from prison, one might even say that Bonhoeffer is guilty here of "*Offenbarungspositivismus*," a positivism of revelation. Suicide is wrong, Bonhoeffer says, because there is a living God, the Creator, to whom the decisions of life and death belong (194). Suicide is wrong because it is the human attempt at self-justification, rather than the dependence on God for justification (195–96). Ultimately, his case is that suicide is wrong because God says so. "Take it or leave it!" (*Friss Vogel oder stirb!*)[23] Therefore, it is suggestive that when Bonhoeffer's theology and philosophy do not concur, it is theology which is decisive. This strengthens the case for assuming that even if Bonhoeffer argues primarily in non-theological ways, it is his theology that more fundamentally informs his thinking.

However one may best construe the reasons for Bonhoeffer's mode of argument, there are at least some preliminary conclusions to be drawn. The first is that this way of discussing particular subjects does not relate to a deontological ethic, where one might expect more discussion of rules, or, in a Christian context, more citation of (scriptural) laws or commands (196–98).

Secondly, his mode of argument is never consequentialist in that his concern is not the outcome of actions, let alone the notion of the "greatest happiness for the greatest number." In contrast with this, he is often concerned to preserve the good of the individual over the perceived good of the society, as in his comments regarding euthanasia (187–89).

Thirdly, it would seem that in many instances the factor that holds most sway (apart from the relationship of the Creator to the natural rights)

---

23. See *DBW* 8:415, 404, and 481. See also his discussion of sterilization and his surprising use of scripture there, *DBW* 6:212.

is the motive for the action. It is worth noting how often Bonhoeffer refers to what is an evil as "arbitrary," suggesting that it is the lack of an adequate or acceptable rationale or motivation that causes an action to be wrong. So "arbitrary killing" is wrong, whereas there may well be acceptable reasons for killing (as in warfare, or killing a criminal, 183–84); similarly "arbitrarily robbing" someone's freedom is wrong (215–16), with the implication that there are appropriate reasons for imprisoning persons. Also, Bonhoeffer leaves open the question of whether abortion may be appropriate if the motive is saving the mother's life (204, his note 4). Similarly in his discussion of contraception, motive plays a large role in that he recognizes both a need for responsibility in determining how many children there are in a family, and the need for spouses to have sexual communion even when further children are not intended (205–7). Likewise it is a matter of motive (as well as the pragmatic question of whether other means might be available) that decides whether voluntary sterilization may be admissible (210). However, noting the repeated treatment of motive as an important if not decisive factor in his assessments does not yet make it easy to claim that Bonhoeffer is engaging in some form of virtue ethics. Situation ethics might also regard the motivation to be important, yet the lack of concern for outcomes, and his rejection of using an overarching criterion that would be decisive in the situation (such as the question of what might be the most loving thing to do) make the case for seeing Bonhoeffer as a situation ethicist is weak.[24]

Thus from the examination of Bonhoeffer's method of arguing, it seems that he operates from a Christian theological viewpoint, but most frequently arguing philosophically, and overtly stating only fairly general theist positions. This, I take it, tells us more about his intended readership than it does about how his positions are actually formed and informed. Nonetheless, his way of treating specific issues is not obviously deontological, utilitarian or situationist, and his emphasis on motives makes a relationship to virtue ethics more likely than any of the other schools of ethical thought.

---

24. Bonhoeffer rarely discusses the specifics of any situation, though note the exception of the case of a ship where effective quarantine is impossible and there is an outbreak of the plague. In this instance Bonhoeffer allows that euthanasia may be admissible, *DBW* 6:191.

5.2: Mode of Ethical Discourse in the Letters and Papers from Prison

Even if one grants that Bonhoeffer's way of arguing his case when dealing with specific themes in the *Ethics* shows more affinity to virtue ethics than other forms, one may yet rightly ask whether there are any other examples of concrete ethics in his late writings, and if so how he goes about his discussion there. Certainly, given that much of his writing even in prison seems to have been related to his "*große Arbeit*"—his large work, or perhaps his magnum opus, namely on ethics—it would be surprising if there were no examples of concrete ethical discussion.[25] It is all the more important to look for such instances because Bonhoeffer has been seen as an impulsive thinker, and it may be thought that Bonhoeffer might have changed his tack. As Gerhard Jacobi, a pastor and the president of the Confessing Church in Berlin, put it, "Some of his spontaneous definitions he wrote down. He would have declined to develop from them as it were a whole theology. Even though his thoughts were clearly and precisely defined, they often became questionable again to him, especially when expressed in print or writing."[26] Thus I turn now to an instance of a specific ethical issue treated in the prison writings.

The one sustained treatment of an ethical issue in this period is his essay, "What does it mean to tell the truth?"[27] Here his argument is that we are taught to tell the truth by our parents and to our parents and so "this demand applies strictly only within the family circle" (619–20). Moreover the demand to tell the truth is dependent on the role within the family relationships: a child cannot demand truthfulness from the parent, and the truthfulness from parent to child is of a different order. "The question must be asked whether and in what way a person is entitled to demand speech in accordance with truth of another." Speech differs according to the relation of the persons speaking, thus communications between, for instance, husband and wife, parent and child, friends, teacher and pupil, authority and subject, or enemies are by nature different, and therefore a different truth conveyed (620). To the possible objection that truth is not owed to a person but to God, Bonhoeffer counters that God is not a general principle but the living God, and serving him is service in the real

---

25. On his "große Arbeit," see for example *DBW* 8:147, 182, 200, and 428.
26. *I Knew Dietrich Bonhoeffer*, 72. See also Barth's remarks in *World Come of Age*, 89–90.
27. *DBW* 16:619–29, to which all citations in brackets in this section refer.

world in which Jesus Christ became incarnate (620–21). "The truthfulness of our words that is owed to God must assume a concrete form in the world. Our word should not be in principle but concretely in accordance with the truth. Something not concretely in accordance with the truth is, before God, not at all in accordance with the truth" (621).

Bonhoeffer then uses the concept of reality to explore what "telling the truth" might entail in complex circumstances. "The real must be expressed in words. Therein consists speech in accordance with reality. It is always concerned with the 'right word.' Finding this is an issue of long, earnest and ever progressive effort on the basis of experience and recognition of the real. To say how something really is, i.e. to speak in accordance with reality, perception and thinking must direct themselves toward how reality is in God and through God and towards God" (622).

Yet Bonhoeffer considers it superficial to imagine that some circumstances require truthful speech while others do not.

> Every word that I ever speak stands under the demand to be true; completely irrespective of the truthfulness of its content, the relationship between me and another person that is expressed in it is true or untrue. ... The individual word is always a part of a whole of reality that wants to be expressed. According to whom I address, by whom I am questioned, about what I speak my word, if it is to be according to the truth, it must be a different one. The word that is in accordance with the truth is not a quantity that in itself is constant, but is as alive as life itself. Where it looses itself from life and from the relationship to the concrete other person, where the "truth is told" without observing to whom I say it, there it has only the appearance but not the essence of truth. (622–23)

The one who does not make these distinctions Bonhoeffer calls a cynic. While such a person claims to tell the truth to everyone always in the same way, he "wounds shame, profanes mystery, breaks trust, betrays the community in which he lives, and laughs arrogantly about the wasteland that he has caused, about the human weakness that 'cannot bear the truth.' He says that truth is destructive and demands its sacrifice, and he feels himself to be a god over the weak creatures and does not know that he serves Satan" (623).

Bonhoeffer then contrasts the truth that is of Satan and God's truth. "There is a truth that is of Satan. Its essence is that it denies all that is real under the pretence of truth. It lives from hatred of the real, of the world that is created and loved by God. It gives the appearance of executing

Mode of Ethical Discourse

God's judgment of the sinful Fall of the real. But God's truth judges out of love for the created, which Satan's truth judges out of envy and hatred. God's truth has become flesh in the world, is alive in the real; Satan's truth is the death of all that is real" (623-24).

The first question to ask in this context relates to the nature of Bonhoeffer's argument. It is clear from the preceding that his discussion is not especially theological. Although he uses the language of "God" and "Satan" and assumes a particular relation of each to truth, his argument does not in fact depend upon the acceptance of this position. Rather his discussion hangs on certain assumptions about appropriate behavior in various circumstances and the distinctiveness of various kinds of relating. Perhaps it also depends upon the shared observation of "truth" being used in many situations as a weapon to wound others. At all events, this discussion falls under the broad category of "philosophical" rather than theological.

Having said this, it is also important to ask what kind of ethic this is? It can hardly be Kantian, since he rejects the form of truth-telling that one might call a "categorical imperative" as "cynical" and "of Satan." It would seem that he is adopting some form that is more malleable, but how is it best understood? It might seem relativist, in that the truth to be told seems to be a relative one. Yet there is no appeal to what conscience might dictate, nor to what appears to be right to the agent. In fact, it would seem that the truth to be told is not so much "relative" as something that parents can teach their children in terms of what is appropriate: "Educationally it is therefore of the greatest importance that parents somehow (which is not to be discussed here) make understandable to the child the differentiation of these spheres of life [family, school, friends, etc.] and his responsibilities" (621).

Many, as we have already seen, have argued that his ethics is situationist, and it would seem that he is here appealing to the specifics of situation. However, two things need to be highlighted. First, the aspect of the given situation that Bonhoeffer mentions over and over again is the relationship between the two parties in conversation, which seems to me to be quite particular and may relate best to other forms of ethics, especially virtue ethics and relational ethics. Secondly, there is no appeal to some guiding principle, such as asking what the most loving thing to do is.

What seems to be the case is that Bonhoeffer is arguing here along similar lines to those he advocates in the *Ethics* when he treats the notion of *suum cuique*, asking specifically what is owed to whom. This becomes more pronounced when he offers a specific case.

> An example: a child is asked in front of the class by his teacher whether it is true that his father often comes home drunk. It is true, but the child negates it. He has been brought into a situation by the teacher's question for which he is not prepared. Indeed he feels that an unjustified invasion in the order of the family is occurring that he must resist. What happens in the family does not belong [in discussion] before the school class. The family has its own secret that it has to protect. The teacher has disregarded the reality of this order. The child should find a way in his answer in which the orders of the family and of the school are equally upheld. He cannot do that yet; he lacks the experience, the perception and the ability for the right expression. Although the answer is untrue, in that he simply negates the teacher's question, yet it gives expression to the truth, nevertheless, that the family is an order *sui generis* in which the teacher was not justified to intrude. Although one can call the child's answer a lie, nonetheless this lie contains more truth, i.e. it is more in accordance with reality than if the child had betrayed his father's weakness in front of the class. The child acted rightly according to the measure of his perception. The blame for the lie rebounds solely on the teacher. An experienced person in the child's place could have, while correcting the questioner, also avoided the formal opposition to the truth of the answer, and thereby have found the "right word" in the situation. (625)

One of the things that is interesting about Bonhoeffer's "case study," if I may call it that, is that the aspects of the situation that seem to be salient in his treatment are the questions of who the agent is, with whom she is dealing, what the setting is, and how the actions are done. It is important that the agent is a child, whose experience of life has not yet afforded him the understanding to be able to do what Bonhoeffer thinks should be done, namely correct the teacher's behavior while still answering without the "formal" lie or any betrayal of the father's drunkenness. According to the child's ability, he has acted correctly. Yet it is not only the child's own capabilities that matter; Bonhoeffer makes much of the fact that the teacher is interfering, that the blame for the "lie" told therefore falls on him, and that although there is a relationship of authority that Bonhoeffer would surely assume is to be respected,[28] a more experienced person would nonetheless correct the teacher's inappropriate questioning. Similarly, although Bonhoeffer does not make much of the fact, the setting of asking such a

---

28. On relationships of authority, see e.g. *DBW* 6:377, 394–96, 400, and *DBW* 7:32, 112.

question before the whole class is significant, for if there might be circumstances in which it is appropriate for a teacher to ask about private matters (and I think in our society this is much more likely to be the case), it is not in front of the whole class where the child may then suffer taunts or bullying from the others, and where it may expose the family to gossip. Finally, it seems important in Bonhoeffer's account to consider the motivation for how the child acts, in this case to protect his family from wrongful interference. What is interesting about all of these considerations is that they are all part of what Aquinas considers to be important aspects surrounding an act that help determine what is the right course to take (or how a completed action is to be judged).[29] Furthermore, it is clearly the case that Bonhoeffer is deeply concerned with what Thomas would call prudence, and what he refers to in terms of experience, perception (or discernment, *Erkenntnis*) and capability. In this case it would seem that Bonhoeffer praises the child's perception that his first loyalty is to his family and that the teacher's question is out of line, even if his experience and capability are not yet developed enough to allow him to handle the situation as well as might be. It seems to me that these features of his example are quite telling, and place his mode of reasoning again in the vicinity of virtue ethics.

Also noteworthy is his emphasis on the role of development for learning to act well. We have already seen that he is interested in the part parents should play in teaching their children to recognize what is appropriate in the different areas of their lives. Here we see again that Bonhoeffer assumes that the ability to act well is learned over time and with experience. This is, of course, one of the basic assumptions of classical virtue ethics, that the capacity to act well is taught, trained, disciplined, and learned over time.

From all this it seems safe to say that Bonhoeffer's mode of arguing did not change greatly after he wrote his *Ethics* manuscripts in terms of the use of "philosophical" and theological arguments regarding concrete issues. Furthermore in this short case study Bonhoeffer's account seems to have real affinity with virtue ethics.

5.3: Conclusions

In this chapter we have seen that when Bonhoeffer does write about specific issues, when he is concrete, there are at least some observable influences from Roman Catholic moral theology, which make a certain

---

29. See e.g., *ST* I-II, question 7.

proximity to virtue ethics seem less improbable than it otherwise might. Here he affirms the natural life and develops a Protestant theological position for incorporating much from Catholic thought whilst also correcting its rule-based manuals tendencies. His mode of argument is often philosophical rather than overtly theological, and when he does argue from a specifically theological stance, it is often of low level, even theist, nature. These factors suggest that Bonhoeffer hoped to be persuasive to a wide range of people, not just Christians, reminiscent of Roman Catholic moral teaching addressing all people of good will, rather than simply "the faithful." More important than such signs of influence, however, in writing about specific issues Bonhoeffer argues in ways that show real affinity with virtue ethics, with a focus on who the agent is as well as the circumstances involved and the motivation for acting. In these ways Bonhoeffer's concrete ethics seems to be in close proximity to virtue ethics, and rather harder to align with other forms of ethical thought. Finally, although there are strong links with relational ethics, especially in his treatment of lying, there are many features of his ethics (apart from human interrelatedness), such as the agent's motive for her action, which are not necessarily a part of relational ethics. Taking all this into consideration, Bonhoeffer's way of making his case on concrete issues would place him closer to virtue ethics than any other mode of ethical discourse.

Yet it would be rash to claim that Bonhoeffer was really expounding virtue ethics under another guise, or without using the term. Even if there are many elements that relate well to virtue ethics, and many others that seem even "virtue-ethical," there is still a large question regarding the influence of Karl Barth and his divine command ethics that must be addressed. To this I now turn.

6

Divine Command and/or Virtue Ethics

6.1: Introduction

HAVING LOOKED AT VIRTUE ETHICS AND RELATED THEMES IN BONHOEFfer's *Ethics*, it is now necessary to ask how virtue ethics relates to the other major strand of ethical thinking identified in these manuscripts, namely, divine command ethics.[1] To do this, I shall first of all trace his usage of this latter motif in the *Ethics* (6.2). This should show clearly the extent of his usage of this mode of considering ethics, and thereby establish the need to consider the place of divine command in any proposal for understanding his *Ethics* as related to virtue ethics.

Secondly, I shall engage more fully than hitherto with the proposals by Larry Rasmussen and Stephen Plant regarding how these two strands of ethical thinking within Bonhoeffer's *Ethics* might be related (6.3). Because these two significant commentators who have discussed divine command and conformation as the key motifs in Bonhoeffer's *Ethics* have different understandings of the relationship between them, it is good to explore their interpretations and consider the strengths and weaknesses of each proposal before continuing with my own examination of the issues at stake.

In this examination, I shall explore issues that are treated in both of these modes of ethical thought (6.4). Here I hope to discover what, if any, difference is made to the concerns he addresses by the form of his ethical thought. This should help to clarify the strengths and weaknesses of Plant's and Rasmussen's respective positions. From this it should be possible to

---

1. I speak of "virtue ethics" in this context as a reminder that the virtue-ethical aspects of Bonhoeffer's *Ethics* are broader than the theme of conformation. Rasmussen and Plant, however, speak of "conformation" and refer to this theme rather than the wider associations with virtue.

draw conclusions about these two strands in Bonhoeffer's *Ethics*, and what the role of virtue ethics is in this work (6.5).

6.2: Divine Command in Bonhoeffer's *Ethics*

In exploring Bonhoeffer's use of divine command in his *Ethics*, it is necessary to distinguish between a more general influence of Barth's theology on Bonhoeffer and specific dependence on divine command ethics. Bonhoeffer's use of Barthian language is so pervasive that an attempt to discuss all such influence would require a study devoted to that.[2] Instead I am interested simply in how Bonhoeffer uses Barth's notion that God's command comes afresh to the Christian in a given moment. So understood, divine command ethics can be said to be both actualist (focused on the *act* in response to command) and particularist (focused on the *concrete* moment, not presuming continuity between what has been commanded in the past and what will be commanded in the present).[3] As such, this is in strong contrast both to a deontology that assumes a set of stable rules and to virtue ethics, which focuses on the agent and her development of qualities over time that enable her to live well.

For this study, then, I shall focus on key terms that may suggest the dependence on this form of divine command, especially "command" (both as noun, *Gebot*, and verb, *gebieten*), "obedience" (*Gehorsamkeit*, or obey, *Gehorsam leisten*), and references to "God's will" (*der Wille Gottes*). Clearly, the use of these words is not sufficient to assert that Bonhoeffer is using divine command theory in relevant passages; however, such language is central to this motif and should enable its usage to be highlighted.

6.2.1: *Divine Command Language in the Early Manuscripts*

6.2.1.A: COMMAND

The first thing to note here is that in the earlier manuscripts (where virtue-ethical aspects are frequently observable), there is little mention of "command." However, in the first passage where he treats the notion of the mandates, Bonhoeffer states, "Not because work, marriage, authority,

---

2. Regarding Barth's influence on Bonhoeffer, see 21 n. 11.

3. Some have tried to uncover ways of interpreting Barth as less particularistic than I suggest. See Webster, *Barth's Moral Theology*; also his *Barth's Ethics of Reconciliation*; Mangina, *Karl Barth on the Christian Life*; and Werpehowski, "Narrative and Ethics in Barth." See also Biggar, *Hastening*; and Helm, ed., *Divine Command and Morality*.

church *is*, is it divinely *commanded (geboten)*; rather because it is *commanded* by God, therefore it *is*, and only so far as its being—consciously or unconsciously—submits to the divine task, is it a divine mandate" (56, his emphases).[4] Here the language of command is used as well as submission, which implies obedience in this case. Given that the discussion is about areas of life (as addressed by the mandates) this is, however, not precisely the actualist or particularist form of divine command ethics one might expect.

Also in his discussion of "Ethics as Formation" Bonhoeffer introduces the language of command (and obedience) without necessarily depending on divine command theory: "Ethics as formation is thus the venture to speak, neither abstractly nor casuistically, neither programmatically nor purely speculatively, of the form of Jesus Christ taking form in our world. Here concrete judgments and decisions must be risked. Here the decision and act can no longer be pushed off on the individual's conscience, but rather here there are concrete commands and directions for which obedience is demanded" (89).

Here too commands (and directions) are given for which obedience is required, but not in the manner of divine command ethics, but rather in the context of Christ winning form in the believer, conforming her to himself. This implies a degree of continuity of agency, and a focus on the agent rather than her isolated acts.

Finally, and more closely related to Barth's conception is the first discussion of "simplicity and cleverness," where Bonhoeffer states that the simple person "is the man of undivided heart. Because he knows and has God, he clings to the commands [or commandments], to the judgment and to the mercy that proceed daily anew from the mouth of God" (67).[5] Here we have not simply the language of command, but the Barthian notion that commands come to the Christian ever afresh from God. This surely is a clear instance of Bonhoeffer's use of this motif, not expounding it as such, but using it to discuss the (God-given) attributes of the person, simplicity and cleverness.

From these passages it is clear that Bonhoeffer does use the language of command, sometimes including the Barthian emphasis on its coming always afresh, though more often simply as the motif of command and obedience. This is the case even when his emphasis is most clearly on the

4. All references in brackets in the main text in this section refer to *DBW* 6.
5. The German "Gebot" may be rendered "command" (as a noun) or "commandment," depending on the context. In this case it is not obvious that any great difference would be made by these translations, but it is worth bearing this point in mind throughout the discussion.

formational (virtue-like) aspects of ethics, as seen when he addresses his notion of mandates, when he defines what appear to be something like infused virtues (simplicity and cleverness), and within his notion of ethics as formation.

6.2.1.B: OBEDIENCE

As with "command," there are also only a few references to "obedience" in the early manuscripts, one of which we have already seen. Two more occur in his discussion of the mandates, where he says that "marriage is not only the place of the conception but also the teaching of children to obey Jesus Christ" (58). Likewise, in discussing the divine mandate of authority, he states, "legislation and the power of the sword preserves . . . the world for the reality of Jesus Christ. Everyone owes obedience to this authority—for Christ's sake" (59). These examples show usage of the notion of (command and) obedience, but do not depend on Barthian divine command as such.

6.2.1.C: THE WILL OF GOD

Finally, the will of God, like the notions of command and obedience, is only rarely mentioned in the early manuscripts. The first reference to it, however, occurs in his justly famous opening sentence: "It is an incomparable imposition that must be addressed to everyone who wants even to look at the problem of a Christian ethic, namely the imposition to abandon from the outset as inappropriate to the issue both questions that lead him to be concerned with the ethical problem at all—'how can I become good?' and 'how can I do something good?'—and instead to ask the question about the will of God" (31).

He picks up this theme again later in the manuscript:

> We discussed at the beginning that the question of the will of God must take the place of the question of one's being good and doing good. The will of God, however, is nothing other than the becoming real of the reality of Christ among us and in our world. The will of God is thus neither an idea that demands realization first; it is much more itself already reality in the self-revelation of God in Jesus Christ. The will of God is however not simply identical with that which exists such that subjection to what exists might be its fulfillment; it is much more a reality that, in what exists and against what exists, wants ever afresh to become real. . . . After the appearance of Christ, ethics can only

> be concerned with one thing, namely with receiving a share of the reality of the fulfilled will of God. But also this receiving a share is only possible because of the fact that, in the fulfillment of the will of God in Christ, I myself am also included, and that means [I am] reconciled with God. The question of the will of God does not inquire about something hidden or unfulfilled, but rather about what is revealed, fulfilled. However, therein remains yet a genuine question, whether I myself, and the world that surrounds me, am placed in this question by the fulfillment. (60-61)

From these passages it seems clear that the will of God, while not mentioned often in the earlier manuscripts, plays a decisive role in the first manuscript, which we have already seen has real affinities with virtue ethics. Furthermore, it is not simply that the will of God is central here to Bonhoeffer's conception of ethics; in speaking of the will of God in terms of a reality that "wants ever afresh to become real" Bonhoeffer displays some of the actualist and particularist aspects of Barth's account.

Thus it is possible to say that in the first manuscripts, which overtly have more in common with virtue ethics than divine command ethics, there are relationships with divine command ethics that require further exploration.

6.2.2: Divine Command Language in Later Manuscripts

Tracing the language of divine command in this detail in the manuscripts written after Bonhoeffer had acquired Barth's *Church Dogmatics* II/2 would be more demanding, for the concept of command most particularly is almost omnipresent in these later writings.[6] Therefore, I shall concentrate on the major themes with which it is connected (6.2.2.a), and further quotations referring to command will appear in connection with "obedience" (6.2.2.b) and "will of God" (6.2.2.c).

6.2.2.A: COMMAND

First, we have already noted the importance of Christology in the *Ethics*, and divine command ethics is treated Christologically: God's command is revealed in Jesus Christ (383-84, 392, 397). In the final manuscript

---

6. See Rasmussen, *Significance*, 96-101, regarding the dependence of these manuscripts on *CD* II/2. See also *DBW* 6:365, note 2, regarding Bonhoeffer's acquisition of Barth's volume.

Bonhoeffer even makes direct reference to "the command of Jesus Christ" (406). Thus, as with virtue-ethical aspects of Bonhoeffer's *Ethics*, divine command ethics is given Bonhoeffer's characteristic Christological emphasis.

Similarly, command language is used in relation to Bonhoeffer's insistence that ethics must be concrete: "While the 'ethical' is concerned in the final analysis with defining and creating territory for living together [i.e. personal involvement as opposed to the role of observer or judge, 372–73] in the whole fullness of life, the command is concerned with this 'living together' even in its concrete contents and in the human freedom that is enabled within and through these [concrete contents]" (390).

Making this linkage between divine command and concrete ethics clearer is the fact that he planned to follow up this section with a consideration of "the concrete command of God" (391). However, it is worth considering that "command" in this passage does not necessarily refer to something actualistic or particularistic. Instead it refers to "the whole fullness of life," which is related in thought to his earlier notion of "the natural," and to his later discussion of the "latitude of freedom." This example is a good reminder that although the later manuscripts contain much Barthian language, his talk of "command" does not always mean divine command ethics.

6.2.2.B: OBEDIENCE

Given the persistent usage of "command," one might expect to see an equally heightened usage of its corollary, "obedience." This, however, is not the case; instead there are relatively few passages concerned with this notion. One reason for this may be the fact, as just seen, that Bonhoeffer often is using "command" to refer to the whole of life, rather than to actualistic, particularistic events.

However, in the context of speaking about an important theme in his *Ethics*, responsibility, in the second version of "History and the Good," Bonhoeffer draws on the notion of obedience in stark terms: "Jesus stands before God as the obedient one and the free one. As the obedient one he does the will of the Father in blind following of the law commanded him. As the free one, he affirms the will out of his most personal [*eigenster*] recognition" (288).[7]

---

7. The editors of *DBW* 6 include this manuscript (in both versions) in the third writing period, which covers the time in which Bonhoeffer acquired *CD* II/2 (see *DBW*

In this passage Bonhoeffer shows the relationship between responsibility and obedience, and between freedom and determination: "Obedience has fettered hands; freedom is creative. In obedience the person keeps God's Decalogue; in freedom the person creates new decalogues (Luther)" (288). In this instance, "obedience" is centered on the person of Christ and stands in continuity with his Christological emphasis. However, the form it takes is not necessarily divine command ethics, for Bonhoeffer does not make explicit that the person who "creates new decalogues" is doing so in constant attention to the command of God that comes constantly afresh.

Even if Bonhoeffer does not speak of obedience frequently, when he does it is often in stark terms: "God's command is God's speech to the person, and specifically, in its content as well as in its form, [it is] concrete speech to the concrete person. God's command allows the person no room for application, for interpretation, rather only for obedience or disobedience" (382). This idea he repeats later in the same manuscript, "The 'Ethical' and the 'Christian' as a Theme": "God's command as that which is revealed in Jesus Christ is always a concrete speaking *to* someone, never an abstract speaking *about* something or someone. It is always an address, a claim, and that in such a comprehensive and simultaneously determining way that there is no longer the freedom of interpretation and of application, but rather only the freedom of obedience or disobedience" (384, his emphases).

Thus the notion of "obedience" takes on an uncompromising character not seen in the earlier references to it. Unlike the preceding passages, however, here divine command ethics is surely being expounded. God's address is named as "command," obedience or disobedience are the only possible responses, and from the context it is reasonable to suggest that it is not the written command that Bonhoeffer has in mind, but the command that comes always newly from God to the believer.

6.2.2.c: The Will of God

Unlike the notion of "obedience," "God's will" is almost a leitmotif in the final manuscripts, and most powerfully so in the manuscript "The Love of God and the Decay of the World," where it is of central importance.

6:17, 465; and *DBW* 16:266–67). This makes it hard to be sure whether this manuscript should be included in those which were directly influenced by Bonhoeffer's reading of this volume. However, the internal evidence in terms of the themes addressed and the mode of discussion are strongly suggestive that he wrote at least the second version in the light of reading *CD* II/2. I therefore include it as belonging to the later manuscripts.

Here Jesus is shown to be the one whose very life is to do his Father's will (315). It is, then, in similar terms that Bonhoeffer describes how a Christian should live:

> The knowledge regarding Jesus is absorbed fully in his action, without any reflection. His own good now remains hidden to the person. [It is not] only that the person *need* no longer be the judge of his good; no, he should not even *desire* to know it any longer, moreover he *must* no longer know it; he *knows* it no longer. So unquestioning has his doing become, so wholly dedicated and fulfilled has his doing become, so much is his doing no longer one possibility among many, rather the one, the real, the will of God, that the knowledge [of his own good] can no longer hinderingly intervene, that here, literally, no more time can be lost which would postpone, put in question, judge the doing (320, his emphases).[8]

Interestingly, although the goal is the simple doing of the will of God (*actus directus*, as he called it in *Act and Being*), Bonhoeffer shows this in terms of development over time: at first the person *need not* be aware of her own goodness, then she no longer *desires* to know it, then she *must* not know it, and finally, she simply *doesn't* know it. Such attention to growth and development, as has been seen already, is a concern of virtue ethics. As the passage continues, he brings this theme of doing the will of God without awareness of one's own good into relationship with his earlier notion of simplicity: "It is the liberating call to simplicity, to repentance; it is the call that cancels/raises [*aufhebt*] the old knowledge from falling away [from God] and gives the new knowledge of Jesus, that knowledge which is completely absorbed in doing the will of God" (321).[9]

Despite this insistence that simplicity enables one to know the will of God, Bonhoeffer turns the discussion to discerning it:

> One cannot discern what the will of God is out of one's own resources, from one's own knowledge of good and evil, but rather fully to the contrary, only he can do it, who has lost all of his own knowledge of good and evil and who therefore totally relinquishes knowing the will of God from his own resources: the one who already lives in unity with the will of God because the

---

8. See also *DBW* 6:322, 334 and 356.

9. Regarding the difficulty of translating *aufheben* (because it can mean either to cancel or to raise, or it can be used deliberately with this ambiguity), see the translator's preface to Barth, *On Religion*. See *DBW* 3:84, 114 regarding knowledge of good and evil as a result of the Fall.

will of God has already effected itself in him. Discerning what is God's will is only possible because of the knowledge of God's will in Jesus Christ. (325)

The will of God he defines as the "will of the *living* God" and as such must always be discerned anew (329). "However," he writes, "in no case is the new unity with the will of God, the simplicity of doing, thereby cancelled or even only disturbed." This he seeks to demonstrate with reference to doing (*das Tun*), which he distinguishes from an isolated deed, (*die Tat*): The Scriptures "do not desire that a person's own deed should be placed alongside the deed of God—whether it be out of thanks or sacrifice—but rather [the Scriptures] place the person completely inside the doing of God and subordinate human doing to this doing of God" (329).

Thus his emphasis here is placed firmly on the doing of God's will, which happens in God-given simplicity and not in any contradiction to the acknowledged need for discerning what it is. It is, however, striking that his emphasis on *doing* rather than on individual deeds implies some degree of continuity, both in divine and human actions.

From these passages we see that the notion of the "will of God," as well as occurring with much greater frequency in the later manuscripts, is at least in some cases clearly used in ways one would expect within divine command ethics. Moreover, Bonhoeffer's treatment of it is Christ-centered and related to his concern for concrete ethics. However, it is also apparent that his talk of "doing" rather than of individual acts, as well as his concern to show the development of acting in simplicity, makes his use of the motive less actualistic and particularistic than might be assumed.

6.2.3: *Some Provisional Conclusions*

From this exploration of Bonhoeffer's treatment of important themes in divine command ethics, namely "command," "obedience," and "God's will" it is undoubtedly the case that all three are present in early as well as later manuscripts, though the emphasis on these themes only really comes after he had read Barth's *Church Dogmatics* II/2. However, both in earlier and later manuscripts his use of the language does not always imply full adherence to the actualistic, particularistic account of divine command ethics one might expect.[10]

Conversely, in examining evidence for virtue-ethical themes, the first manuscripts showed much greater affinity, and in the manuscripts from

---

10. See 164 n. 3.

the final period of writing such references were rare, though these manuscripts included virtue-ethical modes of argument (4.5).[11] What then are we to make of these two strands of ethical thought in this work?

6.3: Rasmussen's and Plant's Interpretations

To try to answer this question I shall begin by looking at the proposals of Larry Rasmussen and Stephen Plant, who offer quite different interpretations.

6.3.1: Rasmussen: Conformation as More Enduring and Original

Larry Rasmussen speaks of the major "methodological themes" (modes of ethical thought) in Bonhoeffer's *Ethics* as conformation and command. He considers both to have a long history in Bonhoeffer's thought, but finally asks if what we have are two "methods" or one. To answer his question he looks at the differences and similarities within these two ways of envisioning ethics. In both he sees an emphasis on concrete ethics as well as an "ethic of reality and realization."[12] Moreover, he sees in both modes a contextual and relational ethics that "becomes increasingly 'filled,'" moving from atomistic to coherent ethics (109). In conformation as well as command ethics Bonhoeffer uses the notion of mandates, and in both the ethical is seen as "peripheral" (109). "In both, moral action is the same. Obedience to the command of God is, for moral content, identical with conformation to Christ" (109). Additionally, in both Rasmussen sees the direction moving from the indicative (asking "How is Christ taking form?" or "What is God commanding?") to the imperative (asking "What action conforms to Christ's action?" or "What action is in keeping with this command?"). Likewise, in both, ethical discernment requires all one's faculties (109). "In both, the underlying assumption for Christian ethics is reconciliation, that is, the recovered unity of God and the world in Christ" (109). In command as well as conformation, the "point of departure for Christian ethics is the body of Christ" (109–10). Finally, in both strands of

---

11. See 128–38. Although it may appear that the conformation is simply the earlier motif and command the later, this is inaccurate, as will be seen when I discuss the case for the integration of these themes, 207–15.

12. Rasmussen, *Significance*, 108. Further references appear in brackets in the main text.

ethical thought Rasmussen identifies the themes of deputyship, vicarious action and deeds of free responsibility, where only God may judge such deeds and the agent must depend on grace (110).

Having discussed so many areas that he sees as similarities, Rasmussen asks, "Is there one method or two? The more cautious answer would be that this remains an open question because Bonhoeffer's theology and ethic remain open-ended" (110). However, the

> riskier, but probably more precise, conclusion is that Bonhoeffer's is an ethic of reality and realization which finds methodological expression in two basic motifs, one of which is both more original and more enduring. In the end, ethics as command should be regarded as a genuine motif, but a subordinate one. Both are authentic but ethics as formation is in better tune with Bonhoeffer's christocratic vision of humanity, nature, and history. Its "fit" is better. Still, it would be an unwarranted projection backward from *Letters and Papers from Prison* to name ethics as formation the method of Bonhoeffer's ethics. By his own testimony, his ideas were unfinished. (110)

What should one make of Rasmussen's account? First, the similarities he notes are largely well-founded, which means that in both modes of expression Bonhoeffer addresses many of the same issues and concerns. However, I have some reservations about speaking in terms of an "ethic of reality and realization," since Bonhoeffer explicitly rejects the notion of "realization," and speaks instead consistently of "becoming real."[13]

I have greater concerns about his statement that Bonhoeffer was engaged in contextual and relational ethics that moved from being atomistic to being coherent. Although his ethical thought is based on a relational anthropology, and he certainly intended to write for his context, it is not "contextual and relational ethics" in the normal way these terms are used, which would surely indicate a form of situation ethics. Since he speaks neither of the particular contours of situations nor of any guiding notions, this is not accurate.

More substantively, however, I query Rasmussen's notion that Bonhoeffer's ethic becomes more "filled," moving from a more atomistic account to one that shows continuity. The earliest manuscripts show an emphasis on the agent and continuity, making this a hard claim to

---

13. See, e.g., *DBW* 6:61. What is at stake is Bonhoeffer's rejection of any notion that human agents "realize" or bring into being God's will; rather persons may participate in God's reality through grace.

substantiate. It would seem Rasmussen made this claim on the basis on the "*Ansatz* theory," despite his awareness of Clifford Green's misgivings regarding the dating of the manuscripts.[14] However, from the meticulous evidence used in the ordering of the manuscripts in *DBW* 6, it would be truer to say that Bonhoeffer's ethic became more, not less, atomistic with his increased dependence on divine command ethics.[15] Yet I believe this claim also would not be fair, for reasons that will be seen later (6.4.4).

Another part of his proposal that seems weak is the suggestion that within both forms of ethics there is a move from the indicative to the imperative. This, however, is a move that Bonhoeffer explicitly rejects.[16] It is also problematic in that the second set of questions Rasmussen offers are not Bonhoeffer's own questions. So even if Bonhoeffer does attend to the (indicative) questions of how Christ is taking form and what God is commanding, he does not speak in terms of discovering what human action might be in keeping with Christ's own action, or what action would be according to what God commands. Indeed, this latter way of speaking is one that Bonhoeffer seemingly spurns, since he avers that God's command leaves no room for interpretation or application.[17]

One final query I would address to Rasmussen is on what basis he claims that "moral action is the same" in both, to wit that "obedience to the command of God is . . . identical with conformation to Christ" (109). Notionally, this must be correct: if the believer is conformed to Christ, whose food is to do the will of God, then action performed as a result of being conformed to Christ must be in accordance with God's will. However, since specific issues are only addressed in a conformation context, we have no evidence for this, and so the claim might be worded more guardedly.

Bearing in mind these points of disagreement with Rasmussen's analysis, is it nevertheless possible to agree with his conclusions? Despite his intention of expressing himself cautiously on the matter, it is a strong claim indeed to assert that "ethics as command should be regarded as a genuine motif, but a subordinate one." By his own account, the theme of command is found in other of Bonhoeffer's works, though it seems to me that he discounts too easily the weight of command, for instance

---

14. Rasmussen, *Significance*, 89. Regarding the *Ansatz* theory, see 45 n. 77.
15. See 164 n. 3.
16. *DBW* 6:34.
17. *DBW* 6:382, 384.

suggesting that there is no real use of the theme in *Discipleship* (96–101).[18] Given that many have criticized the work for depicting Christ too often as commanding, it seems hard to defend this position.[19] Even if one grants his assertion that the theme of command is largely borrowed from Barth, that does not give sufficient support to his claim that the motif is subordinate to conformation. For one thing, it would be difficult to disentangle Bonhoeffer's theology from Barth's because of the latter's great influence on the former's thinking. Unfortunately, Rasmussen does not offer a rationale for how command could be subordinate, whether he means it to be understood as a subset of conformation, which I think would be impossible to substantiate, or whether perhaps he uses the word more loosely simply to suggest command is less important, which would require more investigation to demonstrate. For these reasons I hesitate to follow Rasmussen in describing conformation as "both more original and more enduring" without further examination.

6.3.2: Plant: Irreducible Plurality

I turn now to another account of conformation and command in Bonhoeffer's *Ethics*. In his book, *Bonhoeffer*, Stephen Plant looks at Bonhoeffer's writings and explores the theological themes in each, suggesting "that a trajectory can be traced from Bonhoeffer's earliest to his final writings which describe an ethics of responsibility, lived out in obedience to the God who acts most powerfully in 'the silence of the cross.'"[20] In his estimation, "theological ethics are a central concern of Bonhoeffer's theology" (5). Treating Bonhoeffer's *Ethics* more specifically, Plant argues that "character" and "command" are the two "moods" in which Bonhoeffer did ethics (118–24). Furthermore, just as Bonhoeffer insisted on the "both/and" of the individual and society in *Sanctorum Communio*, and of act and being in his habilitation dissertation, he resists any dichotomy between character (being) and commands (acts) in *Ethics* (118–19). In Plant's view, "only in . . . two sections is there what can be called an explicit method,"

---

18. The theme does not come in the form of divine command ethics in *Discipleship*, but the word command (*Gebot*) has twenty-three entries in the index, and obedience to God or Jesus Christ (*Gehorsam gegenüber Gott/Jesus Christus*) has another twenty-eight.

19. See, e.g., the ambivalent comments of the editors, *DBW* 4:319–20, 327. See also Barth's comments regarding *Discipleship*, first strongly positive (*KD* IV/2:603–26), then concerned that the person seems to be marionette-like (*KD* IV/2:891–93).

20. Plant, *Bonhoeffer*, 9. Further references appear in brackets in the main text.

namely in "Ethics as Formation" and "The 'Ethical' and the 'Christian' as a Theme" (119). These two "methods" Plant likens to grammatical moods: the imperative of divine command ethics, and the subjunctive of formation, in which the "ethicist wishes for a particular relation between the ethical subject and the person of Christ" (119–21).[21] As a language requires different grammatical moods to give expression to a wide range of thought, so Bonhoeffer's ethics are strengthened by having both of these "methods."[22] Furthermore, "Setting Bonhoeffer's command based ethics alongside his ethics as formation enables us to see these ethical 'methods' as two sides of a dialectic: the one concerned with being in Christ (conformation to the Gestalt of Jesus), the other concerned to emphasize God's freedom to command particular things to particular people (God's freedom to act)" (122).

Plant's analysis has many merits, which include his attention to all of Bonhoeffer's writings. This allows him to see the development of Bonhoeffer's thought and different themes within it over time. Plant also attends carefully to what is present in the *Ethics* manuscripts without unduly speculating on what they might have become (had Bonhoeffer lived to complete his book). This keeps Plant's reading properly grounded and faithful to what Bonhoeffer did write.

However, the question remains whether it is best to speak of conformation and command as being irreducibly plural, or whether one can be said to be subordinate to the other.

6.4: Discussion of Similar Concerns

To explore the relation of conformation and command, I shall attend to the issues Bonhoeffer treats in both ethical modes. Here I think Rasmussen is correct in many of the similarities he cites. However, rather than listing them in a somewhat random fashion, I would like to group them according to methodological concerns (6.4.1), structures (6.4.2), and content (6.4.3). This is because it seems to me that since there are issues in each of these areas that he handles both in a virtue-ethical and a divine command form, it is surely indicative of a potentially close relationship between the two modes of ethical thought.

---

21. See Plant, *Bonhoeffer*, 122 regarding the significance of command ethics being the later theme he worked on.
22. From a conversation with Plant, December 2009.

Secondly, regarding issues discussed in both modes, it will also be important to discover if the form of ethics being used makes any notable difference to how the issues are treated. This is particularly interesting, because if Bonhoeffer uses the two modes to express the same things it would be possible to see their relationship in one of two ways: either the mode of ethical thought is irrelevant, since the mode used made no great difference; or Rasmussen may be correct, that one mode may be subordinate to the other. However, if in expressing similar concerns in the two different modes the outcome is different, it would then truly raise the question of whether virtue-based and command-based ethics are in some way parallel ("irreducibly plural"), contradictory, or whether they might be in some sense complementary (6.4.4).

6.4.1: *Methodological Concerns*

Under the heading of "methodological concerns" I shall look at two overarching aspects of ethical thought that are of momentous concern to Bonhoeffer in the earlier as well as the later manuscripts. The first is the need to articulate an ethic that is specific to his time and place, concrete ethics; the second is his concern to address the whole of life in his *Ethics*.

6.4.1.A: Concrete Ethics

The need for concrete rather than abstract ethics is discussed throughout the manuscripts. In "Ethics as Formation" Bonhoeffer writes,

> We have seen: in a Christian ethical meaning formation can only be spoken of in view of the form. . . . There is only one formation from and towards this form of Jesus Christ. . . . Christ is not the one proclaiming a system that would be good today, here and for all times. Christ teaches no abstract ethic that, whatever the price may be, must be executed. Christ was not essentially a teacher, lawgiver, but rather a person, a real person such as we are. Therefore he does not want in the first place for us to be students, representatives and defenders of a particular teaching, but rather persons, real persons before God. Christ does not love, like an ethicist, a theory about the good, but rather he loves the real person. He did not have, like a philosopher, an interest in the "generally valid," but rather in that which serves the concrete, real person. He is not concerned with whether "the maxims of acting could become the principle of a general law,"

> but rather whether my acting now helped a neighbor to be a person before God. It does not say: God became an idea, a principle, a program, something of general validity, a law, but rather God became human. That means that the form of Christ, as certainly as it is and remains one and the same, nevertheless wants to win form in real persons in quite different ways. Christ does not cancel/raise [*aufheben*] human reality in favor of an idea that demands realizing against everything real; rather Christ precisely brings reality into effect; he affirms it; he himself is the real person and thus the ground of all human reality. Formation according to the form of Christ includes two things: that the form of Christ remains one and the same, not as a general idea, but rather as that which it uniquely is, the incarnate, crucified and risen God; and that precisely for the sake of the form of Christ the form of the real person remains preserved and that thus the *real person may receive the form of Christ* (85–86, his emphasis and quote marks).[23]

I quote this at some length because it is important in comparing this with similar passages from a command perspective that a full picture is presented regarding what his insistence on concrete ethics entails. Here it is clear that a concrete ethic addresses a person in the here and now (or as he was writing, in the there and then!), but it was to include much more than this.[24] What exercised Bonhoeffer in this passage is the fact that Christ as a real person affirms each person in her individual and quite different reality. Concrete ethics understood as formation underscores her unique being and allows her also to receive Christ's own form. Thus in this passage we see a commitment not simply to a mode of concrete ethics as a method or theory, but to an understanding of ethics that seems intimately concerned with the particularities of the real life of the real person. With his emphasis on the differing ways in which Christ's form may be received, the interpretation of Bonhoeffer's *Ethics* as "contextual" or "situational" is understandable. Nonetheless, this is an understandable *misrepresentation* of what he is saying. Rather than the context or situation giving guidance as to what an agent should do, the distinguishing feature is the (character

---

23. Regarding *aufheben*, see 170 n. 9. See further *DBW* 6:245–46, 251–53 regarding his rejection of abstract ethics. See *DBW* 6:32–33, 39, 54, 125, and 261 regarding his more general rejection of abstract thinking in these early manuscripts. See also *DBW* 6:218–20, 253 regarding his rejection of the abstract agent. See *DBW* 6:235, and 243 regarding Jesus' teaching not fitting in an abstract ethic. All references in brackets in the main text refer to *DBW* 6.

24. See *DBW* 6:88 for more explicit treatment of the here and now.

of the) agent herself. Similarly, although he takes account of consequences, there is no warrant for speaking in terms of consequentialist ethics. The sense in which the neighbor is to be helped is also integral to her being as a real person, namely being helped to be a person before God. From this passage it is possible to say that in his virtue-ethical treatment, Bonhoeffer's notion of concrete ethics has a focus on the real humanity of Christ (even while affirming his person in the dogmatic terms of incarnate, crucified and risen), and on the real humanity of the agent. Concrete, formational ethics emphasizes the agent's being fully human before God, bearing the form of Christ while remaining a unique person.

In the command-based context of "The 'Ethical' and the 'Christian' as a Theme" Bonhoeffer addresses the problem of abstract ethical speech thus:

> A timeless and placeless ethical speaking lacks any concrete authorization, which every genuine ethical speaking requires. It is the youthful, arrogant, usurping declamation of ethical principles, which contradicts—with whatever subjective earnestness it may be presented—the essence of genuine ethical speaking, in ways that are perhaps difficult to define but are nonetheless clearly perceived. Although often nothing may be objected regarding the correctness of the abstractions, generalizations, theories; nevertheless they are deficient in the specific weight of ethical statements. The words are correct but they do not weigh. They must finally be felt to be not helpful but chaotic. (373)

Here his first concern is with the authorization for ethical speech, an issue he did not address in the earlier passage. Abstract ethical speech is likened to "youthful" and "arrogant" declamation, and as the passage continues Bonhoeffer claims that there are problems associated with youth in speaking ethically: It is not appropriate "if a young man declaims ethical generalities before a circle of experienced and older people, and it leads time and again to such frustrating, surprising and incomprehensible situations for the young person, that his word echoes in emptiness while the word of an elderly person, even if it contains nothing substantively different, is heard and has weight" (373–74).

As he continues to consider how ethical speech is authorized, Bonhoeffer says, "Ethical speech cannot be given in a vacuum, that means in abstraction, but only in concrete commitment. Ethical speaking is thus not a system of in themselves correct sentences that are available to everyone at all times and all places; rather it is decisively tied to persons and times and places. In this determination the ethical suffers no loss of significance, rather precisely in it [sc. the determination] lies its [sc. the ethical's] authorization, its weight, while in the indetermination and general availability of the ethical lies its weakness, even impotence" (374).[25]

From these passages several things appear. First, Bonhoeffer addresses an issue that was not present in the conformation passage, namely the authorization for ethical speech, an issue of some importance to him. Secondly, in thinking of ethics as command he addresses the question of how the command is given, who speaks to whom, and here he begins to address notions of "above and below," which remain present in his thought in prison.[26] Thirdly, it is precisely in its specificity that ethical speech has its appropriate "weight" and is heard; the particulars of persons, time and place are all required for ethical speech to be genuine.

Comparing and contrasting the long passage from "Ethics as Formation" with these excerpts several things emerge. First, it is clear that in both instances abstract ethical thought is rejected and concretion is demanded. Yet in the first passage concretion has the name and face of Jesus Christ, and the particularities of the agent come to the fore. In contrast with this, in the command mode concretion appears as the facets of interrelationship, time and place. In itself this has a more theoretical flavor, as does his concern with authorization of ethical speech. Yet I do not point this out to detract from these later passages in any way. Given that some of the issues remain of importance to Bonhoeffer in his prison writings it would be cavalier to treat them as in any way inferior. Nonetheless it seems right to say that the "concretion" of conformation (virtue-like) ethics looks in fact more concrete than the "concretion" shown in command ethics.

However that may be, it is clear that there is not only an overlap between conformation and command regarding the concrete, there is at least difference, which I believe is complementary rather than contradictory in his handling of the issue of concrete versus abstract ethics.

6.4.1.B: Addressing the Whole of Life

In chapter 4 I spoke of Bonhoeffer's "holistic conception of human life" as being integral to virtue ethics (4.4.2). Here I shall explore how he approached this in the earlier and later manuscripts. As was seen in chapter 4, there are many instances in the earlier, virtue ethical manuscripts where

---

25. See also *DBW* 6:399 regarding abstract and concrete confession of sins.
26. See also *DBW* 6:377, and *DBW* 7:32, 112.

Bonhoeffer's holistic conception is manifestly present. One of the chief areas where this comes to the fore is in his discussion of the penultimate, where all of earthly life is, at least potentially, at stake. Similarly, his treatment of "the natural" leaves no doubt that ethics must be concerned with every facet of human living, including the everyday aspects of human existence that he wants to consider neither sinful nor simply creaturely, because of the effects of the Fall (165). Here he claims that the fact that the natural had been ignored in Protestant ethics "means a heavy substantive loss for Protestant thought because one stood more or less without orientation vis-à-vis the practical questions of natural life. The meaning of the natural for the gospel became opaque, and the Protestant church lost the clear direction-giving word regarding the burning issues of natural life" (163–64).

This passage makes evident that at a programatic level Bonhoeffer fully intended to treat the whole of life in his *Ethics*. What is more significant is that he not only gives a theological rationale for the appropriateness of doing so, he also attends to concrete issues in the following sections of this manuscript that address euthanasia, abortion, arbitrary imprisonment, and other topical issues in Nazi Germany.

Although many things could be said about Bonhoeffer's holistic conception of life as shown in the earlier manuscripts, what is most telling in this context is that Bonhoeffer was able to use these conceptions both theologically and practically. Theologically he was able to break fresh ground in Protestant ethics, opening up the notion of "the natural" without downplaying the effects of the Fall. Additionally he attempted to give a theological basis to the concept of human rights. Practically, he was able to address a wide range of issues that were of vital importance in his context, while also acknowledging that life consists of much more than the borderline decisions such issues may demand.

In the later manuscripts there are, as noted before, intimations of his intention to speak of the whole of life. Arguably, the mandates themselves are meant to be a framework for enabling all of life to come under the command of God, but this is not made explicit. Much more direct and interesting for this purpose is to consider the passage from "The 'Ethical' and the 'Christian' as a Theme" where he discusses the character "Auch Einer,"[27] who finds great decisions easy, but daily living more problematic.

---

27. "*Auch Einer*" literally means "also [some]one" in the sense of an "also ran." I leave the name untranslated as the character's name from F. T. Vischer *Auch Einer II*. See *DBW* 6:366 nn. 4–9.

> [I]t is the sphere of the everyday that causes substantial difficulties and which one must have experienced to feel in relation to it [sc. the sphere of the everyday] the inadequacy, inappropriateness, disproportion of the proclamation of general moral principles. Whether I help someone in need, step in the way of an animal abuser, that is no problem for "Auch Einer"—"that is self evident"—but to get to grips with little mundane things, for instance with a "cold" . . . or with the thousands of intersections of the great and in-principle with the tangential, negligible, objectionable, annoying, that is something else. (366-67, his quote marks)

In commenting on this, Bonhoeffer notes that most ethical discourse ignores the reality of everyday human existence (367). Even if he does not wish to contribute to the "ethical phenomenon" that would result in a totalitarian claim (368), it is nonetheless clear that he does want to speak to the mundane aspects of life as well as the momentous issues and decisions. It is in this sense that he comes to speak of command: "The command of God is something different from what we have hitherto called the 'ethical'; it encompasses the whole of life; it is not only unconditional, rather it is also total" (381).

Command encompasses the fullness of human life, though the "flow of life from conception to the grave is incomprehensible for the ethical" (387-88). "The command of God allows the person to be a person before God, it allows the flow of life to take its course, it allows the person to eat, drink, sleep, work, celebrate, play without interrupting him, without questioning him continually whether he may then sleep, eat, work, play, whether he has no more pressing duties" (388).

This, then, is Bonhoeffer's conception of the command that is central to the later manuscripts. It is this "middle and fullness of life," which includes the mundane and even tedious (such as eating, drinking, sleeping, working, celebrating, playing, or having a cold), and stretches from birth to death.

The question that now needs to be answered is how the treatments of the whole of life differ in the earlier and later manuscripts. As noted previously (4.4.2), there are different terms in use: the penultimate and the natural in the more virtue-ethical manuscripts, and the command of God in the later ones. Yet one must still ask what difference his modes of ethical thought make to the substantive material. First, there is more that is ground-breaking in the conformation manuscripts, especially opening up the possibility of speaking of the natural in Protestant ethics, and giving a

Divine Command and/or Virtue Ethics

Christian foundation to human rights. Secondly, it is in the virtue-ethical context of discussing the natural that Bonhoeffer does what he so often says is most needful, namely treating the specific issues that were of monumental importance in his context. Thirdly, and perhaps paradoxically, it is in divine command mode, when treating the notion of "command," that Bonhoeffer addresses more fully the everyday joys, sorrows, amusements and perplexities of being human. These differences certainly do not cancel each other out—instead there is valuable complementarity.

Thus in both areas that I have called "methodological," Bonhoeffer's concern to formulate concrete ethics and his treatment of all of life, there have been similarities as well as differences when he was working with conformation and command, and the differences have been complementary.

6.4.2: Structures of Ethical Life

There are two ways of speaking of structures for ethical life that have relevance both in the virtue-ethical and divine command writings: Bonhoeffer's notion of mandates, and responsibility. I shall look at each of these now to see what difference, if any, the context of conformation or divine command may make.

6.4.2.A: The Mandates

The concept of "divine mandates" makes its first appearance in the earliest manuscript he wrote, "Christ, Reality and the Good," where he introduces the concept, saying, "The world stands in relationship to Christ whether it knows it or not. This relationship of the world to Christ becomes concrete in certain *mandates of God* in the world. Scripture names four things mandates: *work, marriage, authority, church*. We speak of divine mandates rather than divine orders because thereby the character of the divine task stands out clearly compared to that of a determination of being" (54–55, his emphases).

So this is foremost an attempt to show the relationship of these four areas of life to Christ.[28] This is part of his larger argument against the *"zwei-Reiche-Lehre"* specifically, and against dualism more generally in this manuscript. All of this has particular relevance in Nazi Germany because the notion of "orders of creation" and the teaching regarding the distinction between the "two kingdoms" of church and world had left the

---

28. See also *DBW* 6:57–59.

churches little theological ground to oppose the tyranny of the regime or the gross heresies of the "German Christians."[29]

He also shows an interrelationship between the mandates: the task of authority is to keep and protect a right order that allows marriage, work, and church to fulfill their tasks; while the

> mandate of the church extends over all people, and indeed within all other mandates. Just as the person is simultaneously a worker, a husband, and a subject [of authority], just as one mandate overlaps here with another in the person, and just as it thereby concerns the simultaneous fulfillment of all these mandates, just so the ecclesial mandate reaches into all these mentioned mandates, just as, conversely, the Christian is at once worker, husband, subject. Every division into separated spheres is forbidden here. The whole person stands before the whole earthly and eternal reality, as God in Jesus Christ has prepared it for him. Only in the full response to the totality of the offer and of the claim can the person correspond to this reality. Precisely this—that the mandates are not concerned with the division and tearing apart of the person but rather with the whole person before God, the Creator, Reconciler and Redeemer, that thus the reality in all diversity finally is nevertheless one, namely in the incarnate God Jesus Christ—precisely this is what the church has to bear witness to the world. (59–60)

From this passage it is possible to see that a part of his use of the mandates in this virtue-ethical manuscript to combat dualistic thinking is also to insist on concretion, on treating the person as a whole, and on addressing the whole of life in his *Ethics*.

The other important theme with which Bonhoeffer connects the mandates in this first manuscript is that of responsibility (the second structure, which I shall discuss in its own right in the next subsection). In showing how human sinfulness (failing in the task God gives in the mandates) might affect the divine status of the mandates, Bonhoeffer writes, "Individual offences do not grant the right to abolish, to destroy what exists. Much more it can only be concerned here with the return to genuine sub-ordination to the divine mandate, with the restoration of genuine responsibility to the divine task. This genuine responsibility consists in the orientation of the concrete form of the divine mandates to their source, their existence and their goal in Jesus Christ" (56–57).

---

29. Scholder, *Vorgeschichte*, ch. 3, also 533–34; also his *Ernüchterung*, 198.

Here the theme of responsibility does not yet have the full character that Bonhoeffer gives it later. Yet one hallmark is present, that the person is responsible (must give response, account) to God for certain things, in this case, the appropriate fulfillment of the tasks given in the areas of the mandates (covering all of life). I shall say more about responsibility in the next subsection, but it is worth noting here that in treating the mandates in a more virtue-like passage Bonhoeffer touches on this theme.[30]

What we have seen is that in the first manuscript Bonhoeffer uses the structuring notion of the mandates to combat a form of dualism that had rendered the church ineffective in addressing the problems of Nazi Germany. Within that context he also uses the mandates to express his concern that ethics should address the whole person and the entirety of life. And finally in this more virtue-ethical manuscript, Bonhoeffer begins to address another of his most important themes, responsibility.

I turn now to passages from the later manuscripts where Bonhoeffer treats the mandates in the context of a divine command ethic. The opening passage of "The Concrete Command and the Divine Mandates" gives an indication of his concerns in this manuscript: "God's command—revealed in Jesus Christ in his unity encompassing human life, in his undivided claim on the person and the world through the reconciling love of God—encounters us in four different, and only through the command itself unified, forms: in the church, in marriage and family, in culture, in authority" (392).[31]

As in the virtue-ethical context, Bonhoeffer relates the mandates to his concern for concretion: "Not anywhere and everywhere, not in theoretical speculation and not in private enlightenment, not in historical powers and not in coercive ideals is God's command to be found, but rather only there where it presents itself" (392). This suggestion that God's command is not found "anywhere and everywhere" is somewhat disconcerting, given that the mandates as he expounds them would seem to cover all of life. How then could there be some "anywhere and everywhere" that in some way is not part of one or more of the mandates, or part of the broad conception of command seen already (388, 6.4.1.b)? Bonhoeffer does not answer this question, but one can surmise that he is engaged in polemical hyperbole as part of his demand that ethics be specific.

---

30. See also *DBW* 6:297.

31. Here "marriage" has become "marriage and family," and "work" has become "culture." In both changes Bonhoeffer has broadened the horizons.

Bonhoeffer continues by giving a definition of a mandate that involves not only concretion, but authorization for ethical speech, and the notion of representational action. It is "the concrete, divine task (founded in the revelation of Christ and attested to in Scripture); the authorization and legitimation to execute a certain divine command; the granting of a divine authority to an earthly authority. Mandate is at the same time also to be understood as the claim, the requisition and formation of a certain earthly sphere by the divine command. The carrier of the mandate acts in representation, as a representative of the task-giver" (392–93).

His next concern is to distinguish more carefully between his notion of mandates and the more common categories of "creation orders," "estates" and "offices" (393). The first of these is found wanting because of its autonomy rather than dependence on God, the second because of the whiff of privilege, and the last because of its too secular meaning (393). This section is not really new, but a fleshing out of the passage from the first manuscript regarding the mandates.

From here he defines more carefully the relationships created by these mandates as involving an "above" and a "below," with the carrier of the mandate acting as a representative of God (394).[32] In this discussion Bonhoeffer addresses the problems that arise when the "above" is abused and the "below" rebels, namely that the "below" gains power and the roles are reversed. Then "there is no longer any genuine above and below, but rather what is above receives its authorization and legitimation from below" (396). This means, in Bonhoeffer's terms, that there is no longer the appropriate reference to God in the human relationships that have been inverted; for instead of a position of authority and representation given by God and answerable to God, there is now a position of power that has been grasped and does not see itself as accountable to God. "The relationship of above and below is in this stage of inversion and dissolution, and of the deepest enmity, mistrust, betrayal and envy. However, in this atmosphere, the purely personal abuse of being above and being below also flourishes in an otherwise unprecedented way.... The genuine order of above and below lives out of the belief in the task from 'above,' in the 'Lord' of 'lords.' This belief alone banishes the demonic powers that rise from below" (396–97).

---

32. Regarding his awareness of the unpopularity of this notion, see *DBW* 7:32, and 112. See also *DBW* 6:395 and 398 for safeguards against the abuse of power relationships. See *DBW* 6:400–402 for a "worked example" of what "above" and "below" look like in the church.

Divine Command and/or Virtue Ethics

No doubt Bonhoeffer is here depicting the situation of Nazi Germany, which was not one of liberation of the masses by the overthrow of a ruling elite. If one sees the formerly ruling class as authentically living out an ethic of "noblesse oblige," and of being answerable before God for the well-being of the nation (as Bonhoeffer clearly did), then their overthrow by those seeking personal power without any such ethic is indeed an inversion of godly order.

Yet Bonhoeffer is not only interested in the aspect of mandates as showing tasks given by God, but also in their interrelationship:

> Only in their [being] with one another, for one another and over against one another do the divine mandates of church, marriage and family, culture, and authority bring the command of God as it is revealed in Jesus Christ to our attention. None of these mandates exists for itself alone or can assert the claim of replacing all others. The mandates are *with one another* or they are not divine mandates. In their togetherness, however, they are not isolated, separated from one another, but rather oriented towards one another. They are *for one another* or they are not God's mandates. Yet in this [being] with and for one another, the one is limited by the other, and this limitation is necessarily experienced within the [being] for one another as [being] over against one another. Where this [being] *over against one another* is no longer present, God's mandate is no longer [present]. (397, his emphases)

Bonhoeffer's structural concern regarding the interrelationship of the mandates is interesting in at least two ways for this study. First, as seen in his treatment of the mandates in the virtue-ethical manuscript, is his insistence on seeing life as a whole, not allowing various facets to become compartmentalized. Secondly, and more importantly here because it is new, Bonhoeffer uses the mandates in the context of divine command to give the church permission to be "over against" authority.[33] There can be little doubt that Bonhoeffer is pointing to the Nazi regime as not fulfilling the divine mandate of authority, since it can hardly be shown to work *with* or *for* the other mandates, nor to allow the others to be *over against* it. And the state certainly did try to replace at least the mandate of the church (through various laws, through the takeover of the provincial churches, and the imposition of the *Reichsbischof*).[34] So the mandates in this divine

---

33. *DBW* 6:403 for an example of how the church might speak to the state.

34. See Scholder's account of the *Reichskirche, Vorgeschichte*, 369–87; and of some interventions in Prussia, 453–55. See also the state's intervention in family life, *DBW* 6:200 n. 106; 202 n. 110; 209 n. 127; and 210 n. 129.

command manuscript are a place where he sought ways of offering the church some leverage for prophetic proclamation against the state and even for active opposition to the regime. Of course, in the earlier manuscript, relying more on conceptions related to virtue ethics, he also tried to give the church permission to speak out against the state, mostly through arguing against the two-kingdom teaching. Thus, what he is doing in the final manuscript is not radically new, but only a new usage of the notion of the mandates to address a fairly basic concern.

From this comparison of Bonhoeffer's treatment of the mandates in virtue-ethical and divine command contexts, it is clear that there are changes and developments that may or may not be related to the mode of ethical thought with which he was working. My suspicion is that the change of speaking about "culture" instead of "work" and about "marriage and family" instead of simply about "marriage" is most likely a development largely unrelated to whether he was conceiving of ethics more in terms of conformation or command.[35] It seems much more probable that he was broadening the categories so that all of life can be seen as relating directly to at least one of the mandates.[36] What is more significant for this study is the fact that in both manuscripts Bonhoeffer either directly combats dualistic thinking, or indirectly works against the impotence fostered through the two-kingdom teaching. In both he is concerned to treat the whole of life. However, it is only in the virtue-ethical manuscript that he explicitly treats the person in a holistic manner.[37] Conversely, it is only in the command-ethical manuscript that he paints a compelling picture of the ungodly nature of the Nazi regime and offers a theological rationale for active opposition. Thus, although there are some obvious ways in which Bonhoeffer's treatment of the mandates in these two manuscripts is similar, there are complementary differences as well.

---

35. It is also difficult to be sure about what is simply development of his thought and what might be more directly related to the ethical modes since his treatment in the early manuscript is so brief.

36. However, see *DBW* 8:290–92, where Bonhoeffer uses the mandates narrowly in terms of obedience, and speaks more broadly of areas of freedom. It seems to me that his thought was developing and he did not use his terms with the consistency an interpreter would like. Nonetheless, it is clear that whether he speaks of the natural, command, the mandates, or areas of freedom, he wishes to discuss all of life in his ethics, and yet he wishes to distinguish this broader conception from narrower (boundary) issues. For another later reference to the mandates, see *Love Letters*, 161–62.

37. Though, see *DBW* 6:407 for a hint of this in his treatment of the mandate of the church.

Divine Command and/or Virtue Ethics

6.4.2.B: RESPONSIBILITY

In chapter 4 I argued that responsibility is for Bonhoeffer not a human trait that might be seen as a "virtue" in his ethics, but a kind of structure, a given of human relationships and interrelationships (4.3.5). Since it appears both in the manuscripts that rely on a more virtue-like ethic as well as in the later divine command manuscripts, I shall examine how he treats responsibility in both contexts.

As noted above, Bonhoeffer mentions responsibility in the earliest manuscript, "Christ, Reality and the Good," when he introduces the notion of the mandates, where it is clear that the divinely given tasks imply responsibility (56). However, there are only few places where it is mentioned, and it is never given the weight and fullness it receives in the later manuscripts.[38]

In "Ethics as Formation," while arguing against abstract forms of ethics, he says that instead ethics is about "the times and places that direct concrete questions to us, give us tasks and place responsibility upon us" (88). Individualism, he says, is countered by the fact "that we are placed in a particular context of experience, responsibility and decision from which we cannot withdraw without abstraction" (88). From this it is clear that Bonhoeffer takes responsibility to be a given; it is not something an agent may take upon herself (or not), but part of the situation in which she lives. Furthermore, he links responsibility with concretion and sociality.

In another virtue-ethical manuscript, "Ultimate and Penultimate Things," Bonhoeffer rejects a "radical" position in which the Christian does not concern herself with what happens to the world at the judgment, claiming it is none of her responsibility (144–45). He equally dismisses the "compromise" that divorces the reality of the ultimate from the penultimate and in which the Christian accepts responsibility for this world as it currently is, ignoring the judgment to come (145). This passage denotes a caveat to the above: responsibility is part of the (penultimate) situation in which humans live, but the person must always have the ultimate in view also. This means that the Christian, precisely in this sense of responsibility, prepares the way for the coming of Christ in mercy by, for example, feeding the hungry, and hospitality for the homeless. Such things enable the gospel to be heard: "In the first instance the external enabling must be cared for so that the call to [hear the] sermon may be heard and obeyed. That can mean that the human first must become human again before he

---

38. See, e.g., *DBW* 6:69, where it features along with other modes of conceiving of ethics and why they were inadequate in Nazi Germany.

can be addressed in this way. Preparing the way for the coming Lord is not taken seriously where this task is not undertaken. Compassion for people and responsibility before Jesus Christ, who wants to come to all people, demand such action" (159). Here, then, he spells out the basis of responsibility that will be foundational for all that is said in later manuscripts: it is *for* the other *to* Jesus Christ and *to* the other *for* Jesus Christ.

In the early, virtue-ethical manuscripts, then, responsibility is treated as a given of human life, part of the historical contingencies of interrelationships. The person is responsible before God for how she handles the tasks given her in the areas of life Bonhoeffer calls mandates. She is responsible before Christ for preparing the way for his coming in grace, and this means responsible for attending to the basic needs of her neighbors. The content, though brief, is both rich and interconnected with other important themes, and it lays the groundwork for the more detailed treatment given in later manuscripts.

However, the prime locus for responsibility in Bonhoeffer's *Ethics* is the second version of "History and the Good" with its extended passages and subsections relating to responsibility, when he is working more obviously in a divine command mode.[39] Much that is contained in this manuscript would seem to provide further content to what had already been said in the virtue-ethical manuscripts. Thus Bonhoeffer gives a fuller account of responsibility as responding to the life of Jesus Christ, and responding with the totality of one's life (254–56).

More significantly, as a part of this second version of "History and the Good" Bonhoeffer has a section titled, "The Structure of Responsible Living." In this, he opens with an analysis:

> The structure of responsible living is determined through a double: through the bond of life to person and God, and through the freedom of one's own life. It is this bond of life to person and God that places it in the freedom of one's own life. Without this bond and without this freedom there is no responsibility. Only the life that has become selfless in the bond stands in the freedom of one's own most personal living and acting. The *bond* carries the form of *representation* and of [acting in] *accordance*

---

39. That Bonhoeffer had acquired *CD* II/2 in May of 1942 is clear from a letter he wrote to Barth of May 13, 1942, *DBW* 16:266–67. See also Busch's account of Barth's publisher giving Germans unbound copies of proofs to smuggle into Germany, *Karl Barth*, 315. That this manuscript was written after acquiring the volume seems clear not only from its content, but from formal indications of the paper used and the precise color of ink, *DBW* 6:20.

with reality; freedom proves itself in [counting] *oneself responsible* for living and acting, and in *venture* of concrete decision. (256, his emphases)[40]

This passage, then, brings together the notion of responsibility with one of the major themes of the early manuscripts, namely action in accordance with reality (which, of course, is known only in Christ).[41] It also presupposes the anthropology witnessed in the early manuscripts that sees human beings as necessarily involved in interrelations.[42] What is relatively new here is the concern with the "venture" or "risk" (*das Wagnis*) of concrete decision, and the freedom of most personal (*eigensten*) living and acting.

Again, parallel to the statements in the virtue-ethical manuscripts, he speaks of responsibility as a given, and here he explores its parameters determined through the person's creaturely finitude. "Our responsibility is not an infinite, but rather a limited one. Within these limits, of course, it comprises the whole of reality; it does not ask only about a good will, but rather also about a good success of one's acting, not only about the motive but also about the object; it tries to recognize the given whole of reality in its origin, essence and goal; it [sc. responsibility] sees it [sc. the whole of reality] under the divine Yes and No" (267).

However, the agent's responsibility is not only limited by her own creaturely finitude, but also by the responsibility of other agents: "Further, it belongs to the limitation of responsible living and acting that it reckons on the responsibility of other encountered persons.... The responsibility of the father or the statesman is limited through the responsibility of the child or the citizen; indeed the responsibility of the father or the statesman consists precisely in raising awareness of and strengthening the responsibility of the one entrusted to him. There can never be an absolute responsibility that does not find its essential boundary in the responsibility of the other person" (268-69).

Recognizing the limits of responsibility that are formed by God and other is not only a part but is itself the origin of responsible action (269). This material has more that is new than the preceding passages, although the boundaries he considers here may be said to be implied by what he

---

40. See also *DBW* 6:284, where he describes the bonds to God and others as liberating.

41. See also *DBW* 6:219-20, 237-38, and 260-64.

42. See also *DBW* 6:219-20 and 256-58. Regarding representation (*Stellvertretung*) and responsibility see *DBW* 6:266.

had said about interrelationships (if there is genuine mutuality, then there must be an interaction between the agent's responsibility and that of others), and by the limits Bonhoeffer presupposed in considering how far humans may be said to "prepare the way" for Christ's coming in mercy.

His further discussion also takes account of the inevitable fallibility of human decision and judgment, and the fact that this requires the agent to cast herself on the mercy of God. However, trusting in divine grace is only a part of Bonhoeffer's vision of what responsible action will entail, as is shown in material that is startlingly new. For Bonhoeffer claims that the contingencies of living and acting in history, in the real world, will require of her a readiness to take guilt upon herself. Bonhoeffer calls this willingness, along with freedom, the structure of responsible acting (275).[43] After depicting Jesus as the guiltless one who loves the real human too much to leave her in her guilt, Bonhoeffer draws the parallel with responsible human action:

> Whoever wants in responsibility to withdraw himself from taking on guilt detaches himself from the final reality of human existence, detaches himself however also from the redeeming mystery of Jesus Christ's guiltless carrying of guilt, and has no share in the divine justification that rests on this event. He places his personal innocence above the responsibility for people, and he is blind to the more unholy [*heillosere*] guilt with which he—precisely thereby—burdens himself, blind also to the fact that real innocence proves itself precisely in that it, for the sake of the other person, enters into the community of his guilt.[44] That the sinless one, the selfless loving one becomes guilty belongs through Jesus Christ to the essence of responsible acting. (276)

Naturally he offers the proviso that human acting is never sinless but rather in its essence poisoned by original sin, yet he is happy to speak of a "relative sinlessness" that in responsible acting is willing to take on others' guilt (279-80). This is certainly material that is new in this later manuscript, and although it poses certain difficulties for interpreters, the notion of incurring guilt can be said to offer Bonhoeffer and his fellow conspirators a theological rationale for the work they are undertaking, both the lies they constantly tell (280)—and Bonhoeffer knows they may have to tell

---

43. See also *DBW* 6:232–34.

44. The word "*heillos*" is generally translated, as here, as "unholy." More literally in a theological context it may mean "without salvation" or "irredeemable." If Bonhoeffer means this, and he may well, his statement is all the more stark.

such under interrogation[45]—and the intended acts of assassination and overthrow of government. One significant aspect of this rationale is that Bonhoeffer does not seek to provide justification for such acts. As mentioned in the previous chapter, he does not follow Aristotle and Aquinas in suggesting that tyrannicide is not wrong (5.1.4); such a suggestion would, in his terms, be a faithless self-justification. Nor does he follow Barth's own line that if God commands such an act, the agent can perform it with joy, and presumably a clear conscience.[46] Instead he insists that the person in responsibility must act for the well-being of others, and trust in God's mercy. That an agent's conscience may baulk at incurring guilt, and having no absolute proof of the rightness of doing so, is a possibility Bonhoeffer considers. In such a case, she should not go beyond what her conscience (which is freed in Christ) may bear (281–83). Although the element of depending on God's grace rather than constructing a case for the rightness of any particular act is not new, what is significant (because of its relevance to the plans of the conspirators) is the detailed discussion of incurring guilt. Bonhoeffer's use of divine command is not necessarily the important factor for this material, indeed given that it is a departure from Barth's own way of arguing it seems unlikely that it is could be.

Bonhoeffer analyses the notion of responsibility further to speak of it first in its "correspondence" to freedom (283–85) and then in its relation to obedience (285–87). All of this presupposes the freedom of the agent, though Bonhoeffer acknowledges "a profound mystery of history," namely that precisely in acting in freedom out of her most personal responsibility, she may discover that her deed is ultimately God's deed (285). What Bonhoeffer calls a "mystery" is the interaction between divine sovereignty and human freedom, or the question as to how far the human agent is in some sense "determined." He does not delve into this theoretically, but offers simply the paradox that the "free act finally recognizes itself as God's act, decision as guidance/providence, risk as divine necessity" (285).[47] This leads Bonhoeffer to discuss the relationship between responsibility and freedom, showing Christ (as the example of responsibility) to be both the obedient one and the free one. In this context "obedience" certainly takes a divine command form, defined in terms of confirming the will of

---

45. See "What does it mean to tell the truth?" *DBW* 16:619–29, and comments in 5.2, p. 157–61.

46. See 150 n. 17.

47. See Muller, "Ethic of Responsibility," for a misreading of Bonhoeffer's views, 111.

God rather than adhering to any fixed rules (288).[48] This is both new and clearly linked to divine command ethics.

In this manuscript that depends on divine command ethics, then, Bonhoeffer fleshes out the brief statements he had made in earlier manuscripts, both as a given in human relationships, and as a function of connection with God and others. Unsurprisingly, Bonhoeffer grounds much of what he says in the example of Jesus Christ, which he had not done in the earlier manuscripts but which is typical both of his overall christocentric approach and more specifically of the theme of conformation to Christ. Likewise, treating responsibility as being in accordance with reality ties the theme closely to this chief concern in his early manuscripts.

What is new in this manuscript are the notions of taking risks, representation, and incurring guilt. These facets of responsibility are significant in that they enable Bonhoeffer to address more overtly some of the genuinely difficult decisions he and others had to make regarding the conspiracy. It is not clear that these themes are necessarily connected with his greater dependence on divine command ethics, unlike his treatment of freedom and obedience. Given how little material there is on responsibility in the earlier manuscripts, it is difficult to say that the treatment is complementary; in the later manuscript he certainly negates nothing of what he had previously said, but rather he builds upon it. Indeed, I would suggest that nothing of substance would be lost if one simply ignored the earlier material. Nevertheless, I hesitate to ascribe this to the modes of virtue and command being used. Rather it would seem that in the later treatment he brings together themes and concerns from the earlier manuscripts (holistic view of life, interrelatedness, accordance with reality, the example of Christ, dependence on grace) and develops them by the addition of a central concern from divine command ethics, namely obedience to the will of God.

Regarding structures, then, it would seem that there is more genuine complementarity in Bonhoeffer's treatment of the mandates in the earlier and later manuscripts than in his handling of responsibility. In the case of the mandates, different aspects of Bonhoeffer's theology and concerns come to the fore: in the virtue-ethical passages there is a holistic concern for the agent, and her humanity and individuality are tangible; in the treatment based on divine command ethics there is a stark depiction of the evils of Nazism and a theological argument for active opposition. In

---

48. In the following sections responsibility is further clarified, but there are no changes to how it is treated or used.

Bonhoeffer's handling of responsibility he builds on the themes from the early manuscripts and develops them much further, using at least in places the concerns of divine command ethics.

6.4.3: *Content of Ethical Life*

I have argued that in issues of methodological concern that Bonhoeffer addressed in earlier and later manuscripts, namely the need for concretion and to attend to the whole of life, there were both similarities and differences that were complementary. Additionally we have seen that where Bonhoeffer's structural emphases, the mandates and responsibility, occur both in the virtue ethical manuscripts and those based on divine command ethics, the relationship is slightly more complex. There are changes, developments and augmentation that cannot simply be attributed to the ethical mode in which he was working. Nonetheless it was possible to identify some similarities as well as complementary differences in his handling of the mandates, and some real integration of themes and concerns from both modes of ethical thought in his treatment of responsibility. How then are areas of overlap regarding the content of ethical life affected by the ethical mode in which he was working?

6.4.3.A: CHRIST THE CENTER

The first aspect of the content of ethical life that appears in both modes of ethical thinking is the centering of ethical thought and action on the person of Jesus Christ. This is so elemental in Bonhoeffer's thought in general as well as in the *Ethics* that a full consideration of how he treats this would itself be worthy of study in its own right. For the purposes of this enquiry, however, it should suffice to look at the broad contours of how centering ethics on Christ is approached in the two different forms of ethical thought.

As the title of the earliest manuscript, "Christ, Reality and the Good," suggests, one of the first moves Bonhoeffer makes is to define both reality and the good in relation to Christ. Thus, in "Christ we encounter the opportunity to participate at once both in the reality of God and the reality of the world, one not without the other" (40). This appears as a part of his extended argument against the dichotomies of the two-kingdom teaching (40–52).[49] To understand reality, the person must fix her eyes on "the body

---

49. See also *DBW* 6:102.

of Jesus Christ himself, the Incarnate, Crucified, and Risen One" (52–53), and there she will discover God's acceptance of the world in his becoming human, and his judgment of and love for the world expressed through the cross (53–54).[50] Thus Bonhoeffer speaks of Christ specifically in terms of doctrine in defining reality in relation to him.

His way of defining the good in relation to Christ is not so direct. At the beginning of the manuscript, Bonhoeffer throws down the gauntlet: the questions that normally appear at the start of ethical discourse ("How can I be good?" and "How can I do good?") must be abandoned as inappropriate to Christian ethics. Instead the infinitely different question regarding the will of God must be asked (31). Only at the end of the manuscript does he return to this: "We spoke at the beginning about how the question of the will of God must take the place of the question about one's own goodness and of doing good. The will of God, however, is nothing other than the becoming real of the reality of Christ among us and in our world" (60–61). Hence the cryptic relationship between the question of the good and the will of God in the opening passage now has another element, namely the reality of Christ. Moreover, the will of God has been revealed and fulfilled in Christ, and humans have access to the totality of reality only in Christ (61). Thus the question of the good is treated firstly in terms of the will of God, and then in terms of Christ.

In the second virtue-ethical manuscript, "Ethics as Formation," Christ is again at the centre, this time as the form to whom the person is to be conformed. After considering various ways of approaching ethics and showing that each of them has failed in the context of Nazi Germany, Bonhoeffer sees the need "to exchange rusty weapons for shining" ones, which he calls "simplicity" and "cleverness" (67). Yet simplicity and cleverness would seem to be difficult to integrate; indeed this union is only possible because of the reality of the reconciliation of God and the world in Jesus Christ (68-69). Again in this manuscript, Christ is viewed in relation to the doctrines of the Incarnation, Crucifixion, and Resurrection (70–80). "The one who is accepted by God, judged and raised to new life, that is Jesus Christ, that is, in him, the whole of humanity, that is who we are. It is alone the form of Jesus Christ who encounters the world victoriously. From this form proceeds every formation of a world reconciled with God" (80).

---

50. It is interesting that Bonhoeffer does not say specifically how Christ as the Risen One affects how we understand reality. However, much of his discussion centers on the church as the body of Christ, and this may be said to be the outworking of the resurrection.

Divine Command and/or Virtue Ethics

Yet it is not only that formation has Christ as its source and agent, Bonhoeffer also calls it "being pulled into the form of Jesus Christ" or "conformation with the only form of the Incarnate, Crucified and Risen One" (80). Being conformed to Christ in his incarnation means the Christian is accepted in her real humanity; being conformed to Christ the crucified means that she stands under God's judgment; being conformed to the risen Christ means that she too is a new person (82). The Church as the body of Christ is where Christ wins form, but what "is happening in it is happening as an example for and a representation of all people" (84). Yet although Christ is always the same and the Church is one, the form of Christ wants "to win form in the real person, and that means in wholly different ways" (85–86). Therefore it is necessary to speak concretely about "*how Christ is winning form among us today and here*" (87, his emphasis). This he elucidates only by saying that the times and places in question are those "that concern us, in which we have experience, which are realities to us. It concerns times and places that direct questions to us, give us tasks and place responsibility on us," "in the context of our decisions and encounters" (88).

Summarizing the focus on Christ in terms of formation, then, it is possible to say that Bonhoeffer speaks primarily in the dogmatic categories of Incarnation, Crucifixion, and Resurrection. Christ is the source and agent of conformation, and that form will vary in ways relevant to the context in which the person is placed (88). Nonetheless, Bonhoeffer explicitly refuses to treat the context of Germany separately from other Western nations, no doubt to counter the nationalistic fervor of "*Grund und Boden*" ideology and notions of racial supremacy.[51] Perhaps most importantly for this study, for Bonhoeffer Christ is at the center of formational (virtue-ethical) ethics, and his focus on Christ is a part of articulating a concrete ethics that underscores the reality of grace.

The third broad theme in which Bonhoeffer's christocentric approach is most apparent in the early virtue-ethical manuscripts is his notion of the penultimate, preparing the way for the coming of Christ in grace. Penultimate things might be "doing, suffering, walking, wanting, losing, getting up, asking, hoping"; the penultimate is "a time of God's permission, waiting and preparation" (141–42). Yet not all of earthly life can be called penultimate since there are aspects of human life that could be said to put hindrances in the way of Christ's coming to justify sinners (141–42). Rather the penultimate encompasses all of life that is open to and prepares

---

51. See also *DBW* 6:96–97, 100–101, and 133–34.

The Virtue of Bonhoeffer's Ethics

the way for Christ's coming. Once again, the prime categories for understanding Christ, and which are used to discuss the penultimate and the ultimate, are the Incarnation, Crucifixion, and Resurrection. In the Incarnation God shows divine love for creation (thus the penultimate should be taken seriously); in the Crucifixion judgment of all flesh is pronounced (though this is not the destruction of creation); and the Resurrection is evidence of God's will for a new creation (which is already breaking in to earthly life) (149–50). Bonhoeffer speaks of two things as being penultimate, being human and being good (151) and only "the coming of the Lord will bring the fulfillment of being human and being good" (157). Christ is involved both in the ultimate and in the penultimate, for even faith itself is made by Christ, only Christ brings the ultimate, but equally the penultimate "Christian living is the dawning of the ultimate in me, the life of Jesus Christ in me" (160). Moreover, whatever "is human and good that can be found in the fallen world belongs on the side of Jesus Christ" (161), and should be claimed for Christ as an "unconscious remnant of a previous bond to the ultimate" (162).

From all this several things can be said about the centrality of Christ in Bonhoeffer's notion of the penultimate. First, the predominant picture of Christ is in his coming, both in terms of the Incarnation and the eschaton (157), and emphasis is placed throughout on the dogmatic formulations of Incarnation, Crucifixion, and Resurrection. The effect of this is that while human life is shown to be accepted and affirmed (for the sake of the ultimate), Christ himself is hardly pictured in his humanity.[52] Secondly, Christ is nonetheless not distant, he lives in the believer, which makes Christian living (ethical living, sanctification) possible. Christ is seen to be sovereign, and the role of grace is emphasized. Thirdly, what seems most particular is the articulation of the relationship to Christ of "good" people who do not profess faith. The "unconscious remnant" would seem to be his way of understanding the good of those, perhaps especially in the conspiracy, who were not Christians: Christians should see them as already belonging to Christ while patiently helping them to come to a full profession (162).

Drawing together the aspects of Christ's centrality in these early, virtue-ethical manuscripts, the centrality of Christ is such that Bonhoeffer defines reality and good (via the will of God) in relationship to Christ. In his discussions he focuses on the doctrines of the Incarnation, Crucifixion, and Resurrection as the lens for viewing not only Christ himself, but

---

52. Though see comments, 131–32.

Divine Command and/or Virtue Ethics

implications for Christian living. Christ is both the agent of conformation, and the one to whom the believer is to be conformed. Christ is sovereign and active; humans rely on grace. Nonetheless, the Christian is to be active, representing what God is doing and intends to do in the world, engaging in activities that prepare for the coming of Christ in mercy. In these manuscripts there is an emphasis on the historical context, and, in focusing on Christ, Bonhoeffer counters nationalistic ideology and articulates the possibility of seeing "good" people as belonging to Christ, even if they as yet make no profession of faith. Given his overall agenda of writing an ethic for his time and place, these latter points are important. Now I turn to the question of how the centrality of Christ figures in the later manuscripts.

In the later manuscripts based on divine command ethics, one of the most arresting aspects of Christ's centrality is the way in which many things are either defined in relation to Christ or for which Christ is the exemplar. Thus, in the second version of "History and the Good" Bonhoeffer speaks of Christ as "my life," drawing on John 11:25. In this context he can say that good is not some abstraction from life, but "life as what it is in reality, that means in its source, its essence and its goal, thus life in the sense of the word: Christ is my life. Good is not a quality of life, but rather 'life' itself. Being good means 'living'" (252).

Yet Bonhoeffer not only defines life in relation to Christ, in the same context he speaks of Christ as the pattern of responsibility. "Because Jesus,—the life, our life—as the Incarnate Son of God, lived representatively for us, all of human life is, through him, representational life" (257). Christ is the epitome of responsibility and representation (258).

In "The Love of God and the Decay of the World," Christ is also shown to be the example of simplicity:

> The freedom of Jesus is not the arbitrary choice of one of innumerable possibilities, but rather it consists precisely of the complete simplicity of his acting, for which there are never several possibilities, conflicts, alternatives, but rather there is always just the one. This one Jesus calls the will of God. He calls it his food to do this will. This will of God is his life. Jesus does not live and act out of the knowledge of good and evil, but rather out of the will of God. There is only *one* will of God. In it the source is regained, in it freedom and simplicity of all acting is founded. (315)[53]

---

53. See also his notion of *actus directus* e.g. DBW 2:23, 48, 126, and 158-60, or "unreflexive action," *DBW* 6:384.

Thus Bonhoeffer draws together the element of simplicity from the earlier manuscripts, with a focus on Christ. Later in the manuscript, Bonhoeffer even defines acting itself in terms of Christ:[54] "'Without me you can do nothing' (John 15:5). This sentence is to be understood most strictly. There is really no doing without Jesus Christ. All of the manifold things that otherwise give the appearance of doing, all the innumerable duties [*Verrichtungen*] are in the judgment of Jesus as if nothing had been done" (330). Bonhoeffer then refers to all doing apart from Christ as "pseudo-acting" (*Scheintun*). This is a claim consistent with his insistence that all reality is known in Christ, and that all things have their source, essence and goal in him. It is not clear what status in reality such pseudo-actions have. Nevertheless, what is of interest here is to note the many things that Bonhoeffer defines in relation to Christ.

Such understanding continues with love, which is not defined generally, "perhaps in the sense of love's being the offering of life for another. Not this generality, but rather the wholly unique offering of the life of Jesus Christ for us is called love here. Love is inseparably connected to the name of Jesus Christ as the revelation of God. . . . Love is always he himself. Love is always God himself. Love is always the revelation of God in Jesus Christ" (337–38). That this is not an arbitrary or unimportant term to define in relation to Christ is shown by the fact that the title of this manuscript is "The Love of God and the Decay of the World."

Another, even more central, term in Bonhoeffer's *Ethics* that he relates to Christ is "command": "*God's command, which is revealed in Jesus Christ, is issued to us in the church, in the family, in work, and in authority*" (383, his emphasis).[55] In "The Concrete Command and the Divine Mandates," Bonhoeffer puts it like this: "God's command, which is revealed in Jesus Christ, in its unity that encompasses all of human life, in its undivided claim of the person and the world through the reconciling love of God, encounters us concretely in four different forms that are united only by the command itself: in the church, in marriage and family, in culture, in authority" (392). However, so central the notion of command is for Bonhoeffer, placing it in reference to being revealed in Jesus Christ does not give it clear Christological contours. The emphasis in both manuscripts is

---

54. It is wrong to make any distinction between doing and acting. Although the German can distinguish between the nouns *Tat* and *Akt*, for the verbal form in this context there is only *tun* since *agieren* has other connotations.

55. I assume that Bonhoeffer's reference to "work" rather than "culture" is a slip of the pen in this instance, likewise his reference to "family" rather than "marriage and family."

placed on the mandates, rather than on any specific aspect of command that is dependent on its being revealed in Christ.

Thus it is clear that in the later manuscripts Bonhoeffer defines a number of important concepts in relation to Christ: life, responsibility, representation, simplicity, acting, love, and command. Three of these are given greater depth by his claim that Christ is our exemplar: responsibility, representation, and simplicity.

Between the more virtue-ethical and divine command-based manuscripts there is the obvious similarity of Bonhoeffer's move to understand or define many things in relation to Christ: reality and good in the early manuscripts, and life, responsibility, representation, simplicity, acting, love, and command in the later. An additional similarity is his reliance on the dogmatic categories of Incarnation, Crucifixion, and Resurrection when speaking of Christ rather than referring to particular gospel narratives. There is also an overlap of themes, most obviously representation. One interesting difference is that in the virtue-ethical manuscripts, Christ is merely the one who gives the command to be both simple and clever; in the divine command-based manuscript Christ is the example of what simplicity is. A much greater significance, however, lies in the fact that centering on Christ seems to do more work in the early, virtue-ethical manuscripts, where Bonhoeffer uses it to counter nationalism, and to give an account of goodness found in people who are not Christians is to be understood and approached.

Taking all this into consideration, I would first suggest that there are more similarities than differences in how Christ is seen to be central in the virtue-ethical and divine command-based manuscripts. Secondly, it would seem paradoxical that it is in a manuscript that relies more on divine command ethics where Bonhoeffer shows Christ to be the exemplar of simplicity, responsibility, and representation, since the very notion of being an exemplar is much closer to virtue-ethical modes of thought. For this reason, I am loath to account for this difference as being in any way related to the form of ethical thought Bonhoeffer was using. Thirdly, however, the differences that exist are complementary, since they do not contradict one another, nor could the material from either form be ignored without loss.

6.4.3.B: COMMUNION WITH CHRIST

While the notion of communion with Christ does not have the obvious place that other aspects of Christology have in Bonhoeffer's thought, there are a number of references to it in virtue-ethical and divine command-based manuscripts. A telling example occurs in "Ethics as Formation," when he is speaking about what it means to be conformed to the risen Christ: "The new person lives in the world like everyone else; he is distinguished often only in few [things/ways] from other people. He does not aim at giving himself prominence, but only to give Christ prominence for the sake of his brothers. Transfigured [*verklärt*] in the form of the Risen One, he carries here only the sign of the cross and of judgment. In that he carries it willingly, he shows himself to be one who has received the Holy Spirit and who lives united in incomparable love and communion with Jesus Christ" (83). Communion with Christ occurs, then, as a result of being conformed to Christ, which, as we have seen, is accomplished by Christ. Hence it is also an aspect of grace. It is also clear that communion with Christ is something ongoing, in the midst of everyday living in the world, though with the Christian's focus on Christ for the sake of her fellow-Christians. There is no triumphalism here: what is visible is the sign of the cross and judgment. Yet even while emphasizing the role of grace, it is clear that the Christian is to be active and to participate, to carry the sign of the cross and judgment willingly. This voluntary participation is what makes evident the Holy Spirit at work in her life; it is the proof that she lives in the "incomparable love" and communion with Jesus Christ.

In another of the virtue-ethical manuscripts, "Guilt, Justification, Renewal," Bonhoeffer returns to this topic. "Genuine recognition of guilt does not grow up out of the experiences of dissolution and of decay, but rather for us, who encountered him, only out of the form of Christ himself. It [sc. recognition of guilt] presupposes thus a measure of communion with this form. Precisely therefore it is a wonder; for how should the one who has fallen away from Christ still have communion with Christ, unless through the grace by which Christ himself holds tightly the one who has fallen away and preserves the communion for him?" (125–26). This passage underscores the necessity of grace for anyone to have communion with Christ, and yet it goes further, since it opens the possibility that those who have fallen away from Christ may be kept in communion with him, by him. Bonhoeffer considers the recognition of her own guilt to be the first step in the process by which Christ conforms a person to himself. Although this leads on to an extended discussion of confession of

Divine Command and/or Virtue Ethics

guilt within the church, and his unforgettable confession of the sins of the church in Nazi Germany, it is at least possible that this is another place in which Bonhoeffer opens the way for understanding the goodness of those who are not Christians. For if a non-Christian can recognize her guilt, Bonhoeffer would see that as evidence that Christ has begun his work of conforming her to himself.

Thus, in the two passages that treat communion with Christ in the virtue-ethical manuscripts, several things are worth mentioning. The first is that communion with Christ is dependent on grace. The second, however, is that the Christian is to be an active participant, willingly bearing the sign of the cross. Thirdly, and most strikingly, communion with Christ is not only a possibility for the believer, but for those who are being held by Christ and kept in his communion as the first part of his conforming them to himself, perhaps even before a profession of faith may have been made.

Turning to the divine command-based manuscripts, in the section on "The Structure of Responsible Life" in the second version of "History and the Good," Bonhoeffer considers the nature of the conscience in the Christian. "Where Christ, true God and true human, has become the point of unity of my existence (although the conscience still remains—formally—the call from my essential being to unity with myself) this unity, however, can no longer be realized in the retreat to my autonomy of living by the law, but [this unity is realized] rather in the communion with Jesus Christ" (278–79). Here Bonhoeffer's focus is not the grace that enables the Christian to have communion with Christ, though this should be presupposed; it is on how the conscience is transformed from being a call to unity with the self to being a call to unity/communion with Christ. Thus the notion of communion with Christ is being used by Bonhoeffer to develop a more positive understanding of the conscience than is seen in some other passages, and to give an account of its continuing role in the life of the Christian.[56]

In the following section on "The Place of Responsibility," Bonhoeffer returns to his focus on grace: "In the encounter with Jesus Christ the person experiences the call of God, and in that the calling to life in the communion of Jesus Christ. Divine grace befalls the person; it lays claim to him" (290). Here Bonhoeffer is more explicit about the workings of grace: an encounter with Jesus Christ, the call of God, the calling or vocation to life in the communion of Jesus Christ.[57] There is no mention in this

---

56. See also *DBW* 6:292–93.
57. See also *DBW* 6:360.

instance of a call to repentance, or of the recognition of guilt, but again grace is emphasized.

In another divine command-based manuscript, "The Concrete Command and the Divine Mandates," Bonhoeffer takes this notion a step further. Part of the church's mandate is to "bear witness to Jesus Christ as Lord and Savior of his Church and of all the world, and thereby [to] call [others] into his communion" (403). Thus the call to life in communion with Christ may not, as above, be the direct call of God but a call pronounced by the church. This brings the concept of communion with Christ into harmony with Bonhoeffer's long-standing ecclesiological focus. Later in this manuscript Bonhoeffer shows an enhanced role for the church, namely that precisely in its communion with and following of Christ it represents the world: "The Christian Church stands in the place in which the whole world should stand; in so far it serves the world representatively, it is there for the sake of the world. On the other hand, the world comes to its own fulfillment there where the Church stands. . . . In this double representation the church stands wholly in the communion and discipleship of its Lord, who was precisely the Christ in that he was there for the world and not for himself" (408–9). This passage brings together ecclesiology not only with communion with Christ, but also with the important theme of representation.[58]

Thus in the divine command-based passages communion with Christ is, of course, dependent on grace. Yet here Bonhoeffer does more with it: he uses it to give an account of the nature and role of the conscience in the Christian; he explores how God's call comes to a person, including coming through the church's witness, and he suggests even that the church's communion with Christ is part of its representation of the world.

Comparing and contrasting, then, Bonhoeffer's treatment of communion with Christ in the earlier passages with these later ones, the one similarity is the role of grace in enabling a person to live in communion with Christ. The passages depending on virtue-like ethics bring this together with the agent's willing participation. Importantly, the second quote shows Bonhoeffer giving some account of non-Christians being in communion with Christ. Likewise, in the latter passages, Bonhoeffer is also concerned to speak of how one might come to be in communion with Christ, though here he offers a different pattern. Significantly, in these excerpts based on divine command ethics, Bonhoeffer hints at the role of the church, both in voicing God's call to communion with Christ and in

---

58. This also contains the theme of existence for others. See *DBW* 8:558, 560.

being the representative for all humanity in his communion. It is not clear that these differences are linked to his mode of ethical discourse, but the differences are complementary.

6.4.3.c: Simplicity (and Cleverness)

As noted previously (4.5.2.a), simplicity is God-given; additionally, both in the virtue-ethical and the divine command-based manuscripts there is at least a hint that it can be understood only in Christ himself (68; 315). In that context I suggested that simplicity (together with cleverness, since Bonhoeffer describes them as a unity) functions in some way analogous to a virtue, and specifically to prudence. "Because the simple one does not squint at the world alongside God, therefore he is capable of seeing freely and impartially the reality of the world. Thus simplicity becomes cleverness. Whoever sees reality as it is, whoever sees the ground of things is clever. Therefore only the one who sees reality in God is clever" (67). This is the aspect of prudence that enables a person to see a situation or reality aright (67–69). Yet in a classical or Thomist account of virtue ethics, one would expect prudence to enable the virtuous person not only to perceive a situation correctly, but also to apprehend the right course of action. In the virtue-ethical manuscripts this function of prudence hardly seems present.

In the divine command-based manuscripts, there is again evidence of something like prudence at work, namely the possibility of right judgment that comes from the unity with God that is given in Christ (318–19).

However, it is only in discussing what it means to discern the will of God (as seen in 6.2.2) that the fuller aspect of prudence is brought into play. "It is the liberating call to simplicity, to repentance, it is the call that itself cancels [or raises, *aufhebt*] the old knowledge from falling away [from God] and gives the new knowledge of Jesus, that knowledge which is utterly absorbed in doing the will of God" (321). Here right perception (new knowledge) is inextricably bound up in right action (doing the will of God). This is not vastly different from Thomas's account of infused prudence. Moreover, simplicity is the capability to do God's will as an *actus directus*,[59] a direct and unreflective action (322).

As already noted, in the case of simplicity, there is a clear difference between the virtue-ethical and the divine command-based manuscripts. In the former instances, Bonhoeffer focuses solely on the aspect of right

---

59. See *DBW* 2:23, 48, 95–96, 126, 148, and 158–60.

perception of reality; in the latter examples there is a clear move towards expression of the God-given ability to apprehend the right course of action (as well as the ability to execute that). Since Bonhoeffer works with the same language in both modes of ethical thought (simplicity, or simplicity and cleverness, which he has said are really one), it seems to me that this is a case where there is clearly development of the one notion over time. It is, of course, also possible that the divine command ethic framework necessarily brings issues of discernment and action into sharper focus. Yet since it is not possible to be certain what influence the mode of ethical thought had on the development, it is safer merely to note that the difference here is not one of complementarity or contradiction; nothing of substance regarding prudence would be lost if one ignored the earlier passages.

6.4.4: Preliminary Conclusions: Command and/or Conformation

It is now possible to consider the various areas of overlapping material to weigh up what the relationship between them is, and thus to be able to answer more surely how the virtue-ethical aspects of Bonhoeffer's *Ethics* relate to the divine command elements. In the case of Bonhoeffer's methodological concerns regarding concrete ethics and treating the whole of life, there were similarities as well as differences, and the differences were complementary. Regarding structures, the mandates and responsibility, the relationship was slightly more complex: his treatment of the mandates showed development over time as well as complementary differences; the notion of responsibility was greatly developed in the later manuscripts after only brief mentions in the earlier ones. So in these issues there was more evidence of development over time, but also complementarity in his treatments of the mandates. In looking at specific aspects of ethical life, centering on the person of Jesus Christ, communion with Christ, simplicity (and cleverness), and prudential discernment, there were varying mixtures of similarity, and complementary difference. In treating the centrality of Christ, there were more similarities than differences, though the differences were complementary. Again in his handling of communion with Christ there were obvious similarities, but with important and complementary differences: articulating an understanding of how non-Christians may be "good" in the earlier manuscripts, and involving his ecclesiological concerns in the later ones. In the case of simplicity, however, there were obvious similarities as well as development in the later manuscript, which

Divine Command and/or Virtue Ethics

lead me to conclude that in this case the earlier manuscript does not contribute much substance not contained in the later. Thus it is possible to say that it is certainly not the case that the mode of ethical thought made no difference to how Bonhoeffer treated these themes; there were too many and important areas of divergence for this to be so. Additionally, there were no instances where the differences were contradictory and therefore indicative of a radical change of direction or thought. The differences were either seen to be the result of development over time, or the evidence of a complementarity engendered by the richness of drawing on two different modes for considering ethics.

In view of all this, it seems to me that Rasmussen is correct in pointing out the similarity of concerns across the manuscripts using conformation and divine command ethics. However, given the many real differences that may be related to the form of ethical thought in use, Plant is surely correct in his unwillingness to make one mode of ethical discourse subordinate to the other. Yet in distinction from them both, I would like to ask if there is not evidence, given all the areas where there was complementarity in Bonhoeffer's treatment of the material, to suggest some sort of integration of the two modes of ethical thought, rather than considering them to be irreducibly plural, or seeing command as subordinate to conformation.

6.4.5: A Case for Integration

One possibility of a more profound relationship between the virtue-like conformation ethics of the earlier manuscripts and the divine command ethics of the later ones would be that Bonhoeffer was in the process of a kind of dialectical integration of the two. The presence of virtue-ethical themes in the divine-command based passages, and conversely of divine command motifs in the virtue-ethical passages,[60] as well as the complementarity of differences when he addresses the same topics in the two modes, are both suggestive of the possibility of his working towards a dialectical integration. Although there can be no positive proof for such a relationship, since he did not complete the book he intended to write and did not make explicit the relationship between the elements extant in the manuscripts we have, the fact that Bonhoeffer worked with similarly disparate notions in other works to try to achieve a synthesis (most obviously

---

60. See 164–67 and 128–38.

in *Act and Being*) is sufficient reason to examine whether there may be indications that he was intending a synthesis in this case as well.[61]

Although Plant does not go so far as to suggest the possibility of the integration of the two "moods," as he calls them, for conceiving ethics, he is aware of examples of dialectical integration in other works. First, in discussing *Act and Being*, Plant notes Bonhoeffer's language of sin as "being in Adam," which is contrasted with that of "being in Christ." Sin, he tells us, is understood by Bonhoeffer not simply as concrete acts, but as *being* in Adam rather than being in Christ.[62] What, then, is the relationship between good acts and being good? Plant tells us, for Bonhoeffer this cannot be a case of either/or, but of both/and: being and act impinge on one another, whether one is in Adam or in Christ. Yet one may not pursue one's own goodness; one can only seek Christ.[63] Such language has rich resonance for Bonhoeffer's *Ethics*, as we shall see presently.

For in writing generally of Bonhoeffer's *Ethics*, Plant notes an implication for ethics from *Act and Being*, namely that "[d]eeds and character cohere in God, and through faith cohere also in the believer."[64] If taken to its logical conclusion, though Plant does not explore the question, this should mean that in the case of conformation the attention to the person never obscures the question of acting well. Likewise it should mean that when Bonhoeffer depends more on divine command language, the emphasis on specific deeds should not eclipse the character of the person who is acting.

In this section I examine elements within the *Ethics* that provide evidence for an integration of conformation and command: the fact that emphasis on the person does not preclude showing the need to act well in the virtue-ethical manuscripts (6.4.5.a), the fact that character is not obscured in the divine command manuscripts (6.4.5.b), and specific passages that are potentially suggestive of synthesis (6.4.5.c). In looking at "acts" in the virtue-ethical manuscripts and at "person" in the divine command manuscripts, I will be attending to the broad sweep, since I have already looked at the detail (6.2.1. and 4.5), but in looking at passages that support the notion that Bonhoeffer was attempting a synthesis it will be important to attend carefully to the detail. In this discussion, the question

---

61. See Bethge's assessment that Bonhoeffer "sought to mediate between two opposing positions," though he identified these as situation ethics and normative ethics, *Biography*, 717.

62. Plant, *Bonhoeffer*, 74.

63. Ibid., 75.

64. Ibid., 112.

Divine Command and/or Virtue Ethics

should also be kept open whether, through faith, the deeds and character of the believer are seen to cohere.

6.4.5.A: "Acts" in Virtue-Ethical Manuscripts

As one might expect, the manuscripts based on conformation have a person-centered approach, and often stress ways of being more than concrete actions. Thus in the extended "ecce homo" passage in "Ethics as Conformation," being conformed to Christ has implications for the believer in terms of "being a real person" (81), carrying scars and "being a sinner" (82), "being a new creature" (82–83). Yet Bonhoeffer expects that being conformed to Christ will involve the person in her decisions and acts; it will entail commands and directions which demand obedience (89). This is not spelled out in detail in this manuscript, but a look at some of the other virtue-ethical manuscripts may make his intentions clearer.

In "Guilt, Justification, Renewal," written in 1941, he is concerned to emphasize that what the Church needs to confess is not the odd mistake or failing but truly "falling away" from Christ (125). However, when he writes the confession, he refers to very concrete acts and omissions based on transgressing the ten commandments (129–32).

Likewise, in "The Ultimate and the Penultimate," Bonhoeffer is clear that specific acts may either prepare the way for the coming of Christ in mercy or may hinder his coming (155, 159).

However, the most obvious instance where the emphasis on the person does not obscure the need to act well is in his treatment of topical issues in "The Natural Life." Although he does not spell out the "commands and directions which demand obedience," they are implied: do not harm or kill anyone arbitrarily (179); do not imprison anyone arbitrarily (183); do not carry out euthanasia (184–91), and so on. Arguably, had the churches given such commands and had all church members been obedient to them, the Nazi regime would have struggled to find people willing to carry out much of their murderous program.

Therefore, it is safe to say that Bonhoeffer's focus on the person does not come at the expense of indicating the need to act well.

6.4.5.B: "Being" in Divine Command Manuscripts

Just as the virtue-ethical manuscripts naturally emphasize the person, unsurprisingly, the divine command manuscripts speak more readily of acting (usually *handeln*). Nonetheless, in the second version "History and the Good," written after Bonhoeffer had acquired Barth's *Church Dogmatics* II/2, there is a regular emphasis on "life" or "living" rather than atomistic acts (e.g., 245–47, 250, 254, and 278), which is seen most directly in the title of the subsection, "The Structure of Responsible Living" (256–89). Although it may seem questionable to equate "life" or "living" with the ontological understanding of "being," its usage in this way comes more clearly into focus when he uses it repeatedly in the pairing "living and acting" (e.g., 256, 259, 264, and 268).[65] Moreover, Bonhoeffer speaks not only in a holistic way about "living," but also shows the relational character of his concepts of responsibility (253–55, and 256), representation (256–58), and calling (290–91, 293–94). Intriguingly, a person's ability to act responsibly is based on her participation (which is definitely a mode of "being" rather than acting) in Christ's responsible action (279–80).

Additionally, "being" is visible when Bonhoeffer speaks of Jesus' carrying the "self" (*Ich*, which is also Freud's term "Ego") of all humans in himself (257–58). There is a concern for the person's individual characteristics and strengths shown in his treatment of responsibility, such that there is "an infinite variety of responsible decision" (282). Again, Bonhoeffer allows the particularities of the person to become apparent when he speaks of the role of self-examination and the danger of confusing character traits with the call of Christ; however, the person is to keep her eyes on Christ, not herself (295).[66]

However, the strongest form in which "being" comes to the fore in "History and the Good" is in terms of the person of Jesus Christ, who is the life and in whom our life finds its source, being and goal (248, 250). It is telling that it is in this manuscript that Bonhoeffer gives examples from Jesus' life (279).[67] Indeed, large parts of Bonhoeffer's arguments in this manuscript are based on Christ as our exemplar (e.g. 257–58, 269, 275–76, and 288), which I have already discussed in terms of its being a typically virtue-ethical argument.

"The Love of God and the Decay of the World" again depends on a relational anthropology, in this case seen negatively: the outworkings of the Fall are found in the separation of the person from God, others and even herself (301–10). Additionally, as so often with Bonhoeffer, the

---

65. See also *DBW* 6:31, 60, 319, and 388.

66. See also *DBW* 6:328.

67. There are also references to Greek tragedies (264–65) and to a play by Goethe (281), almost suggesting a desire to prevent this manuscript from becoming atomistic.

Divine Command and/or Virtue Ethics

emphasis on the person is seen in the centrality of Jesus Christ, but in this manuscript he is contrasted with the type of the person seeking to be ethical through her own (fallen) knowledge of good and evil, the "Pharisee" (311–21, 329–33). Thus although much of the discussion is about doing the will of God, in fact the focus is on the person and her relationship to her Source, God (e.g., 302, 318–19). Importantly, in a manuscript whose central discussion is about acting, the focus is often more on the agent than on acting as such. There is neither any consideration of an act (such as is found in Thomas's account (see 3.2.3.c) nor on the doing (329–31), instead Bonhoeffer speaks about the "doer" and contrasts her with the "legislator" and the "judge" (330).

The next two manuscripts, "Church and the World" and "Regarding the Possibility of a Word of the Church to the World," are essentially theoretical and hardly treat acts or persons in any detail.[68] However, in "The 'Ethical' and the 'Christian' as a Theme" Bonhoeffer speaks directly about the issue: ethical speech is "decisively tied to persons, times and places" (374), and he rejects outright a more atomistic approach (376–77). As with so many other themes, relationality underlies his treatment of God's command, and it is telling that he uses the relation of child and parents to exemplify his understanding (384–85). Finally, it is important that he states, "God's command allows the human to live before God as a human" two times (387 and 388).

The final manuscript extant, "The Concrete Command and the Divine Mandates," again relies on a relational ontology (395), and the form of relationship is worked out in the case of the church through looking at the relation of the minister and congregation (400–402). As is so often the case, the person is in view primarily in the form of Jesus Christ (403–7), but the Christian is also specifically addressed (407).

From all this it is safe to say that the person is by no means eclipsed when Bonhoeffer relies more on divine command ethics.

6.4.5.C: Passages that Suggest an Integration of Command and Conformation

Perhaps the first indication of a projected integration occurs in the manuscript "Ethics as Formation":

---

68. Though see DBW 6:349–53 for his discussion on falsely fearful Christians, how people find faith, who the "tax collectors" and "prostitutes" might be in his society, and his concern with "good" and "bad" people.

> Only the one who is able here to combine simplicity and cleverness with one another is able to endure [*bestehen*]. But what is simplicity? what is cleverness? How can the two become one? Simple is the one who in the inversion, confusion and twisting of all terms keeps only the plain truth of God in view, who is not a "dipsychos," a man of two souls (James 1[:8]), but rather the man of undivided heart. Because he knows and has God, he clings to the commands, to the judgment and to the mercy that proceed daily anew from the mouth of God. Not fettered by principles, rather bound by love for God, he has become free from the problems and conflicts of ethical decision. They no longer oppress him. He belongs wholly, only to God and God's will. (67)

I have already suggested that simplicity and cleverness fulfill a virtue-like role in that they are human dispositions (infused rather than acquired) that enable right action. Yet in this virtue-ethical passage, the virtuous person is defined in terms related to divine command: she is dependent on God's commands, God's will, and the judgment and mercy that come ever afresh from God. There can be no doubt that Bonhoeffer has, at least in this passage, integrated virtue-ethical elements with aspects of Barthian divine command ethics to create something distinctive.

Another place in which such a creative union may be seen comes later in the same manuscript: "Ethics as formation is thus the venture to speak, neither abstractly nor casuistically, neither programmatically nor purely speculatively, of the form of Jesus Christ taking form in our world. Here concrete judgments and decisions must be risked. Here the decision and act can no longer be pushed off on the individual's conscience, but rather here there are concrete commands and directions for which obedience is demanded" (89). Again in this instance there is a conjunction of the two strands. Ethics as formation, as has already been seen, is in some senses related to virtue ethics. Yet in Bonhoeffer's conception, speaking of ethics as formation necessarily entails concrete commands requiring obedience. In the first passage it is possible to see a logical union of simplicity as prudence and divine command ethics: divine command requires some account of how God's will is discerned, and simplicity may be said to fill this need. In such a case, the "virtue" of simplicity would be secondary to the divine command as the primary mode of conceiving ethics. In this second passage, however, it is not immediately possible to see an internal link between what is necessary for ethics as formation to be coherent and concrete commands. For instance, it is thinkable for an ethic based on formation so to emphasize the variety of ways in which Christ's form shapes different persons that it would be difficult to articulate any (but the most general) command applicable to all. Or, it would be possible to emphasize that the person is so conformed to Christ that she herself wills what God wills, obviating the need for commands and obedience. In context, however, Bonhoeffer's concern is with articulating a concrete, rather than abstract, ethic, and it would seem that the connection between formation and commands in this passage is related to how he conceives of a concrete ethic: one in which specific commands are given and obedience is demanded. Yet even if the connection made is not one of logical necessity, what is important for this study is that for Bonhoeffer the connection is there and is compelling.

These two pointers to the possibility of an intended integration of conformation and command in the virtue-ethical manuscripts have their counterparts, also only few, in the divine command-based manuscripts.

An intimation of virtue ethics in the latter manuscripts has already been mentioned: his repeated depiction of Jesus as the model of faithful living. Christ is the paradigm for what it means to live in responsibility and representation (257–58). He is the exemplar of the simple person (315). He is love (337–38). Of course reference to a virtuous person is a move to be expected within virtue ethics. The presence of such material in the manuscripts dominated by divine command language, however, is suggestive of the two modes of thought being brought together.

One final hint of an intended integration occurs in the manuscript "The Love of God and the Decay of the World":

> How does this testing "what the will of God be" proceed? Decisive here is the clear prerequisite that there is this testing only because of a "metamorphosis," a complete inner change of the form hitherto because of a "renewal" of the mind (Rom 12:2), because of living as children of the light (Eph 5:9). This "metamorphosis" can only be concerned with the overcoming of the form of the person who has fallen away, Adam, and with the conformation to the form of the new person, Christ. That emerges clearly from other biblical uses of these terms. The new form, in whose strength alone the testing of the will of God is possible, has left behind the old person, who in falling away from God was striving for the knowledge of good and evil. It is the form of the child of God, who in unity with the will of the Father lives in conformation to the only true Son of God. (324–25)

The Virtue of Bonhoeffer's Ethics

We have already seen that the "virtue" of simplicity is at work in allowing a Christian to discern the will of God. In this passage it is the notion of being conformed to Christ that is brought into closer relationship with "testing" the will of God. The categories for understanding conformation are subtly changed in that Bonhoeffer does not speak explicitly in terms of Christ's action, his "winning form," (and the believer's passivity). Yet there is still the concern to speak of the Fall in terms of falling away from God (as he did in the conformation manuscript "Inheritance and Decay"), and of desiring to gain the knowledge of good and evil. In this case, however, conformation does not play a secondary role to the will of God as simplicity did. Such a secondary role may, of course, be seen in the fact that it is Christ's form in the believer that allows her to discern God's will. Nonetheless, it would seem that it is God's will that she should be conformed to Christ. Thus the two are brought dialectically such that neither can be said to be subordinate to the other.

Although there are relatively few passages that refer to the themes of conformation and command together, yet there are hints in the virtue-ethical and divine command-related manuscripts that Bonhoeffer was working with both notions in his mind from the beginning. Additionally, there is at least some indication that both simplicity and conformation are used in a supporting role for perceiving, testing, and doing the will of God, but equally that conformation to Christ is God's will. From this it is possible to suggest that the integration Bonhoeffer intended might well have envisaged a dialectic in which simplicity and conformation are instrumental in a conception of ethics based on the will of God, which in turn is to be discussed in terms of conformation to Christ.

At this point it is possible to return to the question of whether it can be truly said that in Bonhoeffer's *Ethics* the deeds and character of the believer cohere through faith.[69] As seen previously (4.4.2), it is in conformation mode in "The Natural" that Bonhoeffer addresses concrete issues in the most sustained manner. Likewise in "The Ultimate and Penultimate" he speaks of specific acts that prepare the way for the Lord's coming in grace (154–56). These are both wide-ranging ways in which it can be claimed that in conformation ethics the focus on character does not obscure deeds. Similarly there are ways in which in divine command the emphasis on deeds does not eclipse the person, such as the fact that interrelationships between persons are brought out more explicitly in the later manuscripts, as are everyday, contingent realities of life. More striking, however, is the

---

69. Plant, *Bonhoeffer*, 112.

fact that it is in speaking of ethics from a divine command perspective that he offers the depiction of Christ as the exemplar of what it means to be simple, to be responsible, and to live representationally. It could be argued that in doing so Bonhoeffer was not so much employing a mode of reasoning from virtue ethics as working out in practice his christocentric theology. However, the point can equally be made, and I believe it is true, that the centrality of Christ in all Bonhoeffer's thought essentially necessitates perceiving ethics in terms that approximate virtue ethics. However one interprets this form of reasoning, it is certainly the case that an emphasis on deeds does not eclipse the person. Thus Plant is right to say that because in Bonhoeffer's conception character and deeds cohere in God, through faith (or, being conformed to Christ) they cohere also in the Christian. This very fact contributes to my conviction that character-based conformation and the deed-focused divine command ethics are not, as Plant suggests, irreducibly plural, but are being brought into a new and distinctive union in which neither is merely subordinate to the other.

6.5: Tentative Conclusions

At the end of chapter 4, it was possible to state firmly that there are virtue-ethical elements of Bonhoeffer's *Ethics*. Here, however, it is necessary to be more cautious, since there is not enough explicit material to be sure of how those elements relate to the parts of Bonhoeffer's writings that depend more on divine command ethics.

Yet, however tentatively, it is necessary to proceed: it is right to attempt a more precise articulation of the relationship between conformation and divine command. From the fact that Bonhoeffer uses divine command language even in the most explicitly conformation-oriented material, and the fact that elements of conformation are present in the later manuscripts, it seems appropriate to conclude that he worked with both of these modes of conceiving of ethics throughout. In examining passages that bring virtue and divine command ethics together, it seemed in some examples that the overarching vision of ethics is framed in terms of the will of God, and that virtue-ethical aspects play a supporting role. Thus the "virtue" of simplicity enables the Christian to perceive reality correctly and to discern the will of God, while being conformed to Christ is the *sine qua non* for testing the will of God.

However, in other ways it seemed that the two modes of conceiving ethics were used dialectically: conformation enables the believer to discern the will of God; and the will of God is that she be conformed to Christ. Similarly, the opening sentence of the first manuscript with its "incomparable imposition" of abandoning the questions of how one might be or do good and asking rather about the will of God (31) places the question of being good (virtue ethics, as it were) as well as doing good (command based ethics) in a secondary position to the will of God. In discussing this passage earlier (6.2.1.c), I assumed that the reference to "the will of God" is related to divine command,[70] but I would like to revisit this passage and its completion at the end of the manuscript to ask if there truly is a link to divine command implied. When he returns to the theme, he states:

> We discussed at the beginning that the question of the will of God must take the place of the question of one's being good and doing good. The will of God, however, is nothing other than the becoming real of the reality of Christ among us and in our world. The will of God is thus neither an idea that demands realization first; it is much more itself already reality in the self-revelation of God in Jesus Christ. . . . After the appearance of Christ, ethics can only be concerned with one thing, namely with receiving a share of the reality of the fulfilled will of God. But also this receiving a share is only possible because of the fact that, in the fulfillment of the will of God in Christ, I myself am also included, and that means [I am] reconciled with God. The question of the will of God does not inquire about something hidden or unfulfilled, but rather about what is revealed, fulfilled. However, therein remains yet a genuine question, whether I myself, and the world that surrounds me, am placed in this question by the fulfillment.
>
> The will of God, as it was revealed and fulfilled in Jesus Christ, encompasses the whole of reality. Access to this whole, without allowing oneself to be torn apart by the manifold [things], exists only in faith in Jesus Christ in whom the whole fullness of the Godhead dwells (Col 2:9, 1:19), through whom all is reconciled, whether on earth or in heaven (Col 1:20), whose body, namely the church, is the fullness of him who fulfils all in all (Eph 1:23). Faith in this Jesus Christ is the only source of all good. (60–61)

The will of God, as discussed here, is surely something much broader than the question of what God wills in any particular instance, what God commands. It is the reality that Jesus has already reconciled the whole world to God. Thus it is not something to be discerned and then done, as

---

70. See 166–67.

Divine Command and/or Virtue Ethics

fulfilling God's command might be. It is rather a cosmic reality that puts the question to each person whether she and the world around her receive a share of this reality through faith in Jesus Christ.[71] Of course this grand vision of the will of God could be used within divine command ethics, just as it could be given as the basis for ethics in a variety of forms. It is, however, not indicative that Bonhoeffer was using divine command ethics as his prime category, with virtue only in a subordinate role. Instead, in these passages, Bonhoeffer places both an ethic based on being good (virtue) and an ethic based on doing good (command) in service of this overarching notion of God's will as nothing less than the reconciliation of all things in Christ. This dynamic is also in play when he writes, "Not that I should become good nor that the condition of the world should be improved through me is of ultimate importance, but rather that the reality of God should prove itself to be everywhere the ultimate reality" (32). Becoming good and doing good are subordinate to the higher concern that the reality of God (that all things have been reconciled to God in Christ) is shown to be the ultimate reality.

Furthermore, it is often apparent that Bonhoeffer's understanding of humanity would not allow for an ethical approach that would separate the agent's being from her doing: "*The person is an indivisible whole not only as an individual in his person and his work, but also as a member of the community of humans and of creatures*, in which he stands"[72] (38, his emphases). In a later manuscript, "The Love of God and the Decay of the World," Bonhoeffer refers to judging as being something a person does not merely "do," but as something bound up with her very being, such that "repentance of the whole person" is required (316). Moreover, judging (whether oneself or others) stands in the way of the simple doing of the will of God (316). Later in this same passage he says, "'Judging' is not a particular vice or wickedness of the divided person [divided through sin from God, neighbor, self], but rather it is his being, which reveals itself in his speaking, his doing, and in his feeling" (318). Here it is telling that particular vices or wickedness might be construed as being something less integral to the person that her "being," or that they might not necessarily reveal themselves in a person's speaking, doing and feeling. Yet this

---

71. See also *DBW* 6:40: "To participate in this reality is the true purpose of the question of the good." See also *DBW* 6:59. In later manuscripts this notion reappears: "out of joy over the completed reconciliation of the world with God" comes the doing of the Christian (*DBW* 6:252). See also *DBW* 6:265–67.

72. See also *DBW* 6:35–36, 126 where he speaks of the person and her work as being originally and essentially one. See also *DBW* 6:37, 60 regarding such unity.

tells us only that Bonhoeffer's notions of vice and wickedness (as we saw in chapter 2 regarding "virtue") do not accord with understandings more generally held, let alone those found in most accounts of virtue ethics. Nonetheless, we see here the unity of being and doing which underlies Bonhoeffer's ethics. This unity of being and doing is underscored in his frequent pairing of "living and acting" (see note 65).

For such reasons, I believe that Rasmussen is not right in suggesting that command is in some way subordinate to conformation. Equally, I disagree with Plant's assessment of conformation and command as irreducibly plural; while the two strands are identifiable and not to be simply conflated, their relationship can be described as one of dialectical union pointing to all reality reconciled to God in Christ. Indeed, it seems likely that Bonhoeffer was consciously bringing together two different modes of conceiving ethics to try to articulate a concrete ethic for his context, honoring the strengths of each and using them to counterbalance the weaknesses inherent in the other, but using them both in service of a more cosmic vision of ethics in terms of the reconciliation of all things to God in Christ.

In the next and final chapter I shall explore how Bonhoeffer's integration of virtue-ethical conformation and divine command ethics may be of import and use in our own context.

7

Conclusion

7.1: Summary

7.1.1: Chapter 1—Introduction

BEFORE ASKING WHAT CAN BE LEARNED FROM THIS STUDY OF VIRTUE ethical aspects of Bonhoeffer's *Ethics*, it is good to return to the backdrop described in the first chapter. There we saw a stage that was divided sharply in two halves. The Roman Catholic half depicted justification both in terms of the remission of sins and sanctification, and eternal life was portrayed as a gift of grace as well as a reward for meritorious works. The Lutheran side of the stage showed justification as God's declaration that a sinner is righteous without reference to her works, and eternal life was displayed solely as given by grace; no works could be seen to be meritorious. Furthermore, the Lutheran and Roman Catholic sides diverged over how humans might know what is good, or how able they might be to will what is good. The ensuing accusations of the two parties left the two sides of the stage utterly divided, with considerable consequences for ethical discourse. The strengths of the Roman Catholic side may be said to lie in the fact that the rationale for moral theology was integral to its most basic theological convictions. Of course there were weaknesses in that language of "merit" and growth in grace was open to abuse, and the reliance on the manuals in the confessional led to a form of legalism. The strengths on the Lutheran side lay on the primacy of grace, and assurance of salvation. The greatest weakness was that there was no theological rationale for how ethics is related to justification by faith, by grace.

This is the setting for considering how Bonhoeffer's *Ethics* relates to virtue ethics. I turn now to a summary of what has been seen of this relation in the preceding chapters. In doing so, I hope to see how Bonhoeffer's use of both virtue-ethical and command-based ethics might affect the scenery just described.

7.1.2: Chapter 2—Bonhoeffer and "Virtue Ethics"

One would quite naturally assume that as a Lutheran theologian in the first half of the twentieth century, Bonhoeffer would keep firmly on the Protestant side of the stage. Quite apart from the anachronism of suggesting that anyone at that time might have regarded herself as a "virtue ethicist," even if her center of moral thought came from classical philosophy or Thomism, it is not plausible to imagine that Bonhoeffer considered himself to be an exponent of what we would now call "virtue ethics." Indeed, as was seen, there are many *prima facie* reasons to suppose that he might have disliked the enterprise of expounding virtue ethics. One example of this is his use of the word "*Tugend*" (virtue), which was almost always with negative, if not derisive, connotations.

Similarly, at first glance it would seem that Bonhoeffer's perception of Thomas Aquinas was largely negative. Since Thomism and classical philosophy are the prime contexts in which virtue ethics were expounded, Bonhoeffer's largely negative assumptions and statements regarding Thomas suggest, at least initially, that Bonhoeffer would have rejected any suggestion that he was a virtue ethicist, and would not have ventured to the side of the stage set for the Roman Catholic position on justification. Instead, these indications would seem to confirm the initial assumption that he would remain decidedly on the Protestant side of the stage.

However, in some places it seems that Bonhoeffer rejects all the prime categories and forms of ethical thought, making it difficult to place him on the stage at all. Nor was the question of the mode of Bonhoeffer's ethical thought clarified by looking at what other commentators have concluded, since there is no widespread agreement regarding this.

Furthermore, internal evidence showed, that whatever form his ethics may be said to take, he was concerned particularly that ethics be concrete rather than abstract, that ethics must focus on Jesus Christ, and that reliance on grace should in no way be undermined. Therefore, it became important to explore the nature of virtue ethics in a Christian context to see how it might meet not only these concerns, but also the negative associations that were implied in several passages where Bonhoeffer spoke of virtue (*Tugend*), such as hypocrisy, being private, and attending too little to fallen human nature. In a sense, this could be seen as asking a complementary question: could virtue ethics wander across the stage to the Protestant side?

7.1.3: Chapter 3—Virtue Ethics in the Christian Tradition

Virtue ethics has been conceived in a variety of ways within Christian thought. Thus it was important to look at some differing forms that have been influential or representative of major strands within the tradition. The first I considered was Augustine, whose early work on ethics, *De moribus ecclesiae catholicae,* treated the moral life within a eudaemonist framework, with God as the supreme good for humans. Within that construct, Augustine used the language of the virtues, though redefined as forms of love. As he matured as a theologian, many of the themes most prominent in his conception of ethics retain their fundamental significance: the teleological framework, virtues as forms of love, and the role of knowledge and human happiness. The most important change that affects his conception of ethics is related to how he perceived the human will. As a result of the Fall, human action cannot be described as being free or autonomous, but is seen as motivated by wrong, sinful desires. Only through grace is the will freed to desire and choose the good, and to will something is to be actuated by love. Thus, in later writings he makes human dependence on grace more explicit and central than it had been when writing *De moribus ecclesiae*. What we have, then, is a distinctively Christian form of virtue ethics that emphasizes the role of grace and which could move across the stage to the Protestant side.

The second example of Christian virtue ethics I examined was that of Thomas Aquinas, whose approach brings together virtue ethics from Aristotle and Christian theology. Like Augustine, he uses a form of eudaemonism that focuses on the beatific vision of God; thus both see human flourishing ultimately in eschatological terms. He is content to borrow classical philosophy's cardinal virtues, even in their acquired form, though he supplements these both with their infused counterparts and with the theological virtues of faith, hope and love, which must be infused. Importantly, these virtues are only directed towards the supernatural end (seeing God face to face and enjoying him for ever) if they exist with love, which is received from God. Therefore it is right to stress that Thomas does have a clear recognition of the role of grace, even if many commentators (perhaps including Bonhoeffer) fail to note it. Thus although theologically it is possible (and in recent years this has happened) for Thomas's ethics to cross to the Protestant side of the stage, it seems unlikely that it is a model Bonhoeffer would have found appealing.

The third account I considered is Alasdair MacIntyre's *After Virtue*, along with other contemporary writers who focus on the character of the agent, on the particularities not only of contingent circumstances but of personal make-up, history and interrelations, on the role of community, and on the sense of meaning embedded in a narrative perspective of life. The specifics of current accounts differ in many ways, yet what they have in common is the insistence that the formation of the agent in habits of virtues is of inestimable importance for living well.

Acknowledging the differences between Augustine's teleological virtue ethic involving virtues as forms of love, and Thomas's combination of Aristotelian cardinal virtues with the theological virtues of faith, hope, and love, and the variety of articulations currently abounding, I offered some criteria that I believe must be met if it is to be meaningful to speak of an account as being "virtue ethical" in a Christian context. Some eschatological teleological foundation is important, such as Augustine's notion of God as the supreme good, or Thomas's beatific vision. An account of human flourishing (and the necessity of grace to achieve this) is also essential. Furthermore, it is important to consider how the transformation of the person may be understood to be part and parcel of her salvation. Beyond these more formal considerations, to speak of "virtue ethics" there should be an emphasis on the person, her character and the formation of her character, as well as a focus on aretaic notions of what are good or excellent traits. In the evaluation of behaviors, a virtue ethic will attend to issues that pertain to the agent, such as her motives. Yet more important than evaluation for virtue ethics is the notion of growth in virtue, or the process of being sanctified.

This look at Christian virtue ethics was necessary to counter the *prima facie* reasons seen for supposing that virtue ethics belongs on the Roman Catholic side of the stage, and that Bonhoeffer could not have been engaged in virtue ethics. In this examination virtue ethics has shown itself to be capable of moving across both sides of the stage. With these matters clarified, it was possible to turn to reasons for seeing some relationship of Bonhoeffer's *Ethics* to virtue ethics.

7.1.4: Chapter 4—Bonhoeffer's Ethics as Virtue Ethical

As seen above, a Christian virtue ethic requires an account of the relationship of justification and sanctification to give some notion of how our final

Conclusion

end is (and is not) related to how we live, or to put it differently, how we are to become who we eternally are and shall be.

In Bonhoeffer's early work, and especially in *Discipleship*, it is clear that he develops the doctrine of sanctification essentially in union with that of justification. In the *Ethics* he rejects any dualism between the work of Jesus Christ (justification) and the Holy Spirit (sanctification), and devotes a manuscript to the relationship between them. Obviously, this emphasis on sanctification is not sufficient warrant to see Bonhoeffer as engaging in virtue ethics.

However, in looking at major themes and concerns in his *Ethics* it was apparent that they could well be part of an account of virtue ethics, though none necessitated seeing his ethics as a type of virtue ethics. Nevertheless, certain aspects do have a particularly close relationship to virtue ethics, such as Bonhoeffer's anthropology, which emphasizes the identity of the Christian both as being in Christ and in relationships of representation with others, "narrative" and holistic aspects to his treatment of the person, and perhaps especially his moral vision for the everyday "middle" of life.

Yet most importantly, it is possible to identify one of Bonhoeffer's two prime categories for discussing ethics as being distinctly related to virtue ethics: namely, ethics as conformation. Here we have emphasis on the agent, and her development not in relation to any abstract account of the virtues or some nominal virtuous person, but in relation to the person of Jesus Christ. Moreover there are elements of Bonhoeffer's *Ethics* that seem to function as or to depend on the presence of virtues, to wit simplicity (and cleverness) and some unspecified notion of prudence that is necessary to make sense of his conception of responsibility. Thus it is surely possible to claim that there are virtue-ethical aspects of Bonhoeffer's *Ethics*.

7.1.5: Chapter 5—Mode of Ethical Discourse

Furthermore, an examination of his method of handling concrete issues showed some real affinities with virtue ethics in its emphasis on the agent and her motives, as well as in arguing from reason rather than an overtly theological perspective, even if his position was formed by and consonant with Christian teaching. From all this it is possible to say that, like certain forms of virtue ethics, Bonhoeffer is able to move across the whole stage.

7.1.6: Chapter 6—Divine Command and/or Virtue Ethics

Yet to claim anything more than that there are virtue-ethical elements in his *Ethics* and affinities with virtue ethics in his treatment of specific issues, it is necessary to see how this virtue-ethical strand of his thought relates to the other major strand in his *Ethics*, Barthian divine command ethics. Both strands are present in the earlier, virtue-ethical and later, divine command-related manuscripts, though the weight of emphasis shifts from the virtue-ethical to command. An examination of issues or concerns treated both in virtue-ethical terms and in command language revealed not only similarities but also complementary differences, such that it would be inappropriate to conflate the two or to identify one strand as more important. Strikingly, Bonhoeffer uses virtue-ethical ideas and themes when he is working with command, and command language when he is treating conformation, and there are indications that he had both strands in mind throughout his writing.

Although there are only a few passages that bring the two strands together explicitly, they are important indicators of how the two modes of considering ethics might be related. In one instance it would seem that the simple (or virtuous) person is to be described in terms related to divine command: she depends on God's commands, and on the justice and mercy that proceed anew daily from God. Similarly, ethics as formation, although in many ways closely related to virtue ethics, is discussed in terms of concrete commands for which obedience is required. As a corollary, when Bonhoeffer is working most obviously with divine command language, he uses a mode of argument from virtue ethics most frequently, namely showing the ideal agent (Jesus) as the example for ethical behavior. Finally, the "virtue" of simplicity is at work in discerning or testing the will of God, and yet it is God's will that the believer be conformed to Christ.

Therefore, although his work was left unfinished and it is necessarily impossible to make definitive claims, it seems to me that Bonhoeffer was engaged in an attempt to bring together two different modes of envisaging ethics into a dialectical synthesis in which the virtue-ethical aspects of simplicity and conformation are instrumental for doing the will of God, which in turn is to be understood in relation to conformation to Christ. It is possible, then, to claim that Bonhoeffer is bringing together Thomist virtue ethics and Barthian divine command ethics, in a distinctive ethic for his own context. Here, in Christ, the deeds and character of the believer cohere. Virtue and command both serve his broader picture of the will of God, namely the reality that Jesus has reconciled all things to God, and that ethics as a whole focuses on the question of whether each person and the world around her receive a share of this reality through faith in Jesus Christ.

In this dialectical synthesis, Bonhoeffer is clearly striding with confidence across both parts of the stage. He embraces the unity of justification and sanctification that had been presented on the Roman Catholic side, without losing the insistence (shown on the Protestant side) on grace as the only way a person may be justified.

Although I hope this study may be of interest simply in illuminating the contours of Bonhoeffer's thought, it is worth considering in what ways my findings may be useful in our much changed context today.

7.2: What Bonhoeffer Can Teach us Regarding Virtue Ethics

Since the publication of MacIntyre's *After Virtue*, the need has become apparent for ethics to address issues concerning the agent, to recognize her as a contingent person in a plethora of relationships and roles, with a past and with hopes for the future, and with a sense of continuity of past, present and future, and with characteristics, whether of besetting sins or shining virtues. Within Christian ethics at least three different trends have been identified: the focus on witness-bearing communities of virtue; the attempt to converse with secular culture using philosophical and social-scientific methods; and the endeavor to connect with debates regarding human life among psychologists and educators.[1] More latterly, another trend seems to have emerged using virtue ethics to treat the specific moral issues related to particular professional fields, such a medical ethics.[2] Although all of these concerns are of interest, it is the more theological situation that is pertinent in this study.[3]

Within theological ethics, there is great diversity of opinion as to the place and value of the treatment of virtue. The number of moral theologians who accord virtue a central place has been growing in recent decades. Yet there remains a large number of Christian ethicists who view character traits or growth in virtue as, at best, of secondary value in support of other

---

1. See Yearley, "Recent Works," 3–4.
2. See for instance Walker et al., eds., *Working Virtue*.
3. It would be of some interest, however, to look at Bonhoeffer's approach to conversation with secular culture alongside some of the debates now, but that would be a different study.

ways of conceiving of ethics. In considering how Bonhoeffer's use of virtue-ethical elements might be of benefit in our current and much-changed context, it may be helpful to look at one current exponent of virtue ethics, David Cunningham, and one ethicist who is decidedly more reserved in his assessment, Oliver O'Donovan. Both are Anglicans, yet their manner of approaching virtue ethics presents a sharp contrast. However, I believe that Bonhoeffer's combination of virtue ethics and divine command has a distinctive contribution to make for both stances, in ways related to the stage backdrop sketched above.[4]

7.2.1: *Virtue Ethics and Grace*

The first contribution I believe Bonhoeffer brings is his clear emphasis on the role of grace that he carries as he treads to the Roman Catholic side of the stage. While it would be quite wrong to perpetuate a sort of Protestant myth that wants to dismiss virtue ethics as "works righteousness," it is still the case that accounts of virtue ethics can often be so concerned with how a person acquires virtues[5] or how they are formed within certain kinds of communities[6] or more technical discussions,[7] such as whether there is a unity of the virtues or not, that God's active role and the person's grateful reception may be underemphasized.[8]

This lack of an emphasis on grace is evident the case in Cunningham's recent work, *Christian Ethics: The End of the Law*.[9] This engaging, clear and wise textbook for undergraduates is based firmly on Christian virtue ethics, as Cunningham makes clear in the introduction. In setting out possible approaches to ethics he begins by mentioning the possibility

---

4. I discuss these aspects of Bonhoeffer's conception from the perspective of a Protestant, since that is my own tradition. I trust that Catholic readers can make the necessary adjustments to see how this account may enrich their tradition.

5. See *ST* I–II.51–52, 63; MacIntyre's notion of practices, *After Virtue*, chapter 14.

6. See e.g. Hauerwas's defense against accusations that *Character and the Christian Life* lacked an emphasis on grace, *Character and the Christian Life*, xxxi.

7. E.g., Crisp, ed., *How Should One Live?*; Foot, *Virtues and Vices*; Hursthouse et al., eds., *Virtues and Reasons;* Slote, *Morality to Virtue*. While one can hardly expect philosophical ethicists to emphasize grace, the very fact that virtue ethics may be treated in non-theological ways may encourage the notion that it is not a Christian form of ethics.

8. I do not mean to suggest, however, that it is only among Catholic moral theologians that Bonhoeffer's emphasis on grace within virtue ethics may be of benefit. This is part of my reason for focusing on Cunningham (as an Anglican) in this discussion.

9. Cunningham, *End of the Law*. References to this are in brackets in the text.

of focusing on duty, and offers a brief outline of Immanuel Kant's ethics. He then refers to the utilitarian conceptions of Jeremy Bentham and John Stuart Mill, as well as Joseph Fletcher's situation ethics. "While these perspectives continue to have their champions, they do not (in the humble opinion of the author of this book) truly provide what we seek in understanding what Christian ethics should be. . . . I want to suggest that their faults are not just a result of the specific assumptions of each system. Rather, the inadequacies of these standard approaches to ethics result from the fact that, when it comes to ethical judgments, rules and principles are extremely difficult to formulate and to apply with any degree of specificity and consistency" (7).

These forms of ethics based on principle are thus rejected. Similarly, Cunningham refuses to countenance an ethic based on rules (9–11). Instead, he claims, Jesus "emphasized a theme that was not at all new to his culture, but may have too often been neglected. His theme was that ethical behavior depends, not just on whether or not one has obeyed the relevant laws, but on *the attitude and disposition* with which a person acts" (12, citing Matthew 5:21–22, 27–28).

With carefully chosen passages from scripture Cunningham then shows Paul's writings affirming the end (both as completion and goal) of the law in Jesus (12–13, citing especially Romans 10:4). At this point Cunningham states his intention to treat ethics based on the *person* of Jesus Christ, an undertaking that he recognizes raises a number of questions about knowledge about Jesus, cultural differences between Palestine 2000 years ago and Western countries now, and so on (13–15). Later he explores developing character as a means of preventing wrong-doing, and attends to aspects of contemporary virtue ethics familiar from MacIntyre and Hauerwas, namely narrative, activities and practices, and community (chapter 1).

Appealing as much of this is, there is a notable absence of sin and grace. Indeed, it seems as if there is even embarrassment about the concept of sin. Thus in speaking about the epistle to the Romans, Cunningham speaks of challenges to the modern reader occasioned by "a number of assumptions that are different from ours." He does not elaborate on the notion of sin in this context, but in the next paragraph says, "Although Paul's account of sin leads some readers to feel put off or excessively chastised, his account of God's grace leads him to end this first half of the letter with what might be described as the most gloriously positive and hopeful sentence in the Bible: 'For I am convinced that neither death, nor life, nor angels, nor rulers, nor things present, nor things to come, nor powers, nor height, nor depth, nor anything else in all creation, will be able to separate us from the love of God in Christ Jesus our Lord'" (83, quoting Romans 8:39).

I imagine the author is trying to offer an attractive account of Christian faith for the modern undergraduate, yet it is disconcerting how little attention he pays to sin and human dependence on grace.[10] What I find most telling here is that Cunningham does not seem to make the connection that should be obvious in Romans: for a lively sense of God's grace and mercy that enabled Paul to write "the most gloriously positive and hopeful sentence in the Bible," a deep conviction of sin and human need for grace is required. It is redemption in Christ that brings about God's purposes not only for humans but for the whole of creation, as Paul writes earlier in the same chapter (verses 18–22). The notion of grace is central to articulating God's will as described here by Paul and echoed in Bonhoeffer's overarching statement regarding the reality of the reconciliation of all things in Christ Jesus.[11]

The second part of Cunningham's book (based loosely the Eucharistic liturgy) contains a chapter that one might expect to remedy the situation, "Forgiveness, Reconciliation, and Nonviolence," and he does indeed take the reality of the fallen world and of human fallen nature seriously. Yet there is only a short paragraph that emphasizes God's mercy and forgiveness (not using the word "grace") before he moves on to the expectation that Christians are likewise to be a forgiving people (130–31). It is also significant that in treating the theological virtues he does not include Thomas's understanding that they must be infused, or grace in any other form; they are "among the most worthy virtues to which Christians could hope to aspire" (160–61).[12] The virtues more generally he considers to be habits that "should be cultivated in order to pursue a happy life, a fulfilled and fulfilling life" (163). Only later does he consider these virtues as related to the very character of God, when he states, "Christians understand the virtues to be those dispositions that *God has by nature*, and in which

---

10. In Part I (based on that part of the Eucharistic service which includes the confession of sins and the pronouncement of God's forgiveness) there are surprisingly few and brief passages relating to sin, forgiveness or grace.

11. It is worth noting that Bonhoeffer's focus on the reality of the reconciliation of all things to God in Christ is a natural link to ethical consideration of how the rest of creation is to be treated. Since consideration of ecological concerns often feels like an optional extra, this could be an important corrective of a different kind.

12. However, he rectifies this, 170–71.

Conclusion

human beings *can participate by grace*" (167, his emphases). Yet here again he moves quickly to the element of human reception and participation: "people can allow the virtues to be cultivated in their lives and, thereby, to form their moral outlook. In doing so, they allow God to bring their own lives into alignment with the divine character" (167). In a later passage he again moves swiftly from God's work in us to human participation: "In other words, although Christians believe God is the supreme cultivator of the virtues in human lives, they also recognize that they are capable (nevertheless) of resisting God's work" (170). Similarly, in speaking of the redemption, Cunningham subtly emphasizes the person of Christ and our imitation of him over the work of Christ (177). These comments are not intended to detract from his overall account, but simply to underscore that Cunningham does not emphasize the role of grace, nor the relationship between the doctrines of justification and sanctification. Such a construal could perhaps fit on the half of the stage decorated for post-Tridentine Catholic theology, and elicit similar complaints from the opposite side.

In Bonhoeffer's conception, however, the reader is constantly reminded both of her need for grace, and of God's action for her and on her behalf. The notion that Christ himself wins form in the believer is a sharp corrective to a virtue ethics that underplays the role of grace. The Christian is conformed to Christ by Christ, not by her imitation of him. Christ wins form in her. Nonetheless, Bonhoeffer never succumbs to a "cheap grace" that makes no demands of the believer; strong challenges to holy living are enunciated.

7.2.2: *Virtue Ethics and Eudaemonism*

The second aspect of Bonhoeffer's account that may be of benefit (especially for Protestants) is the articulation of virtue ethics not in a framework that is focused on what it means for human beings to flourish but rather within the context of asking how we participate in the reality that Christ has reconciled all things to God. Oliver O'Donovan rightly points out the potentially problematic aspect of eudaemonism's accent on self-love.[13] Yet he is also surely correct in pointing out the need for distinguishing between moral theology and "epistemological efficiency," for, as he says, it is not the case that we could discover "the whole of our Christian duty by consulting our self-interest, even though the whole of our Christian

---

13. O'Donovan, *Self-Love*. One could interpret Cunningham as succumbing to this; see, e.g., his account of sin as not advantageous, 77.

duty does serve our self-interest."[14] Irrespective of this defense, a Christian virtue ethic that is not set in a eudaemonist framework but rather one that focuses on the cosmic reality of the reconciliation of all things to God in Christ would avoid the potentially problematic aspect of focusing on human happiness, and simultaneously obviate the need for separating moral theology from epistemological efficiency. Bonhoeffer's focus on participation in this reality could be said to show the Christian both what is required of her (living in a way that shows her reconciliation to God through being conformed to Christ) and that the starting point of ethics is in God's action rather than human happiness. Moving from an overarching concern with what constitutes human flourishing to what is this broad conception of reality places Christian revelation at the outset of ethical discourse, which is perhaps an important change if virtue ethics is to be seen as a compelling form of moral theology in at least some quarters.[15]

7.2.3: *The Role of Virtue*

However, even though O'Donovan was happy to defend Augustine's use of eudaemonism (despite its taint of self-love), it is clear from his later *Resurrection and Moral Order* that he has other deep reservations about virtue ethics.[16] O'Donovan claims that attention to character can only be of use in evaluating a proposed or completed act from the position of the observer; the agent's awareness of her own character cannot helpfully enter into her deliberations of what she should do (chapter 10). In this discussion he rejects the common virtue-ethical question of what, say, the courageous, or compassionate thing to do would be as inappropriately prejudging which virtue is most required in the situation, and unduly limiting the range of choices the agent may make (216). Since this is not a mode of discernment Bonhoeffer employs, his account may appeal to O'Donovan more than some.[17]

14. O'Donovan, *Self-Love*, 157.

15. See O'Donovan's argument with Karl Holl and A. Nygren, *Self-Love*, 141–42, 144–45.

16. The first he voices relates to the role of grace, which has already been discussed. See O'Donovan, *Resurrection*, 17–18, where he speaks of a kind of Pelagianism in Maximus's account, and 89. Further references appear in brackets in the main text.

17. I do not, however, think O'Donovan is necessarily right. Hauerwas's view that the virtuous agent *appropriately* limits her range of possibilities by not considering certain options strikes me as having great merit, "Toward an Ethics of Character," 56. Similarly, Thomas's treatment of (infused) prudence enabling the person to perceive

Conclusion

Another possible form of virtue-ethical deliberation is also excluded in O'Donovan's treatment, namely attention to motivation and intention (215).[18] While he may well be right that motives are more useful in a third-person evaluation than the agent's own deliberations, it seems to me that he misses another facet of how intentions inform considerations of what should be done. For intentions may express the goal the agent hopes to achieve through her actions, and the deliberations may be those of practical reasoning to determine the best method of achieving it. However, when Bonhoeffer focuses on intentions or motivations, it is in the context of evaluating proposed actions, so it may again be that his form of virtue may overcome some of O'Donovan's concerns.

Yet more important than this omission in considering the ways in which virtue ethics may be involved in the agent's deliberations are two other prime ways that O'Donovan does not discuss. The first is the way in which all aspects of the person's life are necessarily shaped by who she is. Thus a Christian, being formed more and more in the likeness of Christ will be shaped not only in the plethora of activities she undertakes but also in her thoughts, plans, hopes, and goals, and may or may not even be aware of how she has been formed and shaped. This is not a matter of her reflection on her character, or her choice to create or perpetuate a certain character, both of which possibilities O'Donovan rightly rejects (213–15), as does Bonhoeffer (*DBW* 6:81). This is simply a fact that who a person is will determine, at least in part, how she perceives a situation, which possible courses of action spring to her mind, and which she will consider to be best. Bonhoeffer speaks of this in terms of simplicity, which is given by God, and in terms of how Christ wins form in the believer.

The second way in which virtue ethics may naturally inform ethical decision-making is through reference to a virtuous person, asking what a virtuous person would do in this situation. For many agents this need not take the form of conscious consideration. Instead it may be that admiration and desire to be like a particular virtuous person affects a person's choices and actions without reflection at the time. I could imagine that if O'Donovan had considered such a possibility it is one he might have rejected also as inappropriately limiting the agent's range of choices. And if the reference is to a virtuous person (who despite all virtues is necessarily still sinful and not perfect in her virtue), such an objection may be correct.

---

the situation aright is important (*ST* I-II.57.5, 6), and O'Donovan does not mention this.

18. He speaks of "intention," though it is clear from his discussion that he means this in terms of "motivation" rather than a goal the agent hopes to achieve.

However, Bonhoeffer's way of using this mode of virtue-ethical consideration is to speak of Jesus himself as the example of simplicity, responsible action, representation, and so on. Although he does not advocate a facile attempt to know what Jesus would do, which of course is fraught with dangers, it is clear that Jesus Christ is the person to whom the believer looks to know what it means to live in obedience to God's will and in the freedom of acting in simplicity.

In both these ways, Bonhoeffer's use of virtue-ethical motifs may counter O'Donovan's statement that notions of character can only inform the evaluation of an act, but not the decision of how to act. Nevertheless, it is clear in some passages that Bonhoeffer is happy to accord to virtue an instrumental role (simplicity enables the believer to discern the will of God), and this may also be helpful.

Thus, I think it is right to say that reading Bonhoeffer's *Ethics* in the light of his distinctive combination of virtue and command in service of the reality that all things have been reconciled to God in Christ would be helpful in our current debates. This is so in at least three ways. First, his emphasis on grace shows that a focus on virtue-ethical concerns need not have a Pelagian feel. Secondly, attending to virtue (and command) without a eudaemonistic framework avoids the possibility of seeing virtue ethics as a form of (problematic) self-love. Thirdly, and finally, the variety of ways in which he uses virtue-ethical argumentation may enable the role of virtue within Christian ethics more generally to be reviewed.

> Following the coming of Christ, ethics can only be concerned with one thing, namely with receiving a share of the reality of the fulfilled will of God. However, even this receiving a share is only possible on the basis of the fact that I myself also am already included in the fulfillment of the will of God in Christ, and that means [that I] am reconciled with God. The question of the will of God does not ask about what is concealed, unfulfilled, but rather about what is revealed, fulfilled. It remains, however, nonetheless a real question, in that I myself, and the world around me, am placed in this question through the revelation, through the fulfillment. (*DBW* 6:61)

Bibliography

Althaus, Paul. *The Theology of Martin Luther*. Translated by Robert C. Schultz. Philadelphia: Fortress, 1966.

Anscombe, G. E. M. "Practical Inference." In *Virtues and Reasons: Philippa Foot and Moral Theology*, edited by Rosalind Hursthouse et al., 1–34. Oxford: Clarendon, 1995.

Aristotle. *Nicomachean Ethics*. Translated by Sarah Broadie and Christopher Rowe. Oxford: Oxford University Press, 2002.

Auden, W. H. "Friday's Child: in memory of Dietrich Bonhoeffer . . ." In *Collected Poems*, edited by Edward Mendelson, 675–77. London: Faber & Faber, 1976.

Augustine, St. *The Catholic and Manichaean Ways of Life (de moribus ecclesiae catholicae et de moribus manichaeorum)*. Translated by Donald A. Gallagher and Idella J. Gallagher. Washington, DC: The Catholic University of America Press, 1966.

Barth, Karl. *Church Dogmatics II/2: The Doctrine of God*. Edited and translated by G. W. Bromiley. Edinburgh: T. & T. Clark, 1957.

———. *Church Dogmatics III/4: The Doctrine of Creation*. Translated by A. T. Mackay et al. Edited by G. W. Bromiley and T. F. Torrance. Edinburgh: T. & T. Clark, 1961.

———. *Church Dogmatics IV/2: The Doctrine of Reconciliation*. Edited by G. W. Bromiley and T. F. Torrance. Translated by G. W. Bromiley. Edinburgh: T. & T. Clark, 1958.

———. *Die kirchliche Dogmatik II/2: Die Lehre von Gott*. Zurich: Evangelischer, 1959.

———. *Die kirchliche Dogmatik IV:2: Die Lehre von der Versöhnung*. Zurich: Evangelischer, 1964.

———. Letter to Landessuperintendent P. W. Herrenbrück, December 21, 1952. Reprinted in *World Come of Age: A Symposium on Dietrich Bonhoeffer*, edited by Ronald Gregor Smith, 89–90. London: Collins, 1967.

———. "Nein! Antwort an Emil Brunner." *Theologische Existenz heute* 14 (1934).

———. *On Religion: The Revelation of God as the Sublimation of Religion*. Translated by Garrett Green. Edinburgh and New York: T. & T. Clark, 2006.

Bell, Richard H., editor. *The Grammar of the Heart: New Essays in Moral Philosophy and Theology*. San Francisco: Harper & Row, 1988.

Berkhouwer, G. C. *Faith and Justification*. Translated by Lewis B. Smedes. Grand Rapids: Eerdmans, 1954.

Berryhill, Elizabeth. "The Cup of Trembling. A Play in Two Acts." Greenwich, CT: 1958.

Bethge, Eberhard. "The Challenge of Dietrich Bonhoeffer's Life and Theology." In *World Come of Age: A Symposium on Dietrich Bonhoeffer*, edited by Ronald Gregor Smith, 22–88. London: Collins, 1967.

———. *Dietrich Bonhoeffer: A Biography*. Rev. ed. Translated by Eric Mosbacher et al. Edited by Victoria J. Barnett. Minneapolis: Fortress, 2000.

Bibliography

Bethge, Renate. "Bonhoeffer and the Role of Women." In *Reflections on Bonhoeffer: Essays in Honor of F. Burton Nelson*, edited by Geffrey B. Kelly and C. John Weborg, 169–84. Chicago: Covenant, 1999.

———. "Bonhoeffer's Family and its Significance for his Theology." In *Dietrich Bonhoeffer: His Significance for North Americans*, by Larry Rasmussen with Renate Bethge, chapter 1. Minneapolis: Fortress, 1990.

———. "Bonhoeffer's Picture of Women." In *Bonhoeffer's Ethics: Old Europe and New Frontiers*, edited by Guy Carter et al., 194–99. Kampen, The Netherlands: Kok Pharos, 1991.

———. "Memories of a Child." In Edwin Robertson, *The Shame and the Sacrifice: The Life and Martyrdom of Dietrich Bonhoeffer*, 11–18. New York: MacMillan, 1988.

Betzler, Monika, editor. *Kant's Ethics of Virtue*. Berlin/New York: Walter de Gruyter, 2008.

Biggar, Nigel. "A Case for Casuistry in the Church." *Modern Theology* 6 (1989) 29–51.

———. *The Hastening that Waits: Karl Barth's Ethics*. Oxford: Clarendon, 1993.

Biggar, Nigel, and Rufus Black, editors. *The Revival of Natural Law: Philosophical, Theological and Ethical Responses to the Finnis-Grisez School*. Aldershot: Ashgate, 2000.

Bismark, Ruth-Alice von, and Ulrich Kabitz, editors. *Love Letters from Cell 92: The Correspondence between Dietrich Bonhoeffer and Maria von Wedemeyer 1943–45*. Translated by John Brownjohn. Nashville: Abingdon, 1995.

Black, Rufus. *Christian Moral Realism: Natural Law, Narrative, Virtue, and the Gospel*. Oxford: Oxford University Press, 2000.

Blum, Laurence. "Community and Virtue." In *How Should One Live?: Essays on the Virtues*, edited by Roger Crisp, 231–50. Oxford: Clarendon, 1996

Bonhoeffer, Dietrich. *Dietrich Bonhoeffer Werke 1: Sanctorum Communio*. Edited by Joachim von Soosten. Munich: Kaiser, 1986.

———. *Dietrich Bonhoeffer Werke 2: Akt und Sein*. Edited by Hans-Richard Reuter. Munich: Kaiser, 1988.

———. *Dietrich Bonhoeffer Werke 3: Schöpfung und Fall*. Edited by Martin Rüter and Ilse Tödt. Munich: Kaiser, 1989.

———. *Dietrich Bonhoeffer Werke 4: Nachfolge*. Edited by Martin Kuske and Ilse Tödt. Munich: Kaiser, 1994.

———. *Dietrich Bonhoeffer Werke 5: Gemeinsames Leben/Gebetbuch der Bibel*. Edited by Eberhard Bethge et al. Munich: Kaiser, 1987.

———. *Dietrich Bonhoeffer Werke 6: Ethik*. Edited by Ilse Tödt et al. Munich: Kaiser, 1998.

———. *Dietrich Bonhoeffer Werke 7: Fragmente aus Tegel*. Edited by Renate Bethge and Ilse Tödt. Munich: Kaiser, 1994.

———. *Dietrich Bonhoeffer Werke 8: Widerstand und Ergebung*. Edited by Christian Gremmels et al. Munich: Kaiser, 1998.

———. *Dietrich Bonhoeffer Werke 10: Barcelona, Berlin, Amerika 1928–1931*. Edited by Reinhart Staats et al. Munich: Kaiser, 1991.

———. *Dietrich Bonhoeffer Werke 11: Ökumene, Universität, Pfarramt 1931–1932*. Edited by Eberhard Amelung and Christoph Strom. Munich: Kaiser, 1994.

———. *Dietrich Bonhoeffer Werke 12: Berlin 1932–1933*. Edited by Carsten Nicolaisen and Ernst-Albert Scharffenorth. Munich: Kaiser, 1997.

———. *Dietrich Bonhoeffer Werke 14: Theologenausbildung: Finkenwalde 1935–1937*. Edited by Otto Dudzus et al. Munich: Kaiser, 1996.

———. *Dietrich Bonhoeffer Werke 16: Konspiration und Haft 1940–1945*. Edited by Jørgen Glenthøj et al. Munich: Kaiser, 1996.

———. *Dietrich Bonhoeffer Works English 6: Ethics*. Edited by Clifford J. Green. Translated by Reinhard Krauss et al. Minneapolis: Fortress, 2005.

Bonhoeffer, Karl. "Lebenserinnerungen." In *Karl Bonhoeffer zum hundertsten Geburtstag am 31. März 1968*, 8–114. Berlin/Heidelberg/NY, 1969.

Boyle, Leonard E. "The Setting of the *Summa Theologiae* of St. Thomas—Revisited." In *The Ethics of Aquinas*, edited by Stephen J. Pope, 1–16. Washington, DC: Georgetown University Press, 2002.

Braaten, Carl E., and Robert W. Jenson, editors. *Union with Christ: The New Finnish Interpretation of Luther*. Grand Rapids: Eerdmans, 1998.

Brock, Brian. "Bonhoeffer and the Bible in Christian Ethics: Psalm 119, The Mandates, and Ethics as a 'Way.'" *Studies in Christian Ethics* 18.3 (2005) 7–29.

Burnaby, John. *Amor Dei: A Study of the Religion of St. Augustine*. The Hulsean Lectures for 1938. Norwich: Canterbury, 1938, reprinted 1991.

Burtness, James. *Shaping the Future: The Ethics of Dietrich Bonhoeffer*. Minneapolis: Fortress, 1985

Busch, Eberhard. *Karl Barth: His Life from Letters and Autobiographical Texts*. Translated by John Bowden. Philadelphia: Fortress, 1976.

Calvin, John. *Institutes of Christian Religion*. Translated by L. Jenkins. Philadelphia: Westminster, 1960.

Carney, Frederick S. "Deciding in the Situation: What is Required?" In *Norm and Context in Christian Ethics*, edited by Gene H. Outka and Paul Ramsey, 3–16. London: SCM, 1968.

Carter, Guy, et al., editors. *Bonhoffer's Ethics: Old Europe and New Frontiers*. Kampen, The Netherlands: Kok Pharos, 1991.

Cavanaugh, William T. "A Joint Declaration? Justification and Theosis in Aquinas and Luther." *Heythrop Journal* 41 (2000) 265–80.

Cessario, Romanus, OP. *The Moral Virtues and Theological Ethics*. 2nd ed. Notre Dame: University of Notre Dame Press, 2009.

Clements, Keith. "Bonhoeffer and the British." *Epworth Review* 33.4 (2006) 23–38.

Coleman, Janet. "MacIntyre and Aquinas." In *After MacIntyre: Critical Perspectives on the Work of Alasdair MacIntyre*, edited by John Horton and Susan Mendus, 65–90. Oxford: Polity, 1994.

Cottingham, John. "Partiality and the Virtues." In *How Should One Live?: Essays on the Virtues*, edited by Roger Crisp, 57–76. Oxford: Clarendon, 1996.

Crisp, Roger, editor. *How Should One Live?: Essays on the Virtues*. Oxford: Clarendon, 1996.

———. "Modern Moral Philosophy and the Virtues." In *How Should One Live? Essays on the Virtues*, edited by Roger Crisp, 1–18. Oxford: Clarendon, 1996.

Crisp, Roger, and Michael Slote, editors. *Virtue Ethics*. Oxford Readings in Philosophy. Oxford: Oxford University Press, 1997.

Cunliffe-Jones, Hubert, editor, with Benjamin Drewery. *A History of Christian Doctrine*. Edinburgh: T. & T. Clark, 1978.

Cunningham, David S. *Christian Ethics: The End of the Law*. London and New York: Routledge, 2008.

Cunningham, Robert L. *Situationism and the New Morality*. New York: Appleton-Century-Crofts, 1970.

Bibliography

Davis, Ellen F. "Preserving Virtues: Renewing the Tradition." *Studies in Christian Ethics* 14.2 (2001) 14–22.

Drewery, Benjamin. "The Council of Trent." In *A History of Christian Doctrine*, edited by Hubert Cunliffe-Jones with Benjamin Drewery, 401–9. Edinburgh: T. & T. Clark, 1978.

———. "Martin Luther." In *A History of Christian Doctrine*, edited by Hubert Cunliffe-Jones with Benjamin Drewery, 311–50. Edinburgh: T. & T. Clark, 1978.

Duchrow, Ulrich. "Dem Rad in die Speichen fallen—aber wo und wie?: Luthers und Bonhoeffers Ethik der Institutionen im Kontext des heutigen Weltwirtschaftssystems." In *Bonhoeffer und Luther: zur Sozialgestalt des Luthertums in der Moderne*, edited by Christian Gremmels, 16–58. Munich: Kaiser, 1983.

Dumas, André. *Dietrich Bonhoeffer: Theologian of Reality*. Translated by Robert McAfee Brown. London: SCM, 1971.

Dunn, James D. G., editor. *The Cambridge Companion to St Paul*. Cambridge: Cambridge University Press, 2003.

Ebeling, Gerhard. *Word and Faith*. Translated by James W. Leitch. London: SCM, 1963.

Elstain, Jean Bethke. "Freedom and Responsibility in a World Come of Age." In *Theology and the Practice of Responsibility: Essays on Dietrich Bonhoeffer*, edited by Wayne Whitson Floyd Jr. and Charles Marsh, 269–81. Valley Forge: Trinity, 1994.

Feil, Ernst. "Aspekte der Bonhoefferinterpretation." *Theologische Literaturzeitung* 117 (1992) 1–15; 81–99.

———. "Bonhoeffer und die Zukunft der philosophischen Theologie." *Neue Zeitschrift für Systematische Theologie und Religionsphilosophie* 35 (1993) 150–75.

———. "Gottes Wort ist konkret." *Renovatio* 52 (1996) 89–100.

———. "Standpunkte der Bonhoeffer-Interpretation." *Theologische Revue* 64 (1968) 1–14.

———. *The Theology of Dietrich Bonhoeffer*. Translated by Martin Rumscheidt. Philadelphia: Fortress, 1985.

———, editor. *Verspieltes Erbe?: Dietrich Bonhoeffer und der deutsche Nachkriegsprotestantismus*. Internationales Bonhoeffer-Forum: Forschung und Praxis 2. Munich: Kaiser, 1979.

Feil, Ernst, editor, with Barbara E. Fink. *Internationale Bibliographie zu Dietrich Bonhoeffer*. Gütersloh: Kaiser, 1998.

Fergusson, David. "Reclaiming the Doctrine of Sanctification." *Interpretation: A Journal of Bible and Theology* 53.4 (October 1999) 380–90.

Figur, Fritz. In *I Knew Dietrich Bonhoeffer*, edited by Wolf-Dieter Zimmermann and Ronald Gregor Smith, translated by Käthe Gregor Smith, 56. London: Collins, 1966.

Fletcher, Joseph Francis. *Situation Ethics: The New Morality*. London: SCM, 1966.

Floyd, Wayne. "Encounter with an Other: Immanuel Kant and G. W. F. Hegel in the Theology of Dietrich Bonhoeffer." In *Bonhoeffer's Intellectual Formation: Theology and Philosophy in His Thought*, edited by Peter Frick, 83–119. Tübingen: Mohr Siebeck, 2008.

Floyd, Wayne Whitson Jr., and Charles Marsh, editors. *Theology and the Practice of Responsibility: Essays on Dietrich Bonhoeffer*. Valley Forge: Trinity, 1994.

Foot, Philippa. *Virtues and Vices and other Essays in Moral Philosophy*. Oxford: Basil Blackwell, 1978.

Ford, David F. *Self and Salvation: Being Transformed*. Cambridge Studies in Christian Doctrine. Cambridge: Cambridge University Press, 1999.

Frick, Peter, editor. *Bonhoeffer's Intellectual Formation: Theology and Philosophy in his Thought.* Tübingen: Mohr Siebeck, 2008.

———. "The *Imitatio Christi* of Thomas à Kempis and Dietrich Bonhoeffer." In *Bonhoeffer's Intellectual Formation: Theology and Philosophy in his Thought*, edited by Peter Frick, 31–52. Tübingen: Mohr Siebeck, 2008.

Geach, Peter. *The Virtues.* Cambridge: Cambridge University Press, 1977.

Gill, Robin, editor. *The Cambridge Companion to Christian Ethics.* Cambridge: Cambridge University Press, 2001.

Glazener, Mary. *The Cup of Wrath: The Story of Dietrich Bonhoeffer's Resistance to Hitler.* Macon, GA: Smith & Helwys, 1994; first printing, Savannah: Frederic C. Beil, 1992.

Godsey, John D. "Barth and Bonhoeffer: The Basic Difference." *Quarterly Review* 7 (1987) 9–27.

———. "Reading Bonhoeffer in English Translation." *Union Seminary Quarterly Review* 23.1 (1967) 79–90.

———. *The Theology of Dietrich Bonhoeffer.* London: SCM, 1960.

Godsey, John D., and Geffrey B. Kelly, editors. *Ethical Responsibility: Bonhoeffer's Legacy to the Churches.* New York: Edwin Mellen, 1981.

Grabill, Stephen J. *Rediscovering the Natural Law in Reformed Theological Ethics.* Grand Rapids: Eerdmans, 2006.

Green, Clifford J. *Bonhoeffer: A Theology of Sociality.* Rev. ed. Grand Rapids: Eerdmans, 1999.

———. "Recent Works about Bonhoeffer in English." *Religious Studies Review* 23 (1997) 226–30.

———. "The Text of Bonhoeffer's Ethics." In *New Studies in Bonhoeffer's Ethics*, edited by William J. Peck, 3–65. Lewiston/Queenston: Edwin Mellen, 1987.

Gregor Smith, R., editor. *World Come of Age: A Symposium on Dietrich Bonhoeffer.* London: Collins, 1967.

Gremmels, Christian, editor. *Bonhoeffer und Luther: Zur Sozialgestalt des Luthertums in der Moderne.* Munich: Kaiser, 1983.

———. "Bonhoeffer und Luther." In *Bonhoeffer und Luther: Zur Sozialgestalt des Luthertums in der Moderne*, edited by Christian Gremmels, 9–15. Munich: Kaiser, 1983.

———. "Rechtfertigung und Nachfolge: Martin Luther in Dietrich Bonhoeffers Buch 'Nachfolge.'" In *Dietrich Bonhoeffer heute: Die Aktualität seines Lebens und Werkes*, edited by Rainer Mayer and Peter Zimmerling, 81–99. Giessen/Basel: Brunnen, 1993.

Gremmels, Christian and Hans Pfeifer. *Theologie und Biographie: Zum Beispiel Dietrich Bonhoeffer.* Munich: Kaiser, 1983.

Greschat, Martin, editor. *Theologen des Protestantismus in 19. und 20. Jahrhundert I.* Stuttgart, Berlin, Cologne, Mainz: Kohlhammer, 1978.

Gruchy, John W. de, editor. *The Cambridge Companion to Dietrich Bonhoeffer.* Cambridge: Cambridge University Press, 1999.

Gustafson, James M. *Protestant and Roman Catholic Ethics.* Chicago: University of Chicago Press, 1978.

Haldane, John. "MacIntyre's Thomist Revival: What Next?" In *After MacIntyre: Critical Perspectives on the Work of Alasdair MacIntyre*, edited by John Horton and Susan Mendus, 91–107. Oxford: Polity, 1994.

Bibliography

Harnack, Adolf von. *Das Wesen des Christentums: Sechzehn Vorlesungen vor Studierenden aller Fakultäten im Wintersemester 1899-1900 an der Universität Berlin*. Leipzig: J. C. Hinrichs'sche Buchhandlung. 1927.

Harrison, Carol. *Augustine: Christian Truth and Fractured Humanity*. Oxford: Oxford University Press, 2000.

———. *Rethinking Augustine's Early Theology: An Argument for Continuity*. Oxford: Oxford University Press, 2006.

Harvey, Barry. "Augustine and Thomas Aquinas in the Theology of Dietrich Bonhoeffer." In *Bonhoeffer's Intellectual Formation: Theology and Philosophy in His Thought*, edited by Peter Frick, 11-29. Tübingen: Mohr Siebeck, 2008.

Hauerwas, Stanley. *A Community of Character: Toward a Constructive Christian Social Ethic*. Notre Dame: University of Notre Dame Press, 1981.

———. *Character and the Christian Life: A Study in Theological Ethics*. 2nd ed. Notre Dame; London: University of Notre Dame Press, 1986.

———. "'The Friend': Reflections on Friendship and Freedom." In *Who Am I?: Bonhoeffer's Theology through his Poetry*, edited by Bernd Wannenwetsch, 91-113. London and New York: T. & T. Clark, 2009.

———. *Performing the Faith: Bonhoeffer and the Practice of Nonviolence*. Grand Rapids: Brazos, 2004.

———. "Toward an Ethics of Character." In *Vision and Virtue: Essays in Christian Ethical Reflection*, 48-67. Notre Dame: University of Notre Dame Press, 1981.

———. *Vision and Virtue: Essays in Christian Ethical Reflection*. Notre Dame: University of Notre Dame Press, 1981.

———. *With the Grain of the Universe: The Church's Witness and Natural Theology*. The Gifford Lectures 2001. London: SCM, 2002.

Hauerwas, Stanley, and Alasdair MacIntyre, editors. *Revisions: Changing Perspectives in Moral Philosophy*. Notre Dame; London: University of Notre Dame Press, 1983.

Haynes, Stephen R. *The Bonhoeffer Phenomenon: Portraits of a Protestant Saint*. Minneapolis: Fortress, 2004.

Helm, Paul, editor. *Divine Commands and Morality*. Oxford Readings in Philosophy. Oxford: Oxford University Press, 1981.

Holl, Karl. *Gesammelte Aufsätze zur Kirchengeschichte vol. 1: Luther*. Tübingen: Mohr/Siebeck, 1932.

The Holy Bible (New Revised Standard Version, Anglicized Edition). Oxford: Oxford University Press, 1995.

Honecker, Martin. "Theologische Ethik in einer säkularisierten Gesellschaft." *Zeitschrift für Theologie und Kirche* 98 (2001) 231-46.

Hoogstraten, Hans D. van. "Ethics and the Problem of Metaphysics." In *Theology and the Practice of Responsibility: Essays on Dietrich Bonhoeffer*, edited by Wayne Whitson Floyd, Jr. and Charles Marsh, 223-37. Valley Ford: Trinity, 1994.

Horton, John, and Susan Mendus, editors. *After MacIntyre: Critical Perspectives on the Work of Alasdair MacIntyre*. Cambridge: Polity, 1994.

Huber, Wolfgang, and Ilse Tödt, editors. *Ethik im Ernstfall: Dietrich Bonhoeffers Stellung zu den Juden und ihre Aktualität*. Internationales Bonhoeffer Forum: Forschung und Praxis 4. Munich: Kaiser, 1982.

Hursthouse, Rosalind, et al., editors. *Virtues and Reasons: Philippa Foot and Moral Theology*. Oxford: Clarendon, 1995.

Hursthouse, Rosalind. "Applying Virtue Ethics." In *Virtues and Reasons: Philippa Foot and Moral Theology*, edited by Rosalind Hursthouse et al., 57-75. Oxford: Clarendon, 1995.

———. "Normative Virtue Ethics." In *How Should One Live?: Essays on the Virtues*, edited by Roger Crisp, 19-36. Oxford: Clarendon, 1996

Innes, Robert "Integrating the Self through the Desire of God." *Augustinian Studies* 28.1 (1997) 67-109.

Jacobi, Gerhard. In *I Knew Dietrich Bonhoeffer*, edited by Wolf-Dieter Zimmermann and Ronald Gregor Smith, and translated by Käthe Gregor Smith, 72. London: Collins, 1966.

Jones, L. Gregory. "The Cost of Forgiveness: Grace, Christian Community and the Politics of Worldly Discipleship." In *Theology and the Practice of Responsibility: Essays on Dietrich Bonhoeffer*, edited by Wayne Whitson Floyd, Jr. and Charles Marsh, 149-69. Valley Forge: Trinity, 1994.

Jonsen, Albert R., and Stephen Toulmin. *The Abuse of Casuistry: A History of Moral Reasoning*. Berkeley: University of California Press, 1988.

Kärkkäinen, Veli-Matti. *One with God: Salvation as Deification and Justification*. Collegeville: Liturgical, 2004.

Kelly, Geffrey B., and C. John Weborg, editors. *Reflections on Bonhoeffer: Essays in Honor of F. Burton Nelson*. Chicago: Publications, 1999.

Kelly, Geffrey B., and F. Burton Nelson. *The Cost of Moral Leadership: The Spirituality of Dietrich Bonhoeffer*. Grand Rapids: Eerdmans, 2003.

Kent, Bonnie. "Augustine's Ethics." In *The Cambridge Companion to Augustine*, edited by Eleonore Stump and Norman Kretzman, 205-33. Cambridge: Cambridge University Press, 2001.

———. "Habits and Vices (Ia IIae, qq. 49-70)." In *The Ethics of Aquinas*, edited by Stephen J. Pope, 116-30. Washington, DC: Georgetown University Press, 2002.

Kerr, Fergus. *After Aquinas: Versions of Thomism*. Oxford: Blackwell, 2002.

Klassen, A. J., editor. *A Bonhoeffer Legacy*. Grand Rapids: Eerdmans, 1981.

Köster, Peter. "Nietzsche als verborgener Antipode in Bonhoeffers 'Ethik.'" *Nietzsche-Studien: Internationales Jahrbuch für die Nietzsche-Forschung* 19 (1990) 367-418.

Kotva, Joseph J. *The Christian Case for Virtue Ethics*. Washington, DC: Georgetown University Press, 1997.

Kuntz, Paul G. "The I-Thou Relation and Aretaic Divine Command Ethics: Augustine's Study of Virtues and Vices in the Confessions." *Augustinian Studies* 16 (1985) 107-27.

Lane, Anthony N. S. *Justification by Faith in Catholic—Protestant Dialogue: An Evangelical Assessment*. London: Continuum, 2006.

Langan, John P., SJ. "Augustine on the Unity and the Interconnection of the Virtues." *Harvard Theological Review* 72 (1979) 81-95.

Lange, Frits de. *Waiting for the Word: Dietrich Bonhoeffer on Speaking about God*. Translated by Martin N. Walton. Grand Rapids: Eerdmans, 2000.

Lehmann, Paul. "Bonhoeffer: Real and Counterfeit." *Union Seminary Quarterly Review* 21.3 (1966) 364-69.

Lehmkühler, Karsten. "Evangelische Ethik und Einwohnung Christi." In *Festhalten am Bekenntnis der Hoffnung*, edited by Christian Herrman and Eberhard Hahn, 317-32. Erlangen: Martin Luther, 2001.

Bibliography

Leibholz-Bonhoeffer, Sabine. *The Bonhoeffers: Portrait of a Family.* London/NY: Covenant, 1971.

———. *Weihnachten im Hause Bonhoeffer.* Wuppertal/Barmen, 1971; Gütersloh 1996.

Lockley, Harold. *Dietrich Bonhoeffer: His Ethics and its Value for Christian Ethics Today.* Swansea: Phoenix, 1993.

Lovin, Robin. "The Biographical Context." In *Bonhoeffer's Ethics: Old Europe and New Frontiers,* edited by Guy Carter et al., 45. Kampen, The Netherlands: Kok Pharos, 1991.

Luther, Martin. *Kritische Ausgabe, Weimar,* 1883ff.

———. "Preface to the Commentary on Romans." (1546/1552), *Luther's Works, vol. 25: Lectures on Romans, Glosses and Scholia.* Edited by Hilton C. Oswald. Translated by Walter G. Tillmanns and Jacob A.O. Preus. St Louis: Concordia, 1972.

———. "Preface to the Epistle of St Paul to the Romans." *Luther's Works vol. 35: Word and Sacrament I.* Edited by E. Theodore Bachman. Translated by Charles M. Jacobs. Philadelphia: Fortress, 1960.

Lutheran World Federation and the Catholic Church. *Joint Declaration on the Doctrine of Justification.* Grand Rapids: Eerdmans, 2000.

MacIntyre, Alasdair. *After Virtue: A Study in Moral Theory.* 2nd ed. London: Duckworth, 1985.

———. "A Partial Response to My Critics." In *After MacIntyre: Critical Perspectives on the Work of Alasdair MacIntyre,* edited by John Horton and Susan Mendus, 283-304. Oxford: Polity, 1994.

———. *Three Rival Versions of Moral Enquiry: Encyclopaedia, Genealogy, and Tradition.* London: Duckworth, 1990

———. *Whose Justice? Which Rationality?* London: Duckworth, 1988.

McClendon, James William, Jr. "Dietrich Bonhoeffer." In *Systematic Theology: Ethics,* 187-208. Nashville: Abingdon, 1986.

Mangina, Joseph L. *Karl Barth on the Christian Life: The Practical Knowledge of God.* New York: Peter Lang, 2001.

Markus, R. A. "Augustine. Human Action: Will and Virtue." In *A Cambridge History of Later Greek and Early Medieval Philosophy,* edited by H. Armstrong, 380-94. Cambridge: Cambridge University Press, 1970.

Marsh, Charles. *Reclaiming Dietrich Bonhoeffer: The Promise of His Theology.* New York: Oxford University Press, 1994.

Marshall, Bruce. "Justification as Deification and Declaration." *International Journal of Systematic Theology* 4.1 (2002) 1-17.

Mayer, Rainer, and Peter Zimmerling, editors. *Dietrich Bonhoeffer heute: Die Aktualität seines Lebens und Werkes.* Giessen/Basel: Brunnen, 1993.

Meilaender, Gilbert C. *The Theory and Practice of Virtue.* Notre Dame: University of Notre Dame Press, 1984.

Miller, David. "Virtues, Practices and Justice." In *After MacIntyre: Critical Perspectives on the Work of Alasdair MacIntyre,* edited by John Horton and Susan Mendus, 245-64. Oxford: Polity, 1994.

Moberly, Jennifer. "'Felicity to the Original Text'? The Translation of Bonhoeffer's Ethics, Dietrich Bonhoeffer Works, Volume 6." *Studies in Christian Ethics* 22.3 (August 2009) 336-56.

Mokrosch, Reinhold. "Das Gewissensverständnis Dietrich Bonhoeffers: Reformatorische Herkunft und politische Funktion." In *Bonhoeffer und Luther: zur Sozialgestalt des Luthertums in der Moderne*, edited by Christian Gremmels, 59–92. Munich: Kaiser, 1983.

Morgan, Robert. "Paul's Enduring Legacy." In *The Cambridge Companion to St Paul*, edited by James D. G. Dunn, 242–55. Cambridge: Cambridge University Press, 2003.

Muller, Denis G. "Bonhoeffer's Ethic of Responsibility and its Meaning for Today." *Theology* 100 (1997) 108–17.

Müller, Hanfried. *Von der Kirche zur Welt: Ein Beitrag zu der Beziehung des Wort Gottes auf die societas in Dietrich Bonhoeffers theologischer Entwicklung*. Hamburg: Herbert Reich Evangelischer Verlag, 1966.

Murdoch, Iris. "On 'God' and 'Good.'" Reprinted in *Revisions: Changing Perspectives in Moral Philosophy*, edited by Stanley Hauerwas and Alasdair MacIntyre, 68–91. Notre Dame; London: University of Notre Dame Press, 1983.

Nickson, Ann L. *Bonhoeffer on Freedom: Courageously Grasping Reality*. Aldershot and Berlington, VT: Ashgate, 2002.

Niesel, Wilhelm. In *I Knew Dietrich Bonhoeffer*, edited by Wolf-Dieter Zimmermann and Ronald Gregor Smith, and translated by Käthe Gregor Smith, 147. London: Collins, 1966.

Northcott, Michael. "'Who Am I?': Human Identity and the Spiritual Disciplines in the Witness of Dietrich Bonhoeffer." In *Who am I?: Bonhoeffer's Theology through his Poetry*, edited by Bernd Wannenwetsch, 11–29. London and New York: T. & T. Clark, 2009.

O'Donovan, Oliver. "Augustinian Ethics." In *A New Dictionary of Christian Ethics*, edited by John Macquarrie and James Childress, 46–49. London: SCM, 1986.

———. *The Problem of Self-Love in St. Augustine*. New Haven and London: Yale University Press, 1980.

———. *Resurrection and Moral Order: An Outline for Evangelical Ethics*. 2nd ed. Leicester: Apollos; and Grand Rapids: Eerdmans, 1994.

———. "Usus and Fruitio in Augustine, *De Doctrina Christiana*." *Journal of Theological Studies* 33 (1982) 361–97.

Ott, Heinrich. *Reality and Faith: The Theological Legacy of Dietrich Bonhoeffer*. Translated by Alexander A. Morrison. London: Lutterworth, 1971.

Outka, Gene H., and Paul Ramsey, editors. *Norm and Context in Christian Ethics*. London: SCM, 1968.

Pangritz, Andreas. *Karl Barth in der Theologie Dietrich Bonhoeffers: eine notwendige Klarstellung*. Westberlin: Alektor, 1989.

———. *Polyphonie des Lebens: Zu Dietrich Bonhoeffers "Theologie der Musik."* Berlin: Alektor, 1994.

———. "Theological Motives in Dietrich Bonhoeffer's Decision to Participate in Political Resistance." In *Reflections on Bonhoeffer*, edited by Geffrey B. Kelly, 32–49. Chicago: Covenant, 1999.

———. "Who is Jesus Christ, for us, today?" In *The Cambridge Companion to Dietrich Bonhoeffer*, edited by John W. de Gruchy, 134–53. Cambridge: Cambridge University Press, 1999.

Peck, William J., editor. *New Studies in Bonhoeffer's Ethics*. Lewiston/Queenston: Edwin Mellen, 1987.

Pfeifer, Hans, editor. *Genf '76: Ein Bonhoeffer Symposion*. Munich: Kaiser, 1976.

———. "Die Gestalten der Rechtfertigung: Zur Frage nach der Struktur der Theologie Dietrich Bonhoeffers." *Kerygma und Dogma* 18.3 (1972) 177–201.

Bibliography

Pieper, Josef. *The Four Cardinal Virtues: Prudence, Justice, Fortitude, Temperance.* Translated by Richard Winston et al. Notre Dame: University of Notre Dame Press, 1954.

———. *Introduction to Thomas Aquinas.* Translated by Richard and Clara Winston. London: Faber & Faber, 1962.

Pinckaers, Servais, OP. *The Sources of Christian Ethics.* Translated by Mary Thomas Noble, OP. Edinburgh: T. & T. Clark, 1995.

———. "The Sources of the Ethics of St Thomas Aquinas." In *The Ethics of Aquinas*, edited by Stephen J. Pope, 17–29. Washington, DC: Georgetown University Press, 2002.

Pincoffs, Edmund. "Quandary Ethics." In *Revisions: Changing Perspectives in Moral Philosophy*, edited by Stanley Hauerwas and Alasdair MacIntyre, 92–112. Notre Dame; London: University of Notre Dame Press, 1983.

Plant, Stephen. *Bonhoeffer.* London and New York: Continuum, 2004.

———. "The Sacrament of Ethical Reality: Dietrich Bonhoeffer on Ethics for Christian Citizens." *Studies in Christian Ethics* 18.3 (*Dietrich Bonhoeffer and Christian Ethics: Centenary Reflections*) (2005) 71–87.

———. "Uses of the Bible in the 'Ethics' of Dietrich Bonhoeffer." PhD diss., Cambridge University, 1993.

Pope, Stephen J., editor. *The Ethics of Aquinas.* Washington DC: Georgetown University Press, 2002.

———. "Natural Law and Christian Ethics." In *The Cambridge Companion to Christian Ethics*, edited by Robin Gill, 77–95. Cambridge: Cambridge University Press, 2001.

Porter, Jean. *Moral Action and Christian Ethics.* Cambridge: Cambridge University Press, 1995.

———. *The Recovery of Virtue: The Relevance of Aquinas for Christian Ethics.* London: SPCK, 1994, first published Louisville: Westminster John Knox, 1990.

———. "Virtue Ethics." In *The Cambridge Companion to Christian Ethics*, edited by Robin Gill, 96–111. Cambridge: Cambridge University Press, 2001.

Prenter, Regin. "Bonhoeffer and the Young Luther." In *World Come of Age: A Symposium on Dietrich Bonhoeffer*, edited by Ronald Gregor Smith, 161–81. London: Collins, 1967.

———. "Dietrich Bonhoeffer and Karl Barth's Positivism of Revelation." In *World Come of Age: A Symposium on Dietrich Bonhoeffer*, edited by Ronald Gregor Smith, 93–130. London: Collins, 1967.

Puera, Simo. "Christ as Favor and Gift (*donum*): The Challenge of Luther's Understanding of Justification." In *Union with Christ: The New Finnish Interpretation of Luther*, edited by Carl E. Braaten and Robert W. Jenson, 42–69. Grand Rapids: Eerdmans, 1998.

Rasmussen, Larry L. "Ethik des Kreuzes am gegebenem Ort." In *Bonhoeffer und Luther: Zur Sozialgestalt des Luthertums in der Moderne*, edited by Christian Gremmels, and translated by Ilse Tödt, 129–66. Munich: Kaiser, 1983.

———. "A Question of Method." In *New Studies in Bonhoeffer's Ethics*, edited by William J. Peck, 103–38. Lewiston/Queenston: Edwin Mellen, 1987.

Rasmussen, Larry, with Renate Bethge. *Dietrich Bonhoeffer: His Significance for North Americans.* Minneapolis: Fortress, 1990.

Ratschow, Carl-Heinz. "Paul Tillich." In *Theologen des Protestantismus im 19. und 20. Jahrhundert I*, edited by Martin Greschat, 303-30. Stuttgart/Berlin/Cologne/Mainz: Kohlhammer, 1978.

Reardon, Bernard M. G. *Religious Thought in the Reformation*. London and New York, Longman, 1981.

Rieger, Julius. In *I Knew Dietrich Bonhoeffer*, edited by Wolf-Dieter Zimmermann and Ronald Gregor Smith, and translated by Käthe Gregor Smith, 95-96. London: Collins, 1966.

Rist, John M. *Augustine: Ancient Thought Baptized*. Cambridge: Cambridge University Press, 1994.

Ritschl, Albrecht. *The Christian Doctrine of Justification and Reconciliation: The Positive Development of the Doctrine*. 2nd ed. Edited by H. R. Mackintosh and A.B. Macaulay. Translated by H. R. Mackintosh. Edinburgh: T. & T. Clark, 1902.

Robertson, Edwin. *The Shame and the Sacrifice: The Life and Martyrdom of Dietrich Bonhoeffer*. New York: Macmillan, 1988.

Robinson, John A. T. *Honest to God*. London: SCM, 1963.

Rumscheidt, Martin. Preface to Ernst Feil, *The Theology of Dietrich Bonhoeffer*, translated by Martin Rumscheidt. Philadelphia: Fortress, 1985.

Sagovsky, Nick. "Bonhoeffer, Responsibility and Justice." Seminar paper given at Durham University, February 28, 2002.

Sanders, E. P. *Paul and Palestinian Judaism: A Comparison of Patterns of Religion*. London: SCM, 1977.

Schneewind, J. B. *The Invention of Autonomy: A History of modern Moral Philosophy*. Cambridge: Cambridge University Press, 1998.

Scholder, Klaus. *Die Kirchen und das Dritte Reich: Band 1 Vorgeschichte und Zeit der Illusionen 1918-1934*. Frankfurt am Main: Propyläen, 1977.

———. *Die Kirchen und das Dritte Reich Band 2: Das Jahr der Ernüchterung 1934*. Barmen: Siedler, 1985.

Slote, Michael. *From Morality to Virtue*. Oxford: Oxford University Press, 1992.

Stahlberg, Alexander. "Dietrich Bonhoeffer." In *Die Verdammte Pflicht—Erinnerungen an 1932 bis 1945*, 101-4. Frankfurt am Main et al, 1987.

Stanton, Graham N. "Paul's Gospel." In *The Cambridge Companion to St Paul*, edited by James D. G. Dunn, 173-84. Cambridge: Cambridge University Press, 2003.

Stayer, James M. *Martin Luther, German Saviour: German Evangelical Theological Factions and the Interpretation of Luther 1917-1933*. Montreal: McGill-Queen's University, 2000.

Stock, Konrad. *Grundlegung der protestantischen Tugendlehre*. Gütersloh: Kaiser/Gütersloher, 1995.

Stout, Jeffrey. *Ethics after Babel: The Languages of Morals and their Discontents*. Boston: Beacon, 1988.

Stout, Jeffrey, and Robert MacSwain, editors. *Grammar and Grace: Reformulations of Aquinas and Wittgenstein*. London: SCM, 2004.

Taylor, Charles. "Justice After Virtue." In *After MacIntyre: Critical Perspectives on the Work of Alasdair MacIntyre*, edited by John Horton and Susan Mendus, 16-43. Oxford: Polity, 1994.

Thomas Aquinas, St. *Summa Theologiae* I. Translation and introduction by Timothy McDermott, OP. Blackfriars with London: Eyre & Spottiswoode; and New York: McGraw-Hill, 1963.

Bibliography

———. *Summa Theologiae 16: Purpose and Happiness* (I–II.1–5). Edited and translated by Thomas Gilby, OP. Cambridge: Blackfriars, 1969.

———. *Summa Theologiae 17: Psychology of Human Acts* (I–II, 6–17). Edited and translated by Thomas Gilby, OP. Cambridge: Blackfriars, 1970.

———. *Summa Theologiae 18: Moral Good and Evil* (I–II.18–21). Edited and translated by Thomas Gilby, OP. London: Eyre and Spottiswoode and New York: McGraw-Hill, 1966.

———. *Summa Theologiae 22: Dispositions for Human Acts* (I–II.49–54). Edited and translated by Anthony Kenny. London: Blackfriars with Eyre and Spottiswoode and New York: McGraw-Hill, 1964.

———. *Summa Theologiae 23: Virtue* (I–II.55–67). Edited and translated by W. D. Hughes, OP. London: Blackfriars with Eyre and Spottiswoode and New York: McGraw-Hill, 1969.

Tödt, Heinz Eduard. "Conscience in Dietrich Bonhoeffer's Ethical Theory and Practice." In *Bonhoeffer's Ethics: Old Europe and New Frontiers*, edited by Guy Carter et al., 46–58. Kampen, The Netherlands: Kok Pharos, 1991.

———."Glauben in einer religionslosen Welt: Muβ man zwischen Barth und Bonhoeffer wählen?" In *Genf '76: Ein Bonhoeffer-Symposion*, edited by Hans Pfeifer, 98–107. Munich: Kaiser, 1976.

Tödt, Ilse. "Paradoxical Obedience." *Lutheran Theological Journal* 35 (2001) 3–16.

Torrance, Thomas F. *God and Rationality*. London/New York/Toronto: Oxford University Press, 1971.

Trillhaas, Wolfgang. "Albrecht Ritschl." In *Theologen des Protestantismus im 19. und 20. Jahrhundert I*, edited by Martin Greschat, 113–29. Stuttgart/Berlin/Cologne/Mainz: Kohlhammer, 1978.

Walker, Rebecca L., et al. editors. *Working Virtue: Virtue Ethics and Contemporary Moral Problems*. Oxford: Clarendon; New York: Oxford University Press, 2007.

Wannenwetsch, Bernd. "'Responsible Living' or 'Responsible Self'? Bonhoefferian Reflections on a Vexed Moral Notion." *Studies in Christian Ethics* 18.3 (*Dietrich Bonhoeffer and Christian Ethics: Centenary Reflections*) (2005) 125–40.

———, editor. *Who am I?: Bonhoeffer's Theology through his Poetry*. Edinburgh: T. & T. Clark, 2009.

Webster, John. *Barth's Ethics of Reconciliation*. Cambridge: Cambridge University Press, 1995.

———. *Barth's Moral Theology: Human Action in Barth's Thought*. Edinburgh: T. & T. Clark, 1998.

———. *Word and Church: Essays in Christian Dogmatics*. Edinburgh/New York: T. & T. Clark, 2001.

Wendl, Ernst Georg. *Studien zur Homiletik Dietrich Bonhoeffers*. Tübingen: Mohr/Siebeck, 1985.

Werpehowski, William. "Narrative and Ethics in Barth." *Theology Today* 43.3 (October 1986) 334–53.

Wetzel, James. *Augustine and the Limits of Virtue*. Cambridge: Cambridge University Press, 1992.

Wilken, Robert Louis. *The Spirit of Early Christian Thought: Seeking the Face of God*. New Haven and London: Yale University Press, 2003.

Bibliography

Williams, Rowan. "The Suspicion of Suspicion: Wittgenstein and Bonhoeffer." In *The Grammar of the Heart: New Essays in Moral Philosophy and Theology*, edited by Richard H. Bell, 36–53. San Francisco, 1988.

Wills, Gary. *St. Augustine*. London: Weidenfeld & Nicolson, 1999.

Wind, Renate. *A Spoke in the Wheel: The Life of Dietrich Bonhoeffer*. Translated by John Bowden. London: SCM, 1991.

Wüstenberg, Ralf K. "Dietrich Bonhoeffer on Theology and Philosophy." *Anvil: An Anglican Evangelical Journal for Theology and Mission* 12.1 (1995) 45–56.

———. *A Theology of Life: Dietrich Bonhoeffer's Religionless Christianity*. Translated by Doug Stott. Grand Rapids: Eerdmans, 1998.

Yeago, David S. "Martin Luther on Grace, Law and Moral Life: Prolegomena to an Ecumenical Discussion of *Veritas Splendor*." *The Thomist* 62 (1998) 163–91.

Yearley, Lee H. "Recent Work on Virtue." *Religious Studies Review* 16.1 (January 1990), 1–9.

Zimmerling, Peter. "Dietrich Bonhoeffer—Leben und Werk." In *Dietrich Bonhoeffer heute: Die Aktualität seines Lebens und Werkes*, edited by Rainer Mayer and Peter Zimmerling, 13–40. E. Giessen/Basel: Brunnen, 1993.

Zimmermann, Wolf-Dieter, and Ronald Gregor Smith, editors. *I Knew Dietrich Bonhoeffer*. Translated by Käthe Gregor Smith. London: Collins, 1966.

Index

Abortion, 87, 150, 156, 181
Above/Below, 32, 180, 186
Act, 2–5, 9, 16, 20, 26, 28, 31,
    40–43, 45, 58, 62–64, 66, 67,
    72–78, 83, 84, 86, 90–93, 96,
    100, 103, 109–12, 120–22,
    124–31, 134–37, 139, 142,
    146, 148, 153, 155–56,
    160–62, 164–65, 171–75,
    177–78, 186, 190–93, 195,
    199–201, 205–6, 208–12,
    218, 221, 227, 230–32
  Actus directus, 112, 170, 175,
    199, 205
  divine, 3–4, 45, 50, 103, 108–9,
    114, 170–71, 174, 176, 193,
    199, 214, 229–30
Althaus, Paul, 6, 103–4
Ansatz Theory, 45, 47, 174
Anscombe, Elizabeth, 80
Anthropology (human nature), 13,
    23–26, 30, 32, 52, 60, 62–64,
    75, 79, 97, 99, 123, 140–41,
    173, 191, 210, 220, 223
Aristotle, 12, 26, 55, 57, 62, 70–72,
    75, 78, 85, 88–90, 193, 221
Aquinas, Thomas, 11–12, 15, 20,
    22–25, 53, 69–79, 83–89,
    91, 94–98, 109, 114, 132,
    134–36, 150, 161, 193, 205,
    211, 220–22, 228, 230
Assassination. *See* Tyrannicide
"Auch Einer," 181, 182
Auden, W. H., 40

Augustine of Hippo, 4, 12, 22, 27,
    53–69, 71, 76, 78–79, 87–89,
    91–98, 153, 221–22, 230
Authorization, 31–2, 116, 179, 180,
    186

Barth, Karl, 14, 17–19, 21, 32, 34,
    41, 93–94, 99, 103–4, 111,
    115, 121, 147–51, 155, 157,
    162, 164–68, 170–71, 175,
    190, 193, 210, 212, 224
Being, 3–4, 18–19, 31, 36, 50,
    122–23, 134, 137–38, 148,
    165, 175–76, 178–79, 183,
    203, 208–10, 217–18, 223
Berkhouwer, G. C., 103
Berryhill, Elizabeth, 40
Bethge, Eberhard, 18, 25, 32, 40,
    45–47, 102–4, 145, 151, 208
Bethge, Renate, 11, 40
Bethke Elshtain, Jean, 9, 26, 126
Biggar, Nigel, 92, 94, 121, 164
Black, Rufus, 94
Blum, Laurence, 124
Bonhoeffer, Dietrich (by works),
  DBW 1, *Sanctorum Communio*,
    25, 102, 132, 137, 143, 175
  DBW 2, *Akt und Sein*, 112,
    137–38, 170, 175, 199, 205,
    208
  DBW 3, *Schöpfung und Fall*, 111,
    115, 127, 170
  DBW 4, *Nachfolge*, 103–4, 106,
    110, 112, 114, 133, 138, 175,
    223

Index

DBW 5, Gemeinsames Leben/ Gebetbuch der Bibel, 131

DBW 6, Ethik, (by manuscript)
"Christ, Reality and the Good," 17–18, 22, 29, 106–7, 113, 118, 183, 189, 195
"Church and World," 18, 118
"Ethics as Formation," 19, 28, 29, 50, 107–8, 113, 124, 128–30, 165, 176–77, 180, 189, 196, 202, 211–12
"Guilt, Justification, Renewal," 29, 116–17, 119, 202, 209
"History and the Good," 20, 26, 30, 111, 116–17, 120, 123, 137, 168, 190, 199, 203, 210
"Inheritance and Decay," 22, 116–17, 214
"The Concrete Command and the Divine Mandates," 124, 185, 200, 204, 211
"The 'Ethical' and the 'Christian' as a Theme," 21, 31, 50, 113, 124, 126, 169, 176, 179, 181, 211
"The Love of God and the Decay of the World," 19, 93, 111, 113, 115, 134–35, 169, 199–200, 210, 213, 217
"The Natural Life," 27, 30, 111, 125, 146–47, 209
"Ultimate and Penultimate Things," 108, 113, 125, 189, 214

DBW 7, Fragmente aus Tegel, 20, 32, 121, 137, 160, 180, 186

DBW 8, Widerstand und Ergebung, 11, 24–25, 37, 46, 101–2, 104–6, 118, 121, 126, 138, 155, 157, 188, 204

DBW 10, Barcelona, Berlin, America (1928-1931), 18, 103

DBW 11, Ökumene, Universität, Pfarramt (1931-1932), 21, 103

DBW 12, Berlin (1932-1933), 32

DBW 14, Illegale Theologenausbildung, Finkenwalde (1935-1937), 103

DBW 16, Konspiration und Haft (1940-1945), 25, 92, 143, 157–61, 169, 190, 193

Love Letters, 40, 121, 188

Bonhoeffer, Karl, 40
Boyle, Leonard E., 70–72
Burnaby, John, 54–55, 58–61, 63, 67–69, 93
Braaten, Carl E., 8
Brock, Brian, 121
Burtness, James, 9, 16, 42–44, 108
Busch, Eberhard, 190

Calvin, John, 6–7
Carney, Frederick S., 16
Casuistry, 7, 25, 29, 92
Catholicism, Roman, ix, 3–8, 15, 17, 22–26, 34, 39, 41, 48–49, 79, 92, 102, 143, 146, 154, 161–62, 219, 222, 225–26, 229
Cavanaugh, William T., 8
Cessario, Romanus, O.P., 53, 58, 79, 92
Character, 2, 9, 16–17, 19–20, 36, 54, 62, 88–89, 94–95, 97, 100–101, 124, 126, 128, 130–33, 138, 175, 178, 208–10, 214–15, 222, 224–25, 227, 230–32

Christ as exemplar, 60, 131, 199, 201, 210, 213, 215
Christ, communion with, 202–6
Christology, 16, 23, 78, 114–16, 128, 131, 138–39, 167, 202
Church. *See* Ecclesiology
Church and World, 34, 45, 91, 107, 117–19, 139, 154, 183, 187–88
Cleverness. *See* Simplicity
Coleman, Janet, 83, 85
Command, x, 1, 6, 14, 21, 27, 32, 35, 37, 41, 44, 47–52, 64, 66–69, 90, 92, 99, 112, 125, 127, 135–36, 148–50, 162, 163–218, 220, 224, 226, 232
Concretion, 7, 13, 29–34, 37, 39–41, 44, 48, 50, 95, 97, 103, 111–12, 116–18, 120, 124, 132, 139–45, 149–50, 153, 155, 157–58, 161–62, 164–65, 168–69, 171–73, 177–81, 183–86, 189, 191, 195, 197, 200, 206, 208–10, 212–14, 218, 220, 222–24
Conformation (*Gleichgestaltung*), 1, 13–14, 16–17, 35, 45, 47, 50–51, 58–59, 65, 67, 96, 107–8, 114, 128, 130–32, 135–36, 138, 140–41, 163, 165, 172, 174–76, 180, 182–83, 188, 194, 196–97, 199, 202–3, 206–9, 211, 213–16, 218, 223–24, 229–30
Conscience, 16, 19–20, 28, 74, 108, 128–29, 133, 159, 165, 193, 203–4, 212
Contraception, 25, 92, 150, 156
Cottingham, John, 96
Council of Trent, 3
Crisp, Roger, 142, 226
Cunningham, David, 9, 93, 226–29
Cunningham, Robert L., 39

Davis, Ellen, 53
Drewery, Benjamin, 3
Dualism, 49, 56, 71, 91, 106–7, 109, 118, 139, 183–85, 188, 223
Dumas, André, 16, 108, 119–20
Dunn, James D. G., 6
Ebeling, Gerhard, 9, 104
Ecclesiology, ix, 102, 107, 124, 128, 204, 206
Ethics
    abstract, 29–33, 38, 52, 95–97, 99, 116, 139, 143, 165, 169, 177–80, 189, 212–13, 220, 223
    Barthian command, x, 1, 14, 41, 136, 148–49, 162–218, 224, 226
    deontological, 33, 35, 40, 44, 67, 89, 142, 145, 147, 149–50, 155–56, 164
    relational, 123–24, 146, 159, 162, 172–73
    rights, 24, 27, 34, 110, 125, 135, 145–49, 155, 181, 183
    Roman Catholic, ix, 4–7, 17, 22–23, 25–26, 34, 48–49, 79, 92, 143, 146, 154, 161–62, 219, 226
    situation, 16, 35, 39–45, 50, 143, 146, 149, 156, 159, 173, 178, 208, 227
    utilitarianism (consequentialism), 35, 40, 42–44, 50, 67, 142, 146–47, 149, 155–56, 179, 227
Ettal, 25, 143, 145, 154
Eudaemonism, 55, 61, 64–65, 67, 73, 79, 83, 88, 146, 150, 221, 229–30, 232
Euthanasia, 25–26, 87, 111, 125, 151, 155–56, 181, 209

Faith, 2–7, 9, 18–19, 39, 55–56, 59, 64, 70, 77–78, 102, 104–6,

249

Index

Faith (*cont.*)
  109–10, 113, 137–38, 148
  152, 193, 198–99, 203,
  208–9, 211, 214–17, 219,
  221–22, 225, 228
Fall, 4, 19, 23–24, 26, 52, 62, 64,
  69, 97, 99, 111–13, 115, 129,
  139, 144, 170, 181, 198, 210,
  214, 221, 228
Feil, Ernst, 9–10, 25, 29, 32, 34–35,
  114, 143–44
Fergusson, David, 101, 112
Figur, Fritz, 143
Fletcher, Joseph, 39, 41–42, 44, 227
Floyd, Wayne, 116
Foot, Philippa, 80, 86, 226
Ford, David, 9–10, 38–39, 106
Freedom, 19–20, 22, 24, 30, 37, 50,
  57, 60, 63, 72, 108, 110–11,
  118, 125–27, 133–34, 136–
  38, 151–53, 156, 168–69,
  176, 188, 190–94, 199, 232
Frick, Peter, 32, 130

Geach, Peter, 79, 85–86, 97
Glazener, Mary, 40
Godsey, John D., 10, 16, 21, 26,
  34–35, 102–4, 114
The Good, 4, 18–19, 29–32, 37,
  41–43, 48, 56, 58, 62–65, 69,
  84, 88, 92, 96, 114, 119, 147,
  177, 195–96, 217, 221
Grabill, Stephen J., 5, 94
Grace, 2–4, 6–7, 9, 22, 39, 41, 46,
  49, 52, 54, 59–60, 63–64,
  66, 68–9, 79, 88, 97–101,
  104, 108–15, 125, 132, 134,
  139, 144, 173, 190, 192–94,
  197–99, 202–4, 214, 219–22,
  225–30, 232
  cheap, 104, 109, 114, 138, 229
Green, Clifford, 39, 105, 123, 174
Gremmels, Christian, 9, 39–40,
  101, 104, 109

Guilt, 110, 117, 119, 129, 152, 155,
  192–94, 202–4
Gustafson, James M., 2

Habit, 4, 64–66, 70, 75–76, 95, 222,
  228
Haldane, John, 84
Harnack, Adolf von, 6, 101–2
Harrison, Carol, 55, 61–67
Harvey, Barry, 22
Hauerwas, Stanley, 9, 16, 32, 44,
  80, 87, 89–90, 94, 97–98,
  100, 117, 124, 128, 132, 135,
  226–27, 230
Haynes, Stephen R., 9, 11, 35
Helm, Paul, 164
Herrenbrück, P. W., 17
History, 30, 43–44, 53, 81, 86,
  106–7, 116–18, 123, 131,
  153, 172–73, 192–93, 222
Hitler, Adolf, 19, 36, 38, 40, 43,
  129, 144–45, 150
Holiness. *See* Sanctification
Holl, Karl, 6, 103, 230
Honecker, Martin, 11
Hope, 3, 56, 59, 77–78, 87, 221–22
Horton, John, 82
Hoogstraten, Hans D. von, 35–39
Hughes, W. D., 75–76
Hursthouse, Rosalind, 86, 90, 96,
  226

Incarnation, Crucifixion and
  Resurrection, 115, 124,
  196–98, 201
Innes, Robert, 65–6
Innocence, 150–51, 192
Intention. *See* Motive

Jacobi, Gerhard, 17, 157
Jenson, Robert W., 8
"Joint Declaration on the Doctrine
  of Justification," 8
Jones, Gregory L., 107

Index

Justice, 20, 35–38, 58, 77, 81, 83, 90–91, 110, 119, 145–6, 224
Justification, 2–9, 20, 39, 48, 81, 95, 98, 100–114, 129, 135, 138–39, 141, 152, 155, 192–93, 219–20, 222–23, 225, 229

Kant, Immanuel, 5–6, 81, 159, 227
Kärkkäinen, Veli-Matti, 8
Kelly, Geffrey B., 26
Kenny, Anthony, 70, 75
Kent, Bonnie, 54, 56, 60–62, 68, 75–76
Kerr, Fergus, 70–72, 78–79, 83
Killing, 6, 20, 119, 148, 150–51, 156, 209
Kingdom of God, 21–22, 35, 44–47, 51
Klassen, A. J., 41
Köster, Peter, 32, 147
Kotva, Joseph J., 53, 80, 89
Kuntz, Paul G., 57, 59, 67

Lane, Anthony N. S., 7
Langan, John P., 59, 64–66
Lange, Frits de, 21
Lehmann, Paul, 10
Lehmkühler, Karsten, 41–42, 121, 130
Leibholz, Gerhard, 34
Leibholz-Bonhoeffer, Sabine, 40, 106
Lockley, Harold, 40–41
Love, 3, 6, 12, 20, 42, 44, 50, 55–56, 58–69, 78, 87, 91, 93, 95–96, 98, 102, 110–11, 130, 136, 158–59, 177, 185, 192, 196, 198, 200–202, 212–13, 221–22, 228
Lovin, Robin, 25
Luther, Martin, 2–6, 8, 22, 25, 39, 102–4, 126, 129–30, 133, 143, 169

Lutheranism, 2, 5–8, 22, 49, 54, 68, 90, 101, 104, 118, 219–20

MacIntyre, Alasdair, 2, 12, 16–17, 35–37, 53, 79–92, 94, 96, 117–18, 124, 128, 222, 225–27
MacSwain, Robert, 79
Mandates, 25, 40, 45, 48, 120–22, 124, 127, 139, 164–66, 172, 181, 183–90, 194–95, 200–201, 204, 206
Mangina, Joseph L., 164
Markus, R. A., 59, 61–63, 65
Marsh, Charles, 21, 32
Marshall, Bruce, 8
McClendon, James William, Jr., 9, 41
Meilaender, Gilbert C., 78, 80, 86, 89, 92–93, 98, 135
Melanchthon, 6–7
Mendus, Susan, 82
Mercy, 6, 60, 109, 114, 136, 165, 189, 192–93, 199, 209, 212, 224, 228
Miller, David, 83–84
Moberly, Jennifer, 10
Mokrosch, Reinhold, 104
Morgan, Robert, 6
Motive, 2, 10, 42–43, 60, 63, 65–67, 73–74, 89, 91, 93, 106, 110, 137, 142, 148, 151–53, 156, 161–62, 191, 221–23, 231
Müller, Hanfried, 16, 45, 47–50
Muller, Denis G., 193
Murdoch, Iris, 80

Narrative, 58, 85, 87–88, 124, 139, 222–23, 227
National Socialism (Nazism), 20, 27–28, 32, 43, 85–87, 90, 108, 117–19, 121, 129, 144, 146–47, 151, 154, 181, 183, 185, 187–89, 194, 196, 203, 209

251

Index

Natural, The, 22–26, 41, 48–49, 87, 111, 114, 125, 127, 143–46, 148–50, 154–55, 162, 168, 181–83, 188
Natural Law, 4, 33–34, 39, 52, 67, 89, 94–95, 99, 154
Nickson, Ann L., 16, 34–35, 42, 104–5, 114
Niesel, Wilhelm, 145
Northcott, Michael, 38

Obedience, x, 45, 69, 127, 164–69, 171–72, 174–75, 188, 193–94, 209, 212–13, 224, 232
O'Donovan, Oliver, 9, 61, 66, 93–94, 226, 229–32
Ott, Heinrich, 9, 16, 39–41

Pangritz, Andreas, 21, 40, 103, 131
Particularity. *See* Concretion
Penultimate, The, 43, 49, 107–11, 113–14, 125, 127, 139, 144–46, 181–82, 189, 197–98
Perception (or Recognition or Discernment), 23, 29–31, 34, 62, 69, 79, 115, 126, 129, 133, 135–36, 140, 154, 155, 158, 160–61, 168, 191, 193, 205–6, 214–15, 230–31
Pfeifer, Hans, 9, 16, 21, 40, 44–47
Phariseeism, 19–20, 22, 52, 90, 93, 99, 102, 211
Pieper, Josef, 24, 71–72, 79, 92, 126, 143, 145, 154
Pinckaers, Servais, 7, 53, 70–71
Pincoffs, Edmund, 21
Plant, Stephen, 14, 16, 21, 24, 34, 39, 50, 120, 124, 137–38, 163, 172, 175–76, 207–8, 214–15, 218
Platonism, 27, 55, 58–62, 66, 68, 72, 89
Pope, Stephen J., 70, 94
Porter, Jean, 54–55, 71, 86, 90

Positivism of revelation, 155
Prenter, Regin, 39
Providence, 144, 193
Prudence, 31, 58, 63, 76–77, 115, 128, 132–33, 135–38, 140, 161, 205–6, 212, 223, 230
Puera, Simo, 130

Rasmussen, Larry, 14, 21, 35, 39, 49–50, 130, 163, 167, 172–77, 207, 218
Ratschow, Carl-Heinz, 102
Reality, 7, 16, 18–19, 24, 29–31, 35, 44–47, 51, 106–7, 109, 114, 117, 126, 128–29, 131, 133–35, 158, 160, 166–67, 172–73, 178, 182, 184, 189, 191–92, 194–201, 205–6, 215–18, 224–25, 228–30, 232
Realization, 46–47, 83, 88, 103, 106, 166, 172–73, 178, 203, 216
Reardon, Bernard M. G., 2–5, 7
Reconciliation, 20, 27, 29, 46–47, 57, 59, 114, 131, 134, 136, 167, 172, 184–85, 196, 200, 216–18, 224, 228–30, 232
Representation, 35–36, 38, 45, 120, 122–24, 134, 186, 190–92, 194, 197, 199, 201, 204–5, 210, 213, 215, 223, 232
Responsibility, 16, 20, 26, 28, 41–42, 48, 67, 72–73, 106, 110–11, 120–24, 128–29, 132, 134, 136–37, 139, 156, 159, 168–69, 173, 175, 183–85, 189–95, 197, 199, 201, 206, 210, 213, 215, 223, 232
Revelation, 4, 18–19, 21, 47, 56, 59, 73, 78, 93–94, 114, 142, 155, 166–67, 169, 185–87, 196, 200–201, 216–17, 230, 232

Rieger, Julius, 143
Risk. *See* Venture
Rist, John, 54–56, 58, 60–64, 66–67
Ritschl, Albrecht, 5, 45–47, 51, 102
Robinson, John H. T., 41, 44
Rolf, Sibylle, 6, 129
Rumscheidt, Martin, 10

Sagovsky, Nicholas, 16, 26, 107, 128–30, 138
Sanctification, 3, 5–8, 13, 58–60, 63, 95, 98, 100–114, 136, 138–39, 141, 198, 219, 222–23, 225, 229
Sanders, E. P., 6
Schneewind, J. B., 81
Scholder, Klaus, 121, 144, 184, 187
Simplicity (and Cleverness), 27, 108, 112, 128, 132–38, 140, 165–66, 170–71, 196, 199–201, 205–6, 212–15, 223–24, 231–32
Sin, 3–7, 20–21, 23, 59, 63–67, 74–75, 102, 105, 108–9, 114, 125, 130–31, 137, 144, 150, 152, 159, 180–81, 184, 192, 197, 203, 208–9, 217, 219, 221, 225, 227–29, 231
Slote, Michael, 89–90, 226
Spirit, Holy, 4, 6, 42, 58, 60, 63, 101, 107, 131, 146, 202, 223
Stahlberg, Alexander, 40
Stanton, Graham N., 6
Stayer, James M., 6, 46
Sterilization, 25, 92, 111, 150, 155–56
Stout, Jeffrey, 79–80
Success, 42–43, 105, 144–45, 191
Suicide, 26, 125, 151–53, 155
Suum cuique, 27, 30, 141, 145–47, 159

Taylor, Charles, 83
Temperance, 19–20, 24, 58–59, 77, 126

Thomism, 2, 17, 22–24, 31, 38, 51, 80, 83–85, 88–89, 99, 115, 135–37, 205, 220, 224
Tödt, Heinz Eduard, 9, 21
Tödt, Ilse, 130, 150
Torrance, Thomas F., 21, 114
Toulmin, Stephen, 92
Trillhaas, Wolfgang, 102
Trinity, 58
Truth, 3, 36–38, 55, 57–58, 65, 71, 73, 76, 95, 130, 157–60, 193, 212
Tyranicide, 40–41, 43, 150, 193

Ultimate, The, 43, 49, 107–11, 114, 138–39, 144, 146, 189, 198

Venture, 31, 152–53, 165, 191, 193–94, 212
Vice, 5, 19, 21–22, 39, 52, 55, 59, 64, 75, 77–78, 86, 93, 217–18
Virtues, 3, 5, 7, 12–13, 17, 19, 22, 35–39, 52–53, 55, 58–61, 63–66, 68–71, 75–79, 83–91, 93, 95–98, 113–14, 117, 130, 132–38, 140, 142, 166, 221–23, 225–26, 228–29, 231
   infused, 4, 63–64, 75–79, 87–88, 95, 98, 113–15, 134, 166, 205, 212, 221, 228, 230

Walker, Rebecca L., 225
Wannenwetsch, Bernd, 137
Webster, John, 21, 106, 164
Wendel, Ernst Georg, 9, 28
Werpehowski, William, 164
Wetzel, James, 55, 62–63, 65
Wilken, Robert Louis, 55, 57, 60, 64
Will
   divine, ix, 4, 18, 33, 42–43, 46–47, 64, 107, 111–12, 121, 125, 133–36, 144–49, 164, 166–71, 173–74, 193–94,

Index

Will, divine (*cont.*)
    196, 198–99, 205, 211–17,
    224, 228, 232
  human, 3–4, 31, 42, 55, 62–6,
    69, 73–77, 79, 88, 124, 144,
    147–48, 154, 162, 191, 219,
    221
Williams, Rowan, 38
Wills, Gary, 62
Wind, Renate, 40
Wüstenberg, Ralf K., 9, 21, 32

Yeago, David S., 8
Yearly, Lee H., 80, 225

www.ingramcontent.com/pod-product-compliance
Lightning Source LLC
Chambersburg PA
CBHW050345230426
43663CB00010B/2002